WHO WILL SAVE
THE FORESTS?

*Knowledge, Power and
Environmental Destruction*

THE WORLD INSTITUTE FOR DEVELOPMENT ECONOMICS RESEARCH (UNU/WIDER) was established by the United Nations University as its first research and training centre and started work in Helsinki, Finland in 1985. The principal purpose of the Institute is to help identify and meet the need for global and development problems, as well as common domestic problems and their inter-relationships. This book is an outcome of UNU/WIDER's work examining alternative approaches to technological transformation in the third world.

The United Nations University
World Institute for Development Economics Research
(UNU/WIDER)
Katajanokanlaituri 6, SF-00160 Helsinki, Finland

Who Will Save the Forests?

KNOWLEDGE, POWER AND
ENVIRONMENTAL DESTRUCTION

Edited by Tariq Banuri and
Frédérique Apffel Marglin

A Publication of
The United Nations University
World Institute for Development Economics Research
(UNU/WIDER)

ZED BOOKS
London & New Jersey

Who Will Save the Forests? Knowledge, Power and Environmental Destruction
was first published by Zed Books Ltd, 57 Caledonian Road, London
N1 9BU and 165 First Avenue, Atlantic Highlands,
New Jersey 07716, USA in 1993.

Cover designed by Andrew Corbett

Typeset by Idiom
Printed and bound in the United Kingdom by
Biddles Ltd, Guildford and King's Lynn

A catalogue record for this book is available
from the British Library
US CIP is available from the Library of Congress

ISBN 185649 159 5 Hb
ISBN 185649 160 9 Pb

Contents

Tables

Figures

1. A systems-of-knowledge analysis of deforestation, participation and management

Tariq Banuri and Frédérique Apffel Marglin

Introduction

The subject matter of the case studies assembled here is the analysis of the relationship between knowledge and power in the process of modernisation. This is accomplished by looking at forestry conflicts as conflicts over modes of knowing and over meanings. In other words, we are interested in forestry primarily because it has become an arena of conflict between modern and non-modern systems of knowledge, a conflict with important implications for current environmental debates. We are not primarily interested in the economic and political rights of tribal, peasant, or other communities, important as these are, but in the fact that many of these communities are embodiments of alternative forms of knowledge. Finally, while we make use of conventional analytical categories, such as those based on systems of political or social differentiation, on political or economic interests, or on political conflict and domination, the key conceptual device of this volume is the systems-of-knowledge framework.

As a first approximation it might be fruitful to simplify by sketching modern and non-modern systems of knowledge as ideal types. The distinguishing characteristics of the former are disembeddedness, universalism, individualism, objectivity and instrumentalism, while the latter are characterised by embeddedness, locality, community, a lack of separation between subject and object as well as a non-instrumental approach. It must be emphasised that 'modern' and 'non-modern' are ideological and not empirical categories. They refer to ideal types and not to observable cultural or regional groups. All societies, whether in the East or the West, the North or the South, use both modern and non-modern forms of knowledge. Our objective is neither to defend non-modern societies nor to vilify modern ones, nor is it to portray non-modern knowledge as unequivocally good and modern knowledge as the incarnation of evil. Our aim is to focus on the politics of knowledge and reveal the domination of one type of knowledge over all others.

Yet, and this is the important overlap between ideological and political categories, modernity as a system of knowledge has been used to marginalise as well as disenfranchise the knowledge of rural non-industrial communities. The modern system of knowledge, along with its associated set of values, has been elevated to the highest status, while alternatives are at best viewed as inferior forms of knowledge and, at worst, as non-knowledge. This process of denial and transformation is taking place at various speeds in various parts of the world: cities and their élites in the South, for example, are just as modern as those in the North. While the process has generally been applauded as desirable and progressive, we find much in it that is problematic and undesirable. This volume is an illustration of our argument.

In this work we have taken four examples of forestry practice in declining order of their distance from modernity: Abujhmarh, tribal India; Uttarakhand, peasant India; Forest Karelia, Finland; and Maine, USA. In each instance there are conflicts between various groups and between these groups and the state. Given the differences in the environment, these conflicts also differ considerably from each other, as does their articulation by activists, by the media, by intellectuals, by state agencies and by politicians. What is more to the point are the different methods and approaches adopted by the four case studies. For us, however, these differences are less important than the common underlying theme of the relationship of the conflicts to the construction and use of knowledge. We see these conflicts either as external encounters between the modern system of knowledge and its alternatives, or as internal debates within a system of knowledge, bound by its limitations or imperatives. As we demonstrate below, the external encounter presents itself even in a modern society like Finland. Similarly, internal debates — e.g. class conflicts, conflicts over social control (scientific forestry) versus *laissez-faire* capitalism — are ubiquitous in all regions of the world.

The central message of the volume is that the deterioration of forestry resources and the environmental crisis in general must be viewed from the angle of the politics of knowledge and a critical approach to the dominant, modern system of knowledge. By the same token we see a need to restore the autonomy of local arrangements based on alternative conceptions of reality. We find that societies which treat such alternatives as legitimate and respectable are relatively more successful in conserving the environment and empowering marginalised communities. For in societies where the alternatives are denigrated and marginalised the result is gradual environmental degradation and often the immiserisation of local populations.

The last outcome is particularly widespread in the South where alternatives have consistently been subjected to a form of intellectual and ideological imperialism by politically powerful protagonists of the modern system of knowledge. Today, relatively self-confident communities articulating an alternative system of knowledge remain only in inhospitable terrains, such as the Amazon forest, the Kalahari Desert, the Australian outback or the Indian jungle. Here, too, the living environment has been severely diminished or laid waste because of the political weakness of these communities relative to outside commercial interests, immigrant populations, state functionaries and other missionaries of modernisation. Yet their sustained confidence in their own ways of thinking and behaving distinguishes them from many other communities where the forced march towards industrialisation, political integration and cultural homogenisation is leading to the elimination of local practices and the destruction of local knowledges.

In recent years, the belief in the desirability of this forced march has been shaken. As we shall argue below, the causes of this shift are new — the emergence of the environmental crisis — as well as old — political resistance based on an alternative idiom against instrumentalist attitudes and practices (see Banuri 1990a). The ubiquity and vitality of such protests suggest that alternative perspectives have managed to survive, albeit in latent and unarticulated forms, even in the more so-called hospitable regions of the world. There is a reason to hope, then, that the worst pathologies of the modern system of knowledge can be contained, and that the prevalent instrumentalist attitude towards nature could be replaced with more nurturing conceptions.

In this volume we shall examine a subset of the above issues pertaining to the forestry sector. In particular, we shall look at the various kinds of protests against irresponsible exploitation of forestry resources, and the extent to which these protests indicate an encounter between modern and non-modern systems of knowledge.

We find that even when it works best the modern system of knowledge is fraught with danger and difficulty. But more often than not it does not work best. Scientific forestry — the best that the modern system of knowledge has to offer — has three types of problems. First, in its ideal form which is supposed to take a long view of the situation, scientific forestry is harmful because its claim to privileged status for its mode of knowing legitimises colonisation and exploitation of the *object* of its knowledge. It is a problem inherent in an instrumentalist view of the world. Second, in practice the label 'scientific' is used to justify short-horizon commercial practices rather than the pursuit of genuinely long-run interests (as, for example, in the use of the terms 'valuable', 'desirable' and 'inferior'). Third, direct state control compounds the problem even further because of corruption, inefficiency and waste. The same term, 'scientific forestry', covers all three instances.

Knowledge, technology and deforestation

The above factors have combined to generate a resurgence of interest in local knowledge, not so much to seek answers to local problems, though that endeavour has not abated, but more and more often to look for answers to the environmental crisis in general. This volume is presented to further this pursuit. It must be understood, however, that we advocate not the adoption of non-modern technologies and practices *as such*, but rather the incorporation of the *rationale* behind these technologies and practices into modern systems.

For many reasons, the forestry sector turns out to be particularly suited to this line of research. The bulk of the world's forests are in the tropical South, and these are very much in danger of disappearing. This would be an occurrence so unprecedented that the extent of its disastrous consequences can only be a subject for speculation; indeed, it is likely that most of the extant life forms, including humans, would be unable to survive that event. Another reason for the interest in forests is that many of the indigenous tribes, whose conservationist ways of life contrast so vividly with modern methods, inhabit afforested areas. These tribes, along with the innumerable species of flora and fauna, are in danger of becoming extinct with the recession of the forest cover.[1]

However, mainstream writers tend to see non-modern societies not as a source of solutions to environmental problems (particularly those having to do with deforestation) but as the source of the problems themselves — partly because their rates of population growth are putting pressure on scarce resources, and partly because their systems of collective resource management appear to be incapable of coping with the additional pressure. These writers advocate the slowing down of population growth and the institutionalisation of modern managerial systems (such as scientific forestry) in the South as solutions to the crisis.

We in turn, for reasons elaborated in this and later chapters, find these solutions to be a part of the problem. As mentioned earlier, we find the source of the emerging crisis to be the dominance of the modern system of knowledge itself; namely the instrumental and reductionist attitude towards nature shared by scientific foresters, programme managers and commercial entrepreneurs alike. This attitude contrasts sharply with the passionate commitment to conservation expressed in the beliefs and actions of long-standing local communities. From our perspective, the managerial solution, while it may minimise the worst excesses of *laissez-faire* commercial exploitation, persists in undermining the larger social basis of conservation.

Managerialism, like *laissez-faire* exploitation, is another attempt to control nature, not to conserve nature. Historically this attitude was legitimised and vindicated by its manifest success in improving the material conditions of existence of a large number of people without perceivable social or economic costs. In that innocent period conservationist outlooks were dismissed as inefficient, irrational and unnecessary. The environmental crisis as the result of the industrialisation process is now teaching us a different, more sobering lesson. This lesson is the subject of this book.

Description of the volume

The chapters in this volume were initiated under a research project on systems of knowledge as systems of domination.[2] The overall objective of the project is to examine the impact of modernity — modern technology and knowledge in general, organisation and institutions, individualism, commercialisation — upon the social as well as natural environment of affected communities. It is also to search for ways and means to decouple the adverse effects of this impact from its more positive achievements.

Within this broad mandate the present volume focuses on issues which are relevant to an important aspect of the environmental debate, namely those dealing with the conservation of forests and forestry resources. However, as has been mentioned above, the attempt is not to conduct an examination of technical issues pertaining to forestry or forest management. Rather, the objective is to elicit from the latent or manifest conflicts over environmental issues — the contrasting visions and attitudes towards resource conservation implicit in modern and non-modern societies — the lessons that these visions and practices provide for coping with the environmental crisis.

In order to examine these issues we present four case studies of forest communities selected on the basis of their distance from a modern, individualistic, instrumentalist, disembedded and rationalist world-view. Ranked from the most to the least distant, these are: a hill tribe practising shifting cultivation in India; a peasant community living in a relatively more modernised afforested region of the same country; smallholders and corporations sharing a forest area in a modern state, Finland; and forest workers and foresters from the Maine woods of the United States. We look at the perspectives of people who dwell in the afforested regions, and their interaction with the larger scientific, managerial or bureaucratic personnel. The background issues are spelled out in chapter 2.

In chapter 3, Savyasaachi provides a rich ethnographic description of an alternative system of knowledge. This is the integrated social, cultural and economic life of the Hill Maria, a tribe living in the area called Abujhmarh in Bastar District, located in east-central India, in the state of Madhya Pradesh whose tropical deciduous and semi-evergreen forests are one of the two largest concentrations of forests in India.[3] Tribes here show only a minimal degree of assimilation into the modern world-view; although their cultural integrity is threatened by the recent government-led programme of rural development, they have responded to it with active as well as passive resistance. Savyasaachi brings out the irony in a situation where the dominant knowledge system allows the government to brand the indigenous system as inefficient and environmentally destructive when all evidence points in exactly the opposite direction.

In chapter 4, Ramachandra Guha presents an example of a malign encounter between modern and alternative knowledge systems, the former inefficiently represented by the state forest department and the latter immanent in the protests and actions of the residents of Uttarakhand region — a part of the Indian state of Uttar Pradesh wedged between Nepal and Kashmir in the foothills of the Himalayas. The subtropical pine and oak forests of this area have been managed by the Indian government for over a hundred years. Many local people have shifted to other occupations, some of them working as migrant labourers in the major urban centres of the country. In this period the area has had to reckon with several features and consequences of modernity: mass media, schools, roads, tourists, etc. Yet this area is the birthplace of one of the most well known environmental movements in the world, the Chipko ('hug the tree') Movement which began in 1973 with protests by local women against the wanton destruction of forests by the state bureaucrats and forest contractors, and has since spread to many other parts of the country.[4]

Once again, although the protesters' arguments and demands were far sounder ecologically and revealed a history of effective local management before the institution of state control, the government consistently blamed the local population for the destruction, and has sought to place restrictions upon their use of the forest. Guha sees the emergence of the Chipko Movement as a response to three sets of (interrelated) factors: the demand for peasant access to forests; the limits of scientific forestry and the nature of state–peasant relationship; and the fragmentation of the village community as a result of commercial penetration. The connection between the three factors is important because, in Guha's words, it underscores an 'alternate model of environmentally sustainable and socially just economic development ... whose relevance is *scarcely* restricted to Uttarakhand'.

What unites the first two cases is the denigration and marginalisation of the world-views of local communities by modernising groups, mainly government bureaucrats and commercial entrepreneurs. The third situation, examined by Jukka Oksa, differs from the first two in that it can be termed a benign encounter between alternative knowledge systems. Oksa looks at the Forest Karelia region of Finland where popular resistance and state regulation have combined to maintain relatively favourable environmental conditions. Although Finnish society is modernised in all its outward forms, local rural communities have managed to preserve a good deal of their political vitality. Their world-views, articulated through social and political mobilisation, continue to exert significant pressure on national political decision making.

Oksa documents the resistance on the part of smallholder farmers-cum-lumberjacks to the industrialisation of agriculture and forestry. This shift took place remarkably late in Finland compared to the rest of Europe — in the 1960s and early 1970s — and displaced such a large number of people to the cities in the south that it is referred to as the 'Great Move'. A decay of social and cultural life occurred in the countryside, as the cohesion of the local communities and larger kinship networks was severely damaged. Consequently there was no alternative but greater reliance on the state in all matters, including those related to forest management, where competing interests — particularly those of powerful forest industries — had a greater influence.

Village residents, although reduced in number, have tried to resist adverse actions through political and social organisations — in the form of village committees — and while they have not been successful in stemming the tides of change, the result of their efforts is that Finnish society, as well as the state, still exhibit a strong commitment to the ideal of sustained yield forestry and multiple use of forests, and a resistance to commercial exploitation with its short time horizon. However mitigated, this political strength of Finnish villagers contrasts favourably with the weakness of the American Indian tribes in the United States and the hill tribes in India. Both these groups have been readily sacrificed at the altar of economic development by governments and social groups contemptuous of alternative ways of relating to nature or to other human beings.

Lastly, David Vail provides an example of an internal conflict within the modern system of knowledge. He examines the Maine forests in the United States where, unlike India or Finland, the original local communities, eliminated by European settlers, were replaced by people who shared the modern, instrumentalist world-view. As a result, environmental conflicts in this society have been, as it were, within the same family. Conservationist movements have only recently begun to challenge the seven paper corporations that own almost half of the land, which have for half a century practised policies of 'mining and neglect' that have led to a severe degradation of forest resources.

Vail finds that the Maine timber industry is in a crisis because of past and current actions in which short-run profit considerations systematically prevailed over longer-run concerns. Neither the government nor the social scientists or other academics have succeeded in regulating or challenging these practices because of the political dominance of industrial groups in the area. The result is, he concludes, that 'the dominant system of knowledge in Maine forestry ... stands as a warning rather than a model to Third World nations'. Despite all this, an ecological consciousness similar to that in India (or among the indigenous Amerindian inhabitants of the Americas) has not emerged among Maine foresters. Vail attributes this to the existence of common values of individualism, materialism, self-employment and independence, and a strong property rights orientation among forest workers as well as corporations. The shared system of knowledge also conditions the reach and impact of new technologies and conceptual systems such as scientific forestry.

A note on methodology

The four case studies collected here complement each other in more than one way. Indeed, we believe that because of this complementarity the volume has to be read in its entirety to get the full flavour of the argument. An important source of complementarity emerges from differences in the analytical approaches adopted in the different studies. This is an important point that merits elaboration.

Since our focus is on systems of knowledge, the purpose of the analysis is to bring out the interplay of conflicting systems in a society. These can find expression in a variety of forms, and need to be captured through a variety of methods. The four examples presented in this volume are: (a) an alternative system of knowledge, explicated through an ethnographic and linguistic study of different communities inhabiting the same space; (b) the 'malign encounter', articulated in the form of a sociological analysis of the collective vision implicit in the protest movements of otherwise heterogeneous groups; (c) the 'benign encounter', described in the form of a political-historical analysis in a case where conflicting visions are harmonised by the state; and (d) the 'internal conflict' within modernity, namely the analysis of conflicts based on divergent interests of modern social classes.

Although every concrete situation is a mosaic of these conflicts, one dimension will dominate others and suggest the appropriate analytical approach. For example, in every society including even the most modern ones, local groups tend to possess alternative (and often 'non-modern') conceptions of reality. Even the most heterogeneous groups can articulate a common vision through the medium of popular social movements or, when the state plays a role in harmonising these visions, through normal political channels. Finally, class conflicts may represent not only competing interests but also alternative visions of the good society. Yet, for analytical purposes, it will be found appropriate to focus only on one of these conflicts.

An example may be useful here. In, say, the case of Maine, four different studies could be undertaken. The first would be an ethnographic-linguistic exercise to explicate the knowledge system of the Maine woodsmen: how they perceive their relationship to the forest and to the larger society, and how these perceptions differ from those of corporate executives, state bureaucrats or conservationist activists. A sociological examination of a conflict situation could reveal, through the behaviour of, say, conservationist groups, the vision which lies behind their actions. Historical analyses on the role of the state in co-ordinating and mediating conflicting interests and visions in the situation of a 'benign encounter' would be equally feasible. So would the study of an internal conflict, namely the conflict between competing class interests of foresters and forest corporations. While all these studies are possible, David Vail's choice in chapter 6 of the last-mentioned option seems to make the most sense from a systems-of-knowledge perspective, since it would help bring out the dominant issues of the construction and use of knowledge. Similar arguments could be made about the other four chapters.

Thus the four case studies present four different cases as well as four different methods of approaching the study of the subject. It cannot be overemphasised that underlying this overt difference is a similarity in terms of the real subject matter of the book, namely the relationship between knowledge and power. Each study constitutes a different entry point for approaching the other studies in the volume, and provides clues for additional inferences which could be drawn from the evidence contained there.

Systems of knowledge

To reiterate, this volume is premised on the view that conflicts between systems of knowledge can lead to observed social dysfunctioning. To pursue this idea further, it is important to clarify some definitional questions.

The concept represented in the phrase 'systems of knowledge' comes from an extensive literature in philosophy and anthropology going back at least to Max Weber and Friedrich Nietzsche, and in some respect to Immanuel Kant. The expression 'systems of knowledge' is in the plural to signify that there are multiple ways of defining reality; this is not meant to evoke a multiplicity of *domains* of knowledge (like economics, anthropology, and so forth); rather it refers to a multiplicity of *communities* of knowledge. From this perspective, indigenous and modern communities are not just different political groups aiming to maximise their income or wealth, but embody different systems of knowledge, different ways of understanding, perceiving, experiencing, in sum, of defining reality, which includes the notions of one's relationship not only to the social milieu but also to the natural environment.

Moreover, the expression is meant to refer not only to knowledge self-consciously explicated but also to knowledge which is implicit in all action.[5] The 'knowledge' part of the expression implicitly recognises that all forms of human activity have a cognitive content. The 'systems' part of the expression indicates that human thought and action (or thought in action) is not random.

The dominant modern or scientific knowledge system, though not exclusively Western, enjoys its domination because of certain assumptions deeply rooted in Western civilisation. These assumptions, being background phenomena, remain mostly invisible and are taken for granted and unquestioned. The contrast with various indigenous systems of knowledge reveal these invisible foundational assumptions and allow us to look at them critically. Our contention is that the environmental crisis has emerged precisely because a central element of these invisible assumptions is an instrumental attitude towards nature. This is in sharp contrast with those components of the perspectives and beliefs of indigenous societies which, by imbuing nature with sacredness, allow a relatively more harmonious coexistence. The logic of this argument is demonstrated very clearly by an analysis of the examples provided by the four case studies in this volume.

The first step of the argument relies primarily on Savyasaachi's rendition of the life of the Hill Maria to bring out the contrast between an indigenous system of knowledge and the modern knowledge system familiar to us from many sociological writings. The discussion is not meant to imply that every characteristic of the Hill Maria's world-view will be found in all non-modern societies; indeed, the chief contrast between these two types of knowledge is the plurality of one and the monism of the other. Nor, to reiterate a point made earlier, is it the contention that these characteristics are wholly absent from Western societies. The point is that in so-called modern societies, the knowledge described here as indigenous or local is viewed as inferior and retrogressive. We shall dwell only on those characteristics which define modern knowledge, namely disembeddedness, universality, individualism, mobility and a dichotomy between the subject and object.[6]

This, however, is not enough. Showing that a remote hill tribe has a benign world-view solves only a part of the problem. While it does allow us to argue that the tribe be allowed to pursue its own lifestyle without unnecessary interference by the state or other modernising groups, it does not say anything about the possibility or desirability of transferring this model elsewhere. Such a lifestyle may not necessarily be acceptable to a majority of the world's people. Even if it *were* acceptable in principle, it is not clear whether or how it could in practice be transferred wholesale to an existing community. Our argument, however, goes further than the claim that the Hill Maria also know how to deal with nature, perhaps better than we do, and that therefore they should be left alone. Our claim is that these alternative perspectives exist everywhere, albeit in somewhat circumscribed, degraded and disregarded forms. They are exhibited in a variety of ways, most prominently in protest efforts such as those of the Chipko volunteers in Uttarakhand or of the forest villagers of Sivakka in Finland. The alternative systems of knowledge do not have to be created out of whole cloth; what needs to be done is to allow them to exist, and to accord them the respect and legitimacy they deserve.

It is instructive to note here that in both cases mentioned above the women of the area were in the forefront of the struggle. This is not surprising, since the conservation of local knowledges and systems of value in modernising societies is generally believed to have been entrusted to women who are often viewed as the source of cultural continuity in society.

Embeddedness

Most descriptions of traditional knowledge systems emphasise the fact that they are embedded in the social, cultural and moral milieu of their particular community. In other words, actions or thoughts are perceived to have social, political, moral and cosmological implications, rather than possessing only, say, a purely technical dimension. This observation will apply in equal measure to questions of agricultural production, household work, social functions and rituals, among others. It will thus be difficult for a farmer to describe farming activity in purely technical or economic terms, even if farming does involve the making of economic and technical decisions.

By contrast, the modern system of knowledge seeks to distinguish very clearly between these different dimensions. Technical questions pertain to cause-and-effect relations in the natural environment, and can coexist with many different social, moral, political or cosmological contexts. The productivity of land does not have anything to do with whether it is being tilled by a co-operative group, by plantation workers or by family labour; nor with whether these people are morally virtuous or otherwise.

The authors of this volume provide several examples of an embedded world-view. Savyasaachi presents many detailed descriptions. He shows that community rituals are the activities that regenerate — or reproduce — the social group. These are synchronised with the times when the forest regenerates itself in the fields and the earth recuperates its fertility. The Hill Maria make clearings in the forest in which they plant various food grains. After a cultivation season they let the forest regenerate on the field for a period of six years; a process which regenerates the fertility of the soil. Just as the women at their menses lie fallow and stop all activities, the earth lies fallow too for regular periods of time. The cycles of fallow and productivity of the fields through the regeneration of the forest are like the periodicity of women, the fallow/menstrual time being the guarantor of fertility. Wilderness and non-productivity are necessary to domesticity and fertility/productivity.

Examples from other chapters reinforce this. For example, the use of religious and social symbolism by Chipko activists in talking about economics and ecology is an example of the fact that the realms of social science and religion are not separate in the world-view of the Himalayan highlanders.

An extremely interesting example comes from Jukka Oksa. This is the contrast between the perspectives of farmers from a modern farming village, Rasimäki, and those from a traditional forestry workers' village, Sivakka, both in northeastern Karelia in Finland. In 1975, when population losses from the rural areas were most alarming, women from these two villages participated in a nationwide television programme about the fate of the villages. What was interesting was the different way in which the women of the two villages represented their views. The first group formulated their position in terms of politics, by raising sharp and sometimes angry questions to government officials, but the second group expressed themselves by presenting poems, songs and skits to bring out the 'poverty culture' of the villages. To us, this difference is a striking example of the differences in response to the same situation from a disembedded and an embedded perspective respectively. The second group, it seems to us, were unwilling to conceive of their situation in purely political or economic terms since, for them, these realms were not distinct from the larger cultural context. Note that it is not the case that one group presented the relevant information and the other did not; indeed, both groups were judged by observers to have been very effective in their endeavour. But each of them presented their respective positions in the way which made sense to them.

Embeddedness has another connotation as well, namely the perception of different realms of social life in analogous terms. For example, the Hill Maria see the regeneration of productive land in the forest in the same terms as the regeneration of social life in the village. In the fallow period, the land is unproductive and barren, but the fallowness is also a sign of fertility and the regeneration of productivity. This time corresponds to a fallow period of productivity, when there is no social co-operation in production. However, it is in this very same period that rituals and festivals help to regenerate social relations and thus to restore productivity and fertility. The pace and rhythm of both these sets of activities are governed by the same ritual calendar. Lastly, the villagers see both social and physical regeneration of fertility in terms analogous to the effect of menstruation, which is at the same time the sign of barrenness (or fallowness) and of the regeneration of fertility.

The interlinking of different realms of experience helps make social knowledge accessible to popular control; it also makes it much more difficult to isolate and change something on purely technical grounds. Modern knowledge separates itself into distinct domains mainly on the grounds that this increases efficiency by enhancing the ability to introduce new technology without worrying about its impact on social relations and moral considerations. It is now being realised that built into these external considerations were a set of restraints which helped conserve the social and physical environment for generations. In the past such views were treated with condescension and called mystical, primitive and non-rational. But built into these views was the understanding that human life ultimately rests on all life on earth, that it is cradled within it. What the American Indian Chief Seattle said in 1855 about the relations between man and the beasts could equally be said about humans and trees: 'What is man without the beasts? If all the beasts were gone, men would die from great loneliness of spirit, for whatever happens to the beasts happens also to the man.'[7]

Contextuality

An important consequence of an embedded lifestyle and knowledge system is the contextuality of local knowledge. Unlike modern knowledge, which bases its claim to superiority on the basis of universal validity, local knowledge is bound by time and space, by contextual and moral factors. More importantly, it cannot be separated from larger moral or normative ends. In order to make knowledge universally applicable and valid it is necessary to disembed it from a larger epistemic framework which ties it to normative and social ends. Technical knowledge thus separated from a larger social and environmental context does become universally applicable. Context is local — it anchors technical knowledge to a particular social group living in a particular setting at a particular time. To value universally applicable technical knowledge over local knowledge in which technical know-how is inseparable from larger normative, social and environmental contexts leads one necessarily to deny local human communities the right to continuity.

An important consequence of universal knowledge is a form of bureaucratisation. Once knowledge is meant to be universally applicable, it begins to gravitate into the hands of experts or professionals whom George Bernard Shaw once accused of 'conspiring against the laity'. The interest of the experts in acquiring, creating, promoting or acting upon the basis of such knowledge is increasingly motivated by internal professional considerations, rather than by normative social implications. In fact, under these circumstances, the activity can often become an end in itself and become unmoored even from its narrow technical objectives.

As an example, consult the discussion of the government-sponsored switch from shifting to settled agriculture among the Hill Maria. The prior beliefs of government experts in the separation of forestry from agriculture (in order to facilitate control), and in the economic and other advantages of rice farming, made it impossible for them to see the overall degradation of the environment for which presumably they were responsible, not to mention the impoverishment of the Hill Maria whom they were trying to help. On the contrary, these failures seemed to strengthen them in their conviction that the real obstacles to improvement were the irrational tribals. In other words, the professionals had become alienated even from their narrow economic goals, not to speak of the larger social objectives such as an improvement in the quality of life for the hill tribes.

David Vail has also noted implicitly such a bureaucratisation of knowledge. He criticises experts from Forest Schools for defending and legitimising such industrial practices as clear-cutting and pesticide spraying, despite their demonstrated dangers. Similarly, Ramachandra Guha mentions the role of the experts in the Indian government's forestry department, in allowing and defending a veritable rape of forestry resources over the period of a century.

Individualism

The above aspects of the modern system of knowledge have a counterpart in the psychological sphere in the form of the rise of a profound individualism as a basic value. To illustrate the consequence of this change, we can contrast the use and meaning of the first-person pronoun in the following two statements:

> The sun, the moon, the air, the trees are signs of my continuity ... I was born a part of the Bhum [the world of the Hill Maria]. I will die when this Bhum dies ... I was born with all others in this Bhum; I go with them. That which has created us all will give us food. If there is so much variety and abundance in Bhum, there is no reason for me to worry about food and continuity. [Hill Maria elder, quoted in chapter 3].

> I'm just a machine. I sleep, eat and work ... I'm about the dullest guy my wife's ever met. [Maine logger, quoted in chapter 6].

These quotes capture very succinctly the shift from a situation in which the person's sense of self is embedded in his local context (both social and cosmological) to an individualistic — in this particular case, defeated — sense of self. Such a transformation requires a concomitant shift from a context-sensitive, non-abstract, non-impersonal knowledge system to a context-free, abstract and impersonal knowledge system.

Disembedding the person from his social and natural environment is a precondition for the ability to act in order to maximise one's agricultural productivity. To label such behaviour 'progressive' or 'advanced' or 'modern' is to assume, for example, that material improvement is obviously superior to one's identity as a member of a local community. Similarly, to assume that spending time, energy and resources on marriages, funeral feasts and communal rituals is improvident and irrational is to assume that the 'I' is a separate entity whose reason for existing is productivity. The seeming superiority of these assumptions derives from the dominance of a particular Western-bred world-view, not from their inherent values. Yet, more and more problems are being discovered precisely with this way of looking at the world. According to the American sociologist Robert Bellah and his collaborators, it is precisely the dominance of this type of individualism which is responsible for a score of ills in US society, from an alarmingly high — and increasing — rate of suicide and schizophrenia among the teenage and adult population to urban violence and decay, and the plight of the elderly.[8]

Such a shift has the effect of disintegrating the strength of communities and their life-supporting systems. By atomising these communities into a collection of maximising individuals and by transforming life-supporting systems into natural resources, the outside forces which bring these changes into being create the space necessary for their own operations. If the local people stay and survive, they become mere instruments in the functioning of these impersonal forces, for their strength lay in their communities and their life-supporting systems. When these are eroded, only atomised individuals remain whose time and energies are wholly devoted to the strategies of personal survival within the constraints imposed by outside forces. Yet, as we have seen, these changes are resisted by local communities of long standing. We shall return to the theme of resistance in the concluding section of this chapter.

Subject/object dichotomy

This change in the sense of the self is also related to the perception of nature. If we go back to the statement made by the tribal elder, we can put our finger on this change. For the Hill Maria, the Bhum is the total universe; it is the sky, the forest, the fields in the forest and the social structures of the villages with their clans. There is no separation between nature and culture. As Savyasaachi puts it, 'nature or ecology or environment is not a separate category in Hill Maria social-cultural life'. This, of course, is not the same as saying that the Hill Maria make no distinction between virgin forest, cultivated fields or village space; they do, as the terms *gera* (the fields and the forest) and *nage* (the village space and activities) indicate, but in ways very different from the rational scientific knowledge system. What contrasts most markedly with the modern world-view is the absence of a subject/object dichotomy in the system of thought, the absence of a separation between the observer from what s/he observes, or of the splitting of the universe into 'mere subjectivity' and 'real objectivity'. The elder thinks of his life as inseparable from the life of his universe. The universe lives as he and all other Hill Maria live. He speaks of his life not as the life span of an individual but as the collective life span of a people and their world. The fate of the elder is indissolubly tied to the fate of the group and of their world — 'nature', the forest, are the very conditions of their existence. By contrast, the ideology of 'mastery over nature' is predicated upon a clear separation between nature and culture, the thinking subject having mastery over an unthinking and passive object. There is both separation and hierarchalisation. Such an assumption is necessary if one is to exploit natural resources, rather than attune individual and collective rhythms to the periodicities of the cosmos.

Mobility and commitment

Perhaps the modern value most relevant for a discussion of environmental conservation is that of mobility. While it can be seen to be the consequence of individualism and the instrumental attitude to nature, mobility has acquired the status of one of the highest human values in its own right; it has almost become a fetish. To paraphrase Karl Marx, the modern conception of utopia is the freedom to 'hunt in the morning in Kenya, fish in the afternoon in the Baltic, rear cattle in the evening in Texas, and to criticise after dinner in New York, just as he has a mind'.

The modern elevation of mobility to the highest value is evidenced in the massive and continuing migrations within and across countries that are a universal feature of capitalist society today. These migrations occur not only for the desire for economic progress, or the need to escape from political oppression, but also because life in the village, life at home, has become meaningless. The action is somewhere else, and only the defeated and the cowardly stay behind.[9] The commitment to one's environment necessary to prevent or restrict such a move has eroded and, in many modern societies, does not exist at all. In turn, the move itself erodes the commitment to the environment as a unique and irreplaceable place.

For the Hill Maria, who see the Bhum as their universe, this attitude is scarcely to be believed. To substitute another place of living for their present one is analogous, perhaps, to the desire to substitute another arm for one's own, or someone else's best friend for one's own. It is simply inconceivable. A poignant statement which brings out this incredulity very forcefully was made by an elder of the Krenak, an Indian tribe in Brazil. He was protesting against the take-over of their tribal lands by the government for a development project. He said:

When the government took our land in the valley of the Rio Doce, they wanted to give us another place somewhere else. But the state, the government will never understand that we do not have another place to go.

The only possible place for the Krenak people to live and to re-establish our existence, to speak to our Gods, to speak to our nature, to weave our lives is where God created us. It is useless for the government to put us in a very beautiful place, in a very good place with a lot of hunting and a lot of fish. The Krenak people, we continue dying and we die insisting that there is only one place for us to live.

My heart does not become happy to see humanity's incapacity. I have no pleasure at all to come here and make these statements. We can no longer see the planet that we live upon as if it were a chess-board where people just move things around. We cannot consider the planet as something isolated from the cosmic.[10]

For the Hill Maria, and for the Krenak, the land — their place of living — is irreplaceable. It cannot be substituted for something of equal or greater value because it is not a question of value at all. For the modern individual, it is often only a question of competing values. When Alexis de Tocqueville called Americans 'real estate speculators at heart' he could have been talking about most modern urban people for whom land is not land, but real estate. Nothing is unique or irreplaceable. Everything is a commodity, with its market value which determines what compensation is adequate for its disappearance.

To substitute for this loss, modern society has sought to replace it with the managerial ethic of control. Thus, it could be said that individuals in modern society love nature only in the abstract, while the inhabitants of traditional societies love it only in the concrete; they love only a particular piece of land. The replacement of the love for the concrete with a love of the abstract is, however, an inadequate compensation. No one in modern societies protects their own environment, because that would be a matter of trade-offs, compensation and valuation. People are supposed to protect only the environment in general and mobilise a campaign, now and then, over a particular issue. Even then there are no incentives for individuals to act in this manner.

This can be stated differently. It is well known in economic theory that if everybody behaved in a 'rational' manner, the public goods problem would be insoluble. Since the protection of the environment is a public goods problem, it is adversely influenced by the unfettering of rationality which takes place with development. The solution of some form of public control or regulation, such as scientific forestry, is also problematic because the controllers too have an instrumental attitude towards the environment. Their concern is motivated not by an identification with the forest as an extension of their own life, but simply by a view of the forest as a source of raw materials or touristic pleasure. Thus, at best, modern society replaces a passionate commitment to protect the environment, with a rational or strategic interest in a source of gratification. This 'substitution of ratiocination for feeling', to use Anthony Burgess's phrase, is likely to be rendered ineffective either because of inadequate knowledge or because of the pressure of conflicting objectives such as high revenue demand from the government, short-run profit considerations and so forth.

Modernity and the environment

We have identified some distinctions between indigenous and modern systems of knowledge, and argued that the characteristic features of the former are also to be found in modernising societies, such as rural Finland or India. The next step is to show the relationship of systems of knowledge to environmental health.

Individualism directly implies the emergence of an instrumental attitude towards the environment, the emergence of that 'loveless disregard for things', as Theodor Adorno called it, which necessarily turns against people too. The environment, social or natural, becomes either the source of gratification for the individual, or a constraint to such gratification. In either case, it has to be manipulated and controlled. Protection of the environment ceases to be a value, and becomes mere strategy. The other aspects of modernisation — disembeddedness, universality, subject/object dichotomy and the estimation of mobility — further facilitate this process.

A new dialogue with nature

The creation of a dichotomy between subject and object has resulted in the 'de-souling' of nature, to use the psychologist James Hillman's felicitous phrase.[11] It has enabled us to look at nature as if it were a passive, inert object, which could be acted upon with abandon. As Ilya Prigogine, the 1977 Nobel prize winner in chemistry, and Isabelle Stengers have argued in a recent book:

> Modern science is based on the discovery of a new and specific form of communication with nature — that is, on the conviction that nature responds to experimental interrogation ... [but] the first outcome of this dialogue was the discovery of a silent world ... [Classical] science ... revealed to men a dead, passive nature, a nature that behaves as

an automaton which, once programmed, continues to follow the rules inscribed in the program.[12]

Prigogine and Stengers go on to argue that this 'de-souling' of nature derives essentially from science's denial of time and complexity, the assumption that nature is governed by universal, timeless and simple laws which can be understood by technicians in the same manner as they understand the working of machines. This assumption is belied by recent developments in science as the essential elements of randomness and irreversibility[13] in nature are being discovered.[14] This is leading to a new view in which matter is no longer a passive substance but is associated with spontaneous activity. 'This change is so profound,' say Prigogine and Stengers, 'that we can really speak about a new dialogue of man with nature.'[15] Scientific forestry, it may be remarked, has all the ingredients of the classical science criticised by Prigogine and Stengers, most notably the claims of simplicity and reversibility, claims which were rejected in indigenous modes of knowing, and which are belatedly being discovered to be significant sources of the environmental crisis.

As may be obvious, the treatment of nature as a passive object is facilitated by the disembeddedness of knowledge from its social and moral contexts. The protective ring which local practices had placed around the forest is broken once the knowledge of nature becomes separable from the knowledge of the individual, of the society and of the cosmos. Once restraint becomes illegitimate and excess laudable, the desire to protect nature also becomes suspect, and has to be justified by purely instrumental arguments.

A preservationist attitude towards nature is invariably associated with a non-rational or a trans-economic commitment to a particular piece of land, be it a house, a homestead, a tree or a forest. The modern virtue of mobility weakens this commitment and therefore weakens the effort needed to preserve it against the depredations of humans themselves. But, then, this commitment to the environment derives, among other things, from the very continuity of collective social life in a particular environment, and is a problem for modern life because it is full of such discontinuities. For this reason it is necessary to challenge not only the instrumental values of modernity, but also the virtue of an ancillary value such as geographical mobility. Undoubtedly, the passionate commitment to new environments will also develop among migrant urban populations the world over, but perhaps not immediately. It may require several generations of continuous relationship with a physical environment before people begin to see it as a part of the continuity of their own life. 'The wrinkles of centuries,' as Victor Hugo once wrote, 'are not extemporised.'

The only long-run solution is a continuous questioning of the instrumental attitude towards nature, of the values which underlie modern society, and of the goals which have been used to legitimise these values. This is by no means an easy task, but it is not an impossible one either; it is already being done in many places and in many different ways. Environmental movements, whether in the North or in the South, base their appeal on such a questioning. Many women's movements also stress the importance of 'women's ways of knowing' which often have a non-instrumental core. The anti-nuclear and peace movements in the West also take issue with rationality and scientific thinking. These forms of questioning, like peasant protests, place limits on the modern enterprise of industrialisation, individualism and universalisation.

Many people have raised these issues in the context of the environmental crisis, and particularly in regard to the need for empowering local forest-based communities, often explicitly from alternative perspectives. Our task here is to reveal the rationality behind these protests and to contrast them to the rationality of the dominant modern system of knowledge. This is what this book is about.

Conclusions

The conclusions which emerge from the above discussion can be summarised fairly quickly. They fall into three categories: political, economic and cultural. The first conclusion is a political one, namely the importance of transferring power to local communities, from whom it has slowly been expropriated over the last two centuries. The earlier transfer of power to commercial and bureaucratic interests has in large part been harmful for social relations as well as environmental health in these areas. Effective decentralisation would ameliorate some of the ill-effects of the past and create the basis for a more benign pattern of change in the future.

Decentralisation of power would also be helpful in providing new solutions to the problem of population growth. Local communities, aware of the immediate environmental consequences of their actions, are more likely to find innovative solutions which would allow them to coexist harmoniously with the environment. Centralised actions have not only been ineffective in this respect, they have also been introduced through violence or disinformation, with inevitable ill-effects on social and communal relations.[16]

The second major conclusion is an economic one, namely the need to question the imperatives of modern technology, particularly in the area of forestry and agriculture. Several recent initiatives have sought to introduce alternative perspectives into technological research and innovation, e.g. eco-farming, agro-forestry, the replacement of chemical-based agriculture technology with organic farming methods; applications of these concepts show that the alternatives might be superior to modern methods even in terms of yield. There is a need to shift the focus of research away from modern agriculture or forestry towards these alternative methods. This would be ecologically superior in the long run, lead to better health of the environment as well as the people, and produce technology and social relations in which local communities would have more power.

However, the most important consequence of the above discussion is in the cultural sphere, namely its implication for the debate over modern and non-modern systems of knowledge. It is not only a question of political empowerment or appropriate technology, though these are important questions in their own right. The larger issue subsuming the other two is that the modern system of knowledge is harmful for human society in the long run. The political as well as economic questions are contained within the cultural question because, when all is said and done, the question is that of the relationship between humans and the natural environment, one which has been asked from time immemorial. The modern interpretation of this relationship is based on the axiom of unlimited human potential for control or mastery over nature. It follows reductionist methods of analysis. In this view nature is segmented into parts, a problematic procedure since nature is an endless cycle. Reductionism, as many writers have argued, leads to excess, violence, exclusion and repression. Its belief is that this is the only valid form of knowing and everything else is superstition, obscurantism and irrationality. This way of thinking provides both the desire to control nature and the belief that it is possible, even moral to do so. It has certainly had its share of success, which is the source of its continued dominance and legitimacy, but the successes have come at a high cost, the extent of which we are just beginning to fathom.

Alternative perspectives reject this way of thinking and search for sustainable development in a redefinition of humans' relationship to nature as one of harmony or stewardship rather than of conquest or mastery, in the abandonment of reductionist methods of analysis and understanding, and in the recognition of the legitimacy and importance of pluralist definitions of reality. It is these which need to be legitimised and acknowledged.

The fox, it is said, knows many things, but the hedgehog knows one big thing. The modern system of knowledge, like the fox, has many strengths, as even its worst critics would be willing to admit, but it has at least one flaw, a potentially fatal one: that in its wish to master nature it is slowly but surely destroying the basis of life upon this planet. The traditional systems of knowledge may not know many of these small things, but they were designed to ensure survival of human and other life forms upon this planet, and to maintain a respectful and dignified relation between humans and other life forms; like the hedgehog, they know one big thing, and that may be the thing we need today. A. N. Whitehead once said that in the mechanistic world-view, the world had got hold of an idea which it could neither live with nor live without; one is tempted to add that unless it learns to live without it, it may not be around much longer to live with it.

Notes

1. World Commission on Environment and Development 1987: 114–16, 146–67.
2. This project was supported by and carried out under the auspices of the World Institute for Development Economics Research (WIDER) in Helsinki, an affiliate of the United Nations University.
3. Madhya Pradesh is also the home of the 44 million '*adivasis*' (original inhabitants), who have succeeded in maintaining a distinct lifestyle by virtue of their isolation from the more settled parts of the country.
4. Sunderlal Bahuguna, one of the two major leaders of the Chipko Movement, is actively spreading the ecological message across the country. Other organisations with similar aims have emerged in other parts of India, including for example the Appiko (which also means 'to hug') in Karnataka in 1983. For details, see Center for Science and Environment (CSE) 1985: 84. For an excellent description and analysis of the Chipko Movement, see Guha 1990 and Shiva 1989.
5. For a discussion of 'systems of knowledge' and related issues see especially chapters 1–4 and 7 in Apffel Marglin and Marglin 1990.
6. For a more detailed discussion of the difference between modern and local knowledge, see Banuri 1990: 43–5.
7. Statement made on the purchase of land by the US government in 1855. Quoted in Brown 1986.
8. See Bellah *et al.* 1985.
9. In the literature on migration, this is known as the 'city lights' argument, as opposed to economic or political explanations of migration.
10. Quoted in World Commission on Environment and Development: 1987, 114.
11. See Hillman 1975: chapter 1.
12. Prigogine and Stengers 1984: 5–6. See also Merchant 1983, who makes a detailed and sophisticated argument that the scientific system of knowledge is about power and control, and hence has violence built into it.
13. Prigogine's interest in irreversibility arises in part from his extensive work on entropy, which has provided an alternate way of thinking to mechanics where everything is reversible. The latter provides the dominant metaphor for 'hard' social sciences such as economics. Related to irreversibility is the notion

of excess. Cutting down one tree may not be irreversible in an 'objective' sense, but clear-cutting the whole forest might be.

14. The physicist Herbert Bernstein has argued recently that the latest research in the hard sciences reveals that science is a discourse whose aim is consistency rather than 'truth'. See Bernstein 1987.

15. Ibid.: 9. Going by the Chipko and other experiences, this would more appropriately be entitled 'woman's dialogue with nature'.

16. Hartmann (1987: 91–125) argues on the basis of extensive research and careful documentation that the centralising bias of current population control strategies has had harmful economic, political, health and human rights consequences for the 'target' population.

Bibliography

Apffel Marglin, Frédérique and Stephen A. Marglin (eds) (1990), *Dominating Knowledge: Development, Culture and Resistance*, Oxford: Clarendon Press.

Banuri, Tariq (1990a), 'Development and the politics of knowledge', in Apffel Marglin and Marglin 1990.

Bellah, Robert and Richard Madsen, William M. Sullivan, Ann Swidler, Steven M. Tipton. (1985), *Habits of the Heart: Individualism and Commitment in American Life*, New York: Harper & Row.

Bernstein, Herbert J. (1987), 'Idols of modern science and the reconstruction of knowledge', in Marcus J. Raskin and Herbert J. Bernstein (eds), *New Ways of Knowing: The Sciences, Society, and Reconstructive Knowing*, Totowa, NJ: Rowman & Littlefield.

Brown, Aggrey (1986), 'Communication technology and development: ideological and technical imperative', paper presented at the XVth International Association for Mass Communication Research, General Assembly and Conference, New Delhi.

Center for Science and Environment (1982), *The state of India's Environment: the First Citizens' Report*, New Delhi.

—— (1985) *The state of India's Environment 1984–85: The Second Citizens' Report*, New Delhi.

Guha, Ramachandra (1990), *The Unquiet Woods*, Delhi: Oxford University Press.

Hartmann, Betsy (1987), *Reproductive Rights and Wrongs: the Global Politics of Population Control and Contraceptive Choice*, New York: Harper & Row.

Hillman, James (1975), *Re-visioning Psychology*, New York: Harper & Row.

Merchant, Carolyn (1983), *The Death of Nature*, Harper & Row.

Prigogine, Ilya and Isabelle Stengers (1984), *Order Out of Chaos: Man's New Dialogue With Nature*, New York: Bantam Books.

Shiva, Vandana (1989), *Staying Alive: Women, Ecology and Development in India*, London: Zed Books.

World Commission on Environment and Development (the Brundtland Commission) (1987), *Our Common Future*, Oxford: Oxford University Press.

2. The environmental crisis and the space for alternatives: India, Finland and Maine

Tariq Banuri and Frédérique Apffel Marglin

Introduction

In development studies, as in other areas of social science, different periods seem to be associated with the prominence of different problems. Economic growth, the key issue on the development agenda in the 1950s and the early 1960s, had been displaced by distribution and basic needs by the late 1960s, and these, in turn, by adjustment and debt less than a decade later. Already it seems clear that the central issue during the 1990s will be that of environmental conservation and sustainable development. This should scarcely be a source of surprise. Ecologists and environmentalists have been warning us for decades of a gathering crisis of global proportions, precipitated by the associated processes of industrialisation, urbanisation, modernisation and deforestation, and sanctioned by the contemporary combination of institutional arrangements, state policies and behavioural patterns. The cogency of these warnings has been amply demonstrated by the accumulating evidence of a rapid and perhaps irreversible deterioration of the planet's life-support systems.[1] Finally, it seems, people are beginning to wake up and take notice.

The intensity of the emerging crisis, coupled with the failure of several decades of development efforts to eradicate poverty or reduce inequalities, has challenged many fundamental tenets of modernisation theories and approaches. It has vindicated, on the incontrovertible grounds of sustainability of development, such supposedly 'normative' concerns as distributional equity, energy conservation, resource (particularly labour) compatibility, popular participation, social control of technology, decentralisation, self-reliance, social and economic stability, women's rights and the preservation of species and cultural diversity (Brundtland Report 1987: chapters 5–8). By drawing attention to these issues, it is changing the very definition of progress and development to include a strong preservationist plank, in other words, to 'sustainable' development. It has underscored the fact that economic concerns cannot be treated in isolation from social, moral and cultural issues.[2]

More importantly, it has provided the basis for a far-reaching critique of modern forms of knowledge, modern technology and modern social arrangements. Criteria of efficiency and mastery over nature, which have invariably been adduced as unequivocal and self-evident claims for the superiority of the rational and scientific knowledge system, have been greatly undermined by the threat that environmental degradation poses to the very continuity of life upon this planet. This is added to the fact that the supposedly mystical, irrational and inefficient knowledge systems of indigenous communities are being found to have often been much sounder ecologically than their modern counterparts.[3] As a result, there is now an opening for the unprejudiced examination of alternative development possibilities, including those practised in non-modern societies, instead of an exclusive and uncritical reliance on modern values and modern technology.

A major implication of this line of thinking is the recognition of the rich complexity of issues involved, and the costs of reducing them to a single dimension. It indicates that attention must be given to the moral and political aspects of the issues as well as to the purely economic ones. How a problem is to be defined is not only a cognitive question; it includes the political questions of who will do the defining, and whose definition counts. Moreover, since the rejection of alternative ways of defining a situation must entail cognitive and thus political domination of those whose definitions are disregarded, the issue has obvious moral implications.

The fact that non-modern technologies and social systems are generally dismissed as superstitious, backward and irrational despite the possibility of greater ecological soundness and sustainability than their modern counterparts, reveals the marginalising attitude of economistic analyses towards such moral and political issues. On the other hand, the discovery of this possibility provides support to the earlier, 'cultural ecology' argument, that the annihilation of cultures, like the annihilation of species, threatens the continuity of life in general. Culture, rather than instinct, bears the brunt of inter-generational knowledge transfer, so annihilation of those cultures that have learned to live in harmony with their environment destroys — maybe for ever — the knowledge of how to do so. It is also consistent with the fact that indigenous technologies exhibited a more pronounced embeddedness into their social and cultural milieu; and that such embeddedness, by instilling work with meaning, in ways that the fragmented nature of modern work arrangements seems to be incapable of doing, succeeded in minimising psychological problems emanating from the alienation and anomie of modern existence.[4]

Environment, participation and management

In the South the desire to protect and preserve the natural habitat was for a long time the sole preserve of peasant movements or fringe intellectuals.[5] Elites in the South dismissed these either as politically motivated actions to protect not habitats but incomes, or as irrational or superstitious activities which needed to be firmly extirpated. These élites often used the association of Western environmental movements with 'quality of life' questions — i.e. the impact of industrial pollution, urban blight and the destruction of natural resources on the quality of and opportunity for leisure activities (hiking, trekking, fishing, swimming and so forth) — to argue against the urgency of an environmental programme in their countries because economic growth, poverty eradication and 'catching up with the West' took precedence over such luxuries as the 'quality of human life'. The fact that most governments in the South base their legitimacy, at least in part, on the promise of rapid growth, also made it difficult for them to acknowledge doubts about the wisdom of these goals and policies.

This position, however, has become increasingly untenable in recent years, as it is becoming clear even to ardent developmentalists that, much more than its contribution to the quality of life, ecological health is necessary for the very sustainability of life upon this planet — and, by implication, even for the sustainability of the development process itself! Explicit recognition of this issue at the international level dates back at least to 1972, when the United Nations global conference on the human environment in Stockholm called for a closer link between long-run sustainability and economic growth and development.[6] Simultaneously, the publication of the Club of Rome Report (Meadows, et al. 1972) raised fresh concerns about the possible exhaustion of the earth's non-renewable natural resources.

Since then, environmental issues, instead of being dismissed with scepticism[7] if not outright hostility (among governments in the South at least), have become an inextricable component of the development debate. The United Nations has been particularly active in publicising these issues. The United Nations Environmental Programme (UNEP) was set up in December 1972 in response to the concerns expressed at the Stockholm conference. Most other UN agencies have started taking explicit account of the environmental dimensions of their decisions and recommendations. Most importantly, a committee under the leadership of Prime Minister Gro Harlem Brundtland of Norway was commissioned specifically to examine these issues in detail and to submit their report. The publication of this excellent report in 1987 has done much to raise international consciousness about the environmental threat.

Countries of the South have not only welcomed recent initiatives but have actually moved to the forefront of the struggle for the goal of sustainable development. Planners and policy makers in these countries are beginning to perceive environmental conservation not as an obstacle to economic development, but as a necessary accompaniment of sustained improvement in economic conditions (see, e.g., Runnals 1986.)

The dimensions of the environmental crisis itself are quite well known by now and need not be recounted here in any detail. Briefly, the problems with potentially global implications include: the deforestation around the globe, most alarmingly of the tropical rainforest belt, and the associated processes of desertification, de-vegetation, and soil erosion and sedimentation; loss of species and genetic diversity; the 'greenhouse' warming of the planet because of carbon dioxide emissions as well as tropical deforestation; depletion of non-renewable natural resources;[8] nuclear waste accumulation; acid rain caused by industrial pollution; depletion of the atmospheric ozone layer;[9] and large-scale destruction which can be unleashed by breakdowns of human or mechanical origin in fragile nuclear or chemical technologies.[10]

In contrast to the above, many, but not all, of the serious environmental problems in the South — such as urban pollution and congestion — are local in character because of the limited ability of these societies to impair global conditions. The most outstanding exceptions are the problems of deforestation which is taking place at a sufficiently massive scale, the shift towards monocultural forestry induced by new forestry arrangements (e.g. commercial orientation) and new forest technology (e.g. clear-cutting, mechanical harvesting), and other damage to forest resources and habitats. Besides this, there are the problematic aspects of Green Revolution technology (see, e.g., Glaeser 1987: chapter 1). These include inefficient use of and dependence upon fossil energy, soil degradation due to the use of chemical fertilisers, pesticide build-up in food products, emergence of pest strains resistant to common pesticides, and destruction of benign as well as malign life forms by the use of pesticides.[11] Another set of problems which have caused a great deal of alarm are the consequences of development projects, such as large dams and irrigation systems,[12] or modern livestock projects (see, e.g., Dyson-Hudson 1985).

Global problems caused by industrialisation are a major source of concern precisely because they lead to the questioning of the scientific world-view, as in the wisecrack attributed to John F. Kennedy that the reason that there was no life on other planets was that their scientists were more advanced than ours. Given that science and rationality are widely believed to be the hope of modern society, if a crisis is engendered by the unfettering of science itself, there is obvious room for concern.

Deforestation

The major example of environmental degradation in the South with potentially global consequences is the high rate of deforestation and degeneration of forest resources which has taken place with the emergence of substantial industrial and commercial demand for timber.[13] The Brundtland Report informs us that

> [t]he mature tropical forests that still exist cover only 900 million hectares out of the 1.5–1.6 billion hectares that once stood. Between 7.6 million and 10 million hectares are eliminated outright each year, and at least a further 10 million hectares are grossly disrupted annually. But these figures are from the 1970s, and since then deforestation rates have probably accelerated. (Brundtland Report 1987: 151)

There are fears that the tropical rainforest will disappear entirely by the year 2025 with disastrous consequences.

India lost 3.4 million hectares of forest between 1950 and 1972, and another 9.2 million hectares in the ten-year period between 1972–75 and 1980–82, leaving a total forest cover of only 46.35 million hectares (CSE 1982: 33; CSE 1985: 80). The high rate of deforestation in the Himalayan region of India is by now well known. Chapter 4 brings out the various adverse consequences for the local inhabitants: women have to walk as far as 15 kilometres to collect fuelwood and fodder, there is a greater incidence of flash floods, and there is a general impoverishment of the population. Chapter 3 describes how the government-sponsored switch from shifting millet cultivation to settled rice agriculture in Abujhmarh is destroying the regeneration of the forest on the farmland. Not only are the forests disappearing, local inhabitants report that the water table has dropped to 120 feet below the surface in the span of one generation. The peasants also state that there is only one monsoon nowadays in contrast to two monsoons in the past, but this is probably due to broader ecological processes.

That this is not purely a phenomenon in the South is evident from the emergence of analogous problems in Maine forestry. Chapter 6 reports that the future of these forests looks ominous as they enter their fourth rotation of commercial cutting. Much of the commercially valuable spruce fir forest has been clear-cut in the past twenty years or is stocked with mature, dead or dying trees. That means a glut of softwoods now and an inevitable decline in mature stands for many years beginning in the 1990s. The only exception to these trends are Finnish forests which are reported by Jukka Oksa to be in relatively good health, partly because of the opposition of local farmers to potentially destructive projects or plans of forest industries.

Table 2.1 Forest information on India, Finland and Maine

India	
Land area (thousand sq. km)	3,288
Forest area (million ha)	46.4
Forest cover (%)	
India as a whole	14
Uttarakhand	37
Bastar District	54
Ownership/control (%)	77
State (inc. parks)	17
Unmanaged forests	17
Plantations	6
Finland	
Land area (thousand sq. km)	338
Forest area (million ha)	26.4
Forest cover (%)	65
Ownership (%)	
Finland	
State	32.3
Industrial	7.6
Private	55.8
Forest Karelia	
State	34.4
Industrial	25.9
Private	36.8
Proportion of softwoods (%)	82
Maine	
Land area (thousand sq. km)	86
Forest area (million ha)	6.9
Forest cover (%)	74
Ownership (%)	
State	6
Industrial	47
Private	47
Proportion of softwoods (%)	65

Sources: India: CSE 1982, 1985; Finland: *Finland in Figures 1987*,;
Maine: Vail 1989.

India, Finland and Maine

Some comparative statistics on the forests in the three countries which form the subject of this volume are given in Table 2.1. Finland is almost four times the size of Maine in total area as well as in forest area (and in population as well), with a similar geo-climatic environment, although it is somewhat more to the north and has a slightly more extreme winter. Both have forest cover of over 60 per cent, consisting of spruces, firs and pines. The forest cover in the whole of India is much lower than in either of the two other regions and it is unevenly distributed, ranging from 50 to 60 per cent in the eastern parts of the country to less than 5 per cent in western areas. The forest department reported a forested area of 75 million hectares (22 per cent of the land area) but satellite data show the actual forest cover to be much lower (46 million hectares or 14 per cent) and to be considerably degraded. The two areas studied by the authors of this volume have relatively larger areas under forest cover: 37 per cent in the Uttarakhand region[14] and Bastar District.[15] While these densities are lower than those in Finland or Maine, the differences are not as significant as for the national averages.

The major differences between the three countries are in terms of the distribution of ownership, namely the much greater incidence of corporate ownership in Maine, a smaller but significant proportion in Forest Karelia, and the high level of state ownership and control in India and Finland. In India almost all the large forest areas are under state management.

India

In India, commercial exploitation of the forests is directly under the aegis of the state and has been so for over a century.[16] In the Himalayan region, commercial exploitation was begun by the colonial state during the period of railroad expansion (*c.* 1855 onwards) in order to procure lumber for railroad sleepers (or ties). Not only was this based explicitly on prevalent scientific wisdom, the colonial government actually invited German forestry experts for help. At the advice of these experts, the government nationalised one-fifth of the forest area and enacted legislation '[regulating] peasant access by restricting it to areas of forest not deemed commercially profitable' (see chapter 4) . Under this legislation, punitive sanctions were introduced against transgressors, and a forest department was set up to police the forests in addition to regulating tree-felling in the area brought under government supervision. Notwithstanding the reliance on scientific forestry and the sophisticated legal and bureaucratic infrastructure, the objective of the management remained commercial — i.e. to ensure a steadily increasing revenue to the state. After independence, the industrialisation bias of the post-colonial state further reinforced the objective of intensive resource exploitation.

Forest management is in the hands of a vast bureaucracy of the Forest Department. Every year the officials from this department mark a certain number of trees for cutting according to the regenerative potential of the forest and auction the work to the contractors, the proceeds being paid into the government treasury. The forest officials also police the forest area to ensure that the contractors do not exceed their allocation and that local villagers do not cut down trees illegally. In theory, these actions will result in a constant yield level, but in practice things are otherwise. Guha reports, in chapter 4, that the output of logged material often exceeds the increment to the forest stock because of lack of information, mismanagement or other factors. The contractors are politically and financially powerful enough to be able to bribe or intimidate the low-paid forestry staff, and there are frequent mentions of collusion between the two.

There are problems even in terms of the admitted objectives of the department. The ideal of sustained and commercially valuable yield often translates into the objective of converting mixed forests of conifers and broad-leaved trees into pure stands of commercially valuable conifers, often without taking wider ecological consequences into account. This is evidenced by the very language used to justify departmental priorities. Trees classified as 'valuable' are those which can be used commercially, while those labelled 'inferior' are trees which cannot be marketed. The contribution of these 'inferior' trees, such as oak or rhododendron, to the forest ecosystem or to the people living in or near the forest is ignored, and as a result these species are on the endangered list in Uttarakhand.[17] Notwithstanding the obvious long-run ecological consequences, such a redefinition enabled governments to designate customary users as enemies of the forest and thus to reinforce their own control.

In retrospect, it appears that the state willingly sacrificed the interests of the bulk of the rural population in the belief no doubt that the benefits of modernisation would trickle down to them. Instead of a trickle of riches coming down the mountain, the peasant population was hit by a series of disastrous floods and landslides beginning in the 1970s.[18] This added to the already existing burdens of massive deforestation and impoverishment due to restricted access to the forests and their resources. This was in an area which was described in a government report from the nineteenth century as 'probably better off than any peasantry in India'.[19]

The rural inhabitants were not slow in recognising the 'causal relationship between increasing erosivity and floods on the one hand, and mass scale felling of trees on the other' (chapter 4). Also, the forest is crucial to their survival as a source of fuelwood, medicine, food in time of agricultural dearth, and fodder (since they depend heavily on animal husbandry). The floods were the last straw which triggered a series of non-violent protests against tree fellings in which women took a leading part in hugging trees to prevent cutting.[20] This gave the name to the movement known as Chipko (hug the tree), begun in 1974 and still continuing today.

Savyasaachi's rich ethnographic description of the Hill Maria tribe provides further evidence of the harmful consequences of state intervention. The hill tribes had managed to conserve their forests for centuries through the practice of shifting millet cultivation, allowing the forest to regenerate itself during the extended fallow periods.[21] Inadequate environmental understanding or an inadequate empirical basis, coupled with the bias of scientific forestry towards the separation of forestry and agriculture, seems to have led government agencies to discourage shifting millet cultivation and to encourage settled rice agriculture.[22] This has turned out to be harmful, since after only two or three rice harvests the forest is unable to regenerate itself on the farmland. Government support has gone generally to non-tribal migrants who, although they share the ways and practices of the Hill Maria, have traditionally practised rice cultivation in selected areas, and are therefore willing to reap the advantages of the development programme by extending it to other areas.

Other contrasts between state actions and popular criticisms, unfavourable to the former, could be given. On the point of management, for example, it is instructive to compare the relative failure of the Indian government's forestry initiatives with the success of grassroots voluntary efforts (CSE 1985: 51–2, 61–2). While 85–90 per cent of the saplings planted by volunteer organisations like Chipko are said to survive, the government's afforestation programme claims a survival rate of only 25 per cent — and even this low figure has been challenged by some writers.[23]

The survival rate is said to be higher in the government-sponsored social forestry project in which tree saplings are distributed to farmers instead of being planted by forest department officials, but this programme has become very controversial on account of its adverse social and ecological consequences (CSE 1985: 51–71). A major object of criticism is the mass-scale planting of rapidly growing eucalyptus trees which, according to critics, have extremely harmful and unpredictable ecological effects (CSE 1985: 63–71). *The State of India's Environment* summarises the situation in the following words:

> Forest departments across [India] love [eucalyptus]: nearly half a million hectares have been brought under this exotic species and 80 percent of all seedlings distributed are eucalyptus. But with increasing vehemence, critics describe it as an 'ecological monster' which drains the water table, depletes the soil, prevents all other plants from growing underneath it, and makes cultivation on neighbouring lands impossible. (CSE 1982: 63)

Finland

Finland and Maine, as has been mentioned already, are quite similar in many respects, with the outstanding exception that at the national level very little of the Finnish forests are in the hands of companies, and a significant share is owned by the state. State direction of forestry practices exists, but it is through economic policies rather than through direct management as in India. In Karelia, which is the region of our interest, the distribution of property has greater similarities to Maine than to the rest of the country. Two companies, Gutzeit and Kaukas, own almost 30 per cent of the forest land, and the proportion of smallholders is correspondingly lower.

The successful management of forests in Finland, as described by Jukka Oksa, provides the only bright spot in the discussion of scientific forestry. Although the proportion of hardwoods in the forest has fallen because of selective regeneration, the overall health of the forest is stated to be reasonably good, partly because of the fact that, as in Maine, the demand for timber has always fallen short of the regenerative potential of the forest.

Scientific forestry ideas have influenced Finnish conditions mainly through their effect on academic and policy debates. German ideas on scientific forestry in the nineteenth and early twentieth centuries entered Finnish academic debate. Today, the state and the universities in Finland still collaborate on these issues, and are far more responsive to the needs and plight of the rural population. Jukka Oksa himself is part of a long-term research team of the University of Joensuu in Karelia. Their studies of the rural population and of the lumberjacks of Finland contrast sharply with the extreme paucity of similar studies of the rural wood workers of Maine. Current conditions, however, have been influenced by many other factors besides academic debates over scientific forestry, and in particular by a historical legacy of popular control of forests. Modern Finland is the heir of a long period of time when two-thirds of the forest was in the hands of private rural smallholders who combined farming with working the woods. The strong traditions of multiple use for a forest accessible to all and of a tradition of sustained yield have undoubtedly contributed to the favourable contrast between the environmentally enlightened silvicultural practices in Finland and the predatory use of the forest in Maine. A good example of this is the successful popular opposition to the influential Gutzeit Corporation in Finland (chapter 5).

David Vail sees the Finnish example as evidence of the possibility of using state regulation (and scientific forestry) to decouple forest technology from its negative social and environmental effects. We would emphasise that the possibility of decoupling has emerged from the strength and historical legacy of a non-individualistic, non-exclusively utilitarian view of the forest which can effectively counterpose and restrain not only modern forest technology but also the ability of modern forest organisation to legitimise the unfettered use of this technology. It is this popular tradition which prevents Finland from following the trajectory of Maine or India, not its élite tradition which is very similar to that of the other two countries. It may, however, only be a matter of time until the context-free logic of industrial forestry reverses the relationship between the forest and the people; then they will totally cease to belong to each other and the people will only exist for the exploitation of the forest.

Maine

In Maine, the colonial state began the expropriation of native forest dwellers in the seventeenth century to obtain tall pines for the ship masts of the Royal Navy. These actions had been preceded by a gradual elimination of the native Americans and the extermination of their systems of knowledge.[24] Until early in the century, lumber was the major export commodity. Later, paper corporations bought out the lumber barons' lands and erected grand pulp mills on Maine's rivers. Today, 47 per cent of the forest land in Maine is held by seven paper corporations. Trees are harvested mainly by small contractors using a single truck and skidder. This system has emerged gradually in the post-World War Two period. Before this, company crews harvested most of the volume.

Except in recent years, the government has not tried to regulate or control cutting operations in any significant degree. The influence of conservationist activists was mainly through their writings on environmental matters. These ideas emerged gradually, beginning around the turn of the century, echoing the appeal of national leaders like Gifford Pinchot, to oppose the extant practices of mining and neglect. These proposals were based on principles of scientific forestry, and advocated long-term planning and the application of new biological discoveries to commercial forestry, with the objective of increasing and sustaining timber yields, raising the rental income of progressive landowners and increasing the supply of low-cost raw materials to growing industries. However, the conservation ethic was honoured more in rhetoric than in practice and, until very recently, did not have much effect on state policy. At the same time, however, scientific views have been invoked by defenders of corporate interests to legitimise the actions of the latter. For example, David Vail reports that although the industrial practice of large-scale clear-cutting — i.e. a harvest which removes at least 70 per cent of the timber from a stand and now accounts for two-thirds of the harvest volume — has been known for a long time to lead to a serious depletion of soil nutrients and the endangerment of commercially valuable spruce resources, criticism of corporate practices on these grounds were met by a litany of responses from expert academics from Forestry School faculties claiming to show on scientific grounds that the practice was not harmful. A similar case could be made about the use of chemical pesticides which continues despite its demonstrated dangers.

What is striking, however, is that even the minimal opposition to the harmful effects of industrial practices and the pattern of technological change came from élite groups, or later from 'leisure' interests, who are generally not the inhabitants of the state itself. Local inhabitants and foresters, who have suffered the most from environmental deterioration, have not provided a significant challenge or protest. Vail attributes this lack of resistance to three causes: (a) the ideology of private property rights which has made it difficult for the notion of *common* property rights as well as the notion of land stewardship to emerge; (b) the value of economic progress, measured principally by growth in material production; and (c) the American dream of self-employment, which has influenced relations between corporations and nominally self-employed foresters. To these can be added a general mistrust of government interventions among Americans.

Be that as it may, the result is that in Maine commercial exploitation has been quite harmful to the forest. Despite the fact that potential timber supplies have chronically exceeded the demand, forest resources have deteriorated. Over many decades, the average stump diameter has declined, the fraction of hardwoods has expanded, and the number of dead or defective trees increased to over one-fifth of the total. This deterioration cannot be explained by an absence of property rights. Most of the forest lands are owned by a few corporations and constitute a significant part of their assets. Major paper and timber corporations active in Maine forests carry roughly $1 billion of illiquid forest land assets on their books and have invested several billion dollars in paper mill modernisation and new haul roads since 1970. Yet, resource conservation measures do not figure highly in their order of priorities, primarily because of the predominance of short-term profit considerations in day-to-day decision making as well as in longer-term decisions on investment and technological innovation. The president of the Great Northern Paper Company put it very bluntly: 'there are more important problems than resources ... the company has to think of surviving in the short-term' (chapter 6).

Similar inferences can be made from Vail's discussion of recent technological innovations which would allow whole tree harvesting as an ecologically superior alternative to clear-cutting, but notes that '*in practice* whole-tree harvesting is often used in clear-cutting operations rather than for timber stand improvement' (chapter 6, emphasis in original).

Besides purely environmental effects, the modern forms of social management have also produced adverse consequences for people who participate in related work arrangements. The increasing impoverishment of the rural population in Uttarakhand as a result of the state take-over of the forests has already been mentioned. Vail cites several adverse consequences of new forest harvesting technologies for the Maine foresters, including a gradual impoverishment, high accident rates and health hazards leading to a shortened working life. The role of universities and academic centres has also been unexemplary. A single example will suffice: even though the rate of occupational injuries among loggers in Maine is 37 per cent above national rates for logging and three times the rate for all manufacturing, the extreme paucity of studies on loggers' lives contrasts with the voluminous research produced by both private companies and the state university on all other — non-human — aspects of the forest industry (chapter 6).

The environmental crisis again

After this brief discussion, we can return to the pressing issue of the environmental crisis in order to contrast some conventional explanations with those suggested by our reading of the four cases assembled here. As mentioned above, we see the conservation of nature to be ensured by the strength of local communities who have a direct commitment to their surroundings. This gives us a somewhat different perspective on issues like population pressure, deforestation and scientific management.

Population growth

Many mainstream writers would disagree with the central thesis of this volume, and view indigenous societies not as the source of solutions to environmental problems but rather as the source of the problems themselves. Their argument is, first, that the high rates of population growth in countries of the South are increasing the pressure on global as well as local resources;[25] and, second, that their managerial capabilities are too undeveloped to cope with these pressures. Indeed, some writers go so far as to suggest punitive actions — including the denial of humanitarian support during crises — against societies whose excessive population growth endangers global survival (Hardin 1968).[26]

Since this volume concentrates on the role played by systems of knowledge in environmental management and not on that of population growth, this may be a good time to discuss the latter issue. The argument here is *not* that population growth is not a problem, or that a high rate of population growth is sustainable in the long run. It is simply that the focus on population growth as *the* problem is a mistaken one. More importantly, this focus is a political stance which, though ineffective in eliminating the problem, is quite effective in justifying unnecessarily deleterious practices. The following statement, taken from a policy document of an international aid institution, is typical of the views of government planners, establishment academics, and aid bureaucrats: 'The causes of environmental degradation are as many and varied as its manifestations. But at the heart of the problem is the rapid rate of population growth in many developing countries' (World Bank 1987: 2).[27]

This is an astonishing statement. An unbiased examination of the issue must reveal that the heart of the problem is not the overpopulation of the South but the overconsumption of the North (Brundtland Report 1987; Redclift 1984; Runnals 1986). North Americans, who though 5 per cent of the world's population consume 40–50 per cent of the world's resources, pose a far greater danger to life on this planet than, say, Indians or Africans with their low consumption levels. According to calculations made by Richard Daly, the population of Bangladesh would have to increase to *297 times* its present level for them to match the energy consumption of an equivalent number of Americans (Daly 1977; see also Georgescu-Roegen 1971).[28] This is why environmental activists insist that the primary focus of attention must be the restructuring of the current Western patterns of production and consumption which cannot be sustained beyond the very short run. Lastly, what must be recognised is that although the pressure on global economic resources will certainly rise beyond tolerable levels when populations in the South shift to consumption and production patterns typical of the West, this will happen even if population levels do not increase! Without seeking to be polemical, it must be said that unless the objective is to exonerate the West of its role in the historic (and continuing) plunder of natural resources in all parts of the globe, it is difficult to understand how population growth could be the 'heart of the problem'.

The second problem with this perspective derives from its prescriptive implication of stringent policies for population control. It is widely accepted by now that population growth is as much a consequence of poverty and resource shortage as its cause; that it is not very responsive to official policies; and that these policies are often socially repressive, violent, inegalitarian and generally unsavoury in nature (Hartmann 1987, Mamdani 1972).

To place the issue in some perspective, it may be useful to contrast the profusion of proposals for population control in the South with the paucity of suggestions to restructure Western production and consumption systems. While it is true that a major restructuring in societies used to wasteful lifestyles will be extremely difficult — although some encouraging changes have already begun to take place (Brundtland Report 1987 p.178) — this cannot be any more problematic than the prescribed changes in fertility patterns of societies in which large families are the norm.

Moreover, as the Kenyan journalist Hilary Ng'weno (1988) has suggested, such a restructuring of consumption and production arrangements would not be entirely unprecedented. Ng'weno uses the analogy of 'Third World debt' to say that, just as many countries in the South borrowed from Western financial banks in the last two decades, Northern countries borrowed heavily from the earth's 'ecological bank' for two centuries to finance their development. Just as the IMF, the World Bank and Western governments ask African and Latin American countries to undertake painful 'structural adjustments' to fulfil their financial debt obligations, the people of the world, especially those concerned about the disastrous consequences of the environmental crisis, should ask Western countries to discharge the burden of their environmental debt obligations by going through an analogous, though much less painful, adjustment process.

The idea here is not to suggest that a high rate of population growth is desirable. It is to question the salience with which this issue has been treated in the mainstream literature on environmental problems, and to place it in perspective by examining the other causes which have generally been excluded from the analysis. We are trying to put the blame on those who are present, those who are powerful and those whose ways of thinking and behaving are leading us towards catastrophe.

Local versus commercial demand for forest products
The above discussion is germane to the case of forestry resources. The bulk of the expansion in the demand for wood comes from the demands created in the modern — generally urban — segments of society, yet one is constantly confronted with 'official' estimates which seek to show that the main reason for the rapid deforestation in the South is the high fuelwood demand of local villagers. For example, the Chief Conservator of Forests, the highest forest department authority in Uttarakhand, says, '[i]t is indiscriminate removal of wood (firewood) from forests which causes the havoc ... a day might come when the urban people will invade the forests for getting firewood' (cited in CSE 1985: 94). The mainstream argument — that either the local demand for timber *is* higher in the South, or that the local systems of management are incapable of accommodating the modern pressure on resources — is bolstered by the empirical observation that while the rising demand for timber is worldwide, the most serious cases of deforestation have occurred in the South.

Several points can be raised here. First, a major reason for the differential rates of deforestation between Western countries and those of the South is the lower cost of tree harvesting in the latter: logging operations in American forests are below full capacity because American paper companies cannot compete in the world market, not because their systems of conservation are better. Second, even if this were not the case, it is unclear why the industrial demand for timber should be taken as an unquestionable desideratum, and the demand for fuelwood as the sole undesirable cause of the deforestation.

Third, in any event, none of the available evidence supports the hypothesis of the irresponsible local villager. Rural inhabitants rarely chop down trees; most collect dead branches or lop them from trees, and when fuelwood is in short supply, they tend to economise or to switch to other fuel, such as cow dung, crop stems and husks, and weeds (Brundtland Report 1987: 190; Shiva 1989). The pressure of fuelwood demand comes, if anything, from commercial rather than subsistence consumption. It should also be remembered that these forests were preserved and protected for centuries by the same local villagers, and were decimated (within decades) only when villagers lost control of the forests to urban commercial interests.

On the role of informal slash-and-burn agriculture, however, an observation is necessary. As econometricians have recognised for a long time, it is very difficult to fix causality when more than one factor is responsible for an outcome. One way of assigning causality is static: i.e. by looking at relative numerical magnitudes in the same time period. Another, more dynamic, method is to look at the appearance of causes in historical time. Massive deforestation began with the appearance of commercial intervention — logging, planned farming, fuel cutting — not with the existence of informal activities, farming as well as fuel cutting, which have been in place for hundreds, if not thousands, of years. Indeed, commercial intervention, by disenfranchising local populations, may have exacerbated the problem by taking away the power, and thus also the responsibility for environmental management, from local populations. We focus on commercial causes mainly out of sensitivity to these concerns.

Centralisation, participation and responsibility

It must be clarified here that we see customary arrangements for the management of resources not as static, reified practices, but rather as dynamic systems which responded flexibly and creatively to emerging disequilibria. This is no longer possible, because with the growing influence of the market and the state, most non-modern societies have lost the ability to decide issues which affect their lives. The fact that forest resources have degenerated in recent years is due to the destruction of these systems at the hands of a centralising, bureaucratic system of management, but not due to these managers inherent irresponsibility or inefficiency. The point is that local systems of production and consumption are generally characterised by a conservationist ethic, and it is often the introduction of the commercial calculus which disturbs ecological balance.

This can be illustrated by highlighting a fundamental fallacy in mainstream prescriptions for population control, which rely on centralised state intervention to produce the desired result. Why *should* local communities accept responsibility for their actions when centralised managerial systems imposed upon them from the outside allow them neither to influence decisions that affect their lives nor give them any responsibility for doing so? Just as societal decisions affecting forests or other environmental resources will become more responsible when these resources are returned to the control of local communities from the hands of industrial concerns or state bureaucrats, so also will population patterns become more responsive to environmental limits when decisions are taken by the people themselves.

In other words, the central question for the future is not whether population growth or styles of living place pressure upon global resources. The real question is whether (and how) different societies and different ways of thinking can mitigate the deleterious consequences of these pressures. The modernistic claim is that the only way of doing so is through some form of rational management at which modern societies are clearly better than indigenous ones. The alternative view is that indigenous systems have a more stewardly attitude towards the environment compared with the instrumental and exploitative bent of modern ways of knowing, and therefore that the incorporation of their rationale into modern arrangements is necessary for the recovery of ecological health. This view also holds that environmental degradation in these areas took place as a result of the economic, political and ideological expansion of the modern system of knowledge, and the corresponding political weakness and loss of self-confidence of indigenous societies.

Thus, while it is true that modern systems of management in countries of the South have fared very poorly, and that the need for reform is urgent, this does not mean that managerialism — including what David Vail calls the 'euphemism' of scientific forestry — is the only solution. Notwithstanding the partiality of modernising élites towards such solutions, there are good reasons to doubt that they would perform better in the future than they have in the past.

At an empirical level, as the above discussion has sought to illustrate, environmental health is associated with the strength and influence of local systems of knowledge, and environmental decay with their de-legitimisation and elimination at the hands of an élite, bureaucratic and centralising system of knowledge such as scientific forestry.[29] Managerial initiatives to conserve the environment have always followed rather than led popular expressions of concern over environmental degradation.[30] These initiatives, moreover, have all too often sought to legitimise development from the top down, as it were, and to de-legitimise the actions, beliefs and practices of grassroots movements and community-based popular groups; indeed, in the past, managerialism has been used more often to control those who, on the basis of alternative ways of thinking, protest against wasteful practices, than to restrain those who indulge in such practices. Lastly, even when the managers were inclined, on their own initiative, to introduce necessary protectionist measures, they were severely handicapped by the major gaps in knowledge about forest ecology. These, and the significant differences among scientists and foresters on the long-run consequences of past and present management practices, suggest what Marcel Proust once said about the risk in summoning the wisest of doctors to our assistance, 'that we may be relying on a scientific truth the error of which will be recognised in a few years' time'.[31]

Scientific forestry
Many writers argue that scientific forestry is a superior alternative not only to 'irrational' and 'superstitious' indigenous practices, but also to unfettered commercial exploitation which in the past has led to severe resource deterioration in the West as well as in the South. In this interpretation of the evidence, the relatively better health of Finnish forests would be adduced as proof of this superiority, while the extensive damage to Indian and Maine forests reported in this volume would be explained either by saying: (a) that scientific forestry was not used at all (as in Maine); or (b) that it was used but not very well (as in India). The evidence seems to us, however, to point in an entirely different direction: scientific forestry will always be damaging — because of inadequate knowledge or information, because of mismanagement, or because of the susceptibility of managers to commercial interests, but most importantly because of its basis in an instrumental attitude towards nature. Examples of the beneficial application of scientific forestry represent not its innate effectiveness, but rather the ability of *local* groups to effectively stalemate the instrumental perspective by a vigorous protective effort based on a conservationist attitude. The following pages will try to show why this interpretation makes more sense than the alternative.

Before proceeding further, it may be important to clarify that the term 'scientific forestry' is often used to designate more than one thing. There is an 'ideal' version of scientific forestry which is supposed to bring out the long-run perspective on the interaction between humans and nature. There is a 'practical' version, where the label often justifies short-horizon commercial practices. Finally, there is a 'corrupted' version implemented by incompetent and venial bureaucrats. We include all three definitions in our analysis but believe that all three are harmful; we include the ideal type in this, because it represents the scientific claims of knowledge and certitude, and thus legitimises the colonisation and exploitation of the known. It is a problem inherent in an instrumentalist view of the world.

Ideas about scientific forestry were first developed in Germany beginning in the eighteenth century.[32] From the start, these ideas were based on the belief that the state should be responsible for forest management, since the long time period needed for rational management of forests was thought to be consistent only with control by governments or perpetual corporations.[33] Rational forest management included the separation of forestry and agriculture from each other, the enactment of forest legislation, the establishment of a forest administration and the introduction of police control. The essential idea was that of 'sustained yield' forestry — i.e. unchanged forest area through replacement of cuttings by natural or artificial means — for purposes of industrial mobilisation of wood. Because of ecological as well as aesthetic problems,[34] this view has faced a great deal of criticism, particularly from those with more organic views of the forest. Still, it has continued to provide the basis for collective forest management in Europe as well as North America in the post-World War Two period.

However, some major differences between tropical and temperate forest ecosystems seriously impair the success of scientific forestry even on its own terms in the tropics. These differences include the fact that tropical forests typically have a multitude of species, of which only a few are commercially valuable; they have a far greater complexity of forest–soil–water relationships, and a correspondingly greater fragility of the ecosystem, which cannot withstand the radical modifications introduced by commercial forestry without going into irreversible decline.

Because of these and other factors, scientific forestry has in practice often failed to conform to its ideals of sustained yield harvesting, however deficient these ideals may be on other grounds. This failure can be attributed to three factors: (a) inadequate knowledge of the complex ecological interlinkages or an inadequate statistical base to update this knowledge; (b) responsiveness of the government and scientists to commercial and industrial interests; and (c) sheer mismanagement. This volume provides ample evidence of all three and it would be instructive to highlight some examples before taking up the larger issue of the ideals of scientific forestry.

This discussion brings out another way of making the argument of the book: social science generally looks at society either as composed of *individuals* (with their preferences and endowments, as in neo-classical economics), or of *organisations* (e.g. the state, corporations, unions, etc. — as in some institutional descriptions). One can interpret scientific forestry as saying that individual control was likely to be undesirable, given the short time horizon of individual actors, and that therefore some form of organised control was necessary for good management. Our alternative view would emphasise a third possibility, the role of *communities*, whose long time horizons are inscribed into their rituals, beliefs, and world-views — in other words, into their systems of knowledge. The neglect of this possibility has limited the debate to only two alternatives, both of which are instrumental, and neither of which we find desirable. The actual practice, however, differs from the intellectual debate in that the third possibility is always present; indeed, in our view, this third possibility is what determines whether the outcome will be good or bad.

Local and universal knowledge

What the above descriptions reveal is that, contrary to the claims of modernising groups, it is they, rather than indigenous forest dwellers, who present the greatest threat to the environment. Local systems of knowledge and resource management have often been presented as the cause of resource problems because of their supposed irrationality. By labelling the tribals backward and ignorant, by decreeing that their practices destroy the forest, the protagonists of the dominant system of knowledge ensure that the voices which could challenge them will not be heard. This allows them to proceed self-righteously and uncritically to treat the forest not as a life-supporting system but as a resource to be exploited for commercial use. The briefest unprejudiced look at the evidence reveals matters to be otherwise. As Guha says about the Himalayan population:

> Yet the fragmentary historical evidence that is available tells a different story: it reveals the existence of a highly sophisticated system of conservancy in pre-colonial Uttarakhand.... Through a mix of religion, folklore and tradition, the peasants ... had drawn a protective ring around the forests. As with other forest-dwelling communities, the continuity of their world rested upon a continuity in their relationship with the forest. (chapter 4)

Similar views have also been expressed about the world-views of the indigenous tribes in North America,[35] in Australia, in the Amazon Basin, in Central America, in the deserts of Africa and elsewhere. These people have preserved 'a traditional way of life in close harmony with the natural environment. Their very survival has depended on their ecological awareness and adaptation' (Brundtland Report 1987: 114).

In India massive state intervention, with the adverse consequences already noted, could proceed unchecked because the local hill tribes or the local populations were effectively disenfranchised by the de-legitimisation of their world-view and cultural practices. The conceptual universe of the government officials is the dominant system of knowledge in the world today. It dominates the thinking of development experts globally. From the perspectives given us by the authors in this volume it becomes clear that this dominance necessitates the marginalisation and total devaluation of alternative systems of knowledge. The colonial state as well as the post-colonial developmentalist state was totally convinced of the correctness, as well as beneficence, of its world-view of modernisation — earlier called 'civilisation' — and later of heavy industrialisation. Alternatives were neither respected nor acknowledged as legitimate, and environmentally harmful actions were taken in total disregard of popular feelings and views upon the subject.

A good example of such marginalisation of the local population is the introduction of the government development programme among the Hill Maria which, as mentioned earlier, led to deforestation and other problems. Savyasaachi notes that local officials place the blame for the deforestation entirely on shifting cultivation, even though the Hill Maria say that they have been living in the forests and practising it for generations without any sign of deforestation. For the government officials — known as Koska to the Hill Maria — the forest represents valuable timber and the tribes a primitive nuisance whose agricultural practices destroy the forest. Alice in Wonderland! The state forestry department responsible for the devastating deforestation of the Himalayan and other Indian forests define those people, who have lived in the forests since time immemorial, as the destroyers of the forest. Only supreme self-assurance born of a secure, dominant position can engender such an inverted perception of reality.

In Maine, the ways of thinking of the modern industrial corporations cannot be contrasted with those of local foresters or other inhabitants of the area because, as Vail puts it, forest workers and forest corporations are protagonists rather than opponents in the drive for the mastery of nature. A more appropriate opposition is that which took place 200 years ago between the indigenous American Indian tribes and the colonial settlers. Prior to that forcible expropriation of lands and forests by the settlers, native tribes followed a holistic way of life in the forest, in which 'the forest had more than value; cultural ecology was instrumental much more than sustainable resource recycling' (chapter 6). At the time of that conflict the local inhabitants were branded as barbarian and backward, and their ways of thinking as mystical, superstitious and irrational, and therefore presumably of no account. Most of the population were literally exterminated and the remainder placed in 'reserves'.[36] It is only since the emergence of the environmental crisis that the greater ecological soundness and wisdom of their ways has begun to receive attention and respect.[37]

As for the new local population, de Tocqueville's wry comment was close to the mark: 'Americans may be farmers, merchants and mechanics, but they are all land speculators at heart' (quoted in chapter 6). They share an ideology of rugged individualism and of a utilitarian orientation to the environment. Thus, there were no alternative conceptions of the forest or the environment among the local population and there was consequently no pressure on the state or the forest industry to respond to such alternatives. As a result, the practice of scientific forestry, as well as the advance of technology, took place along the lines determined by a purely instrumental view of nature. In recent years, environmental groups have become active in the area largely on behalf of leisure interests, and the attitude of the state government is beginning to show some signs of change. Yet the new environmental interests are also based on utilitarian views of the forest and often tend to cast the debate in pure economistic terms.

In Finland, the rural population was greatly reduced by the Great Move, its integrity and cohesion lost, and its social and cultural life destroyed, yet unlike the American Indians this population is still there in the normal countryside, not in separate reserves. Unlike the Indian rural population, it is not yet treated or considered as an inferior group, to be dragged, willingly or not, 'into the twentieth century'. It has acquired political strength through the formation of the Rural Party (now the Centre Party) and through its village committees. Its world-view cannot yet be treated as an irrational obstacle to progress. So it is difficult for the state to disregard entirely the perspectives and wishes of the rural population. Oksa indicates, however, that these communities have no future; even now the age profile is turning against them as the younger people move away. It is not clear how long their resistance to a purely commercial use of the forest will continue, and therefore how long the Finnish forests will continue to be sustained at their present level.

The upshot of the discussion is that the preservation of the natural environment in general and of the forests in particular does not depend on the existence of state regulation and protection, which has quite dissimilar effects in India and Finland, nor on pure private ownership, whose consequences in Maine were less than desirable, nor even upon the emergence of a conservation ideology among managerial élites, which has produced very different results in all three countries where it has had a long history. The conservationist effort and effectiveness depend rather on the existence of an effective antidote to the instrumental ideology of industrial and commercial usage, in the form of strong local action. An environmental ethic simply cannot emerge where such local beliefs and initiatives are degraded and de-legitimised as in India, nor where the pervasiveness of the ethic of growth and property rights, as in Maine, inhibits local groups from asserting their views on social matters.

To us, this interpretation of the evidence casts serious doubts on the criteria of efficiency and mastery over nature which have been invoked as self-evident claims for the superiority of the rational, scientific knowledge system. We find that the long-term effects of such efficiency and mastery are major environmental disasters, as well as increasing human poverty and misery for those who live on or near those resources. We are also sceptical of the advantage of centralised approaches to the solution of these problems, such as scientific forestry. Even if it constitutes an improvement over the short time horizon of commercial decision making, it still looks at the forest from the same unidimensional perspective, namely that of yield, and while it may seek to avoid actions which lower the forest yield in the short to medium run, it tends nevertheless to ignore those elements of forest maintenance which do not have an obvious pay-off in yield terms.

Local arrangements, on the other hand, had conservationist attitudes and practices built into their ways of thinking. Their opposition to the state or to corporate interests was based not on political differences or distributional calculations, but on entirely different ways of looking at nature. Ramachandra Guha expresses this idea very well:

This clash between scientific forestry and village management was not merely economic. The conflicting perspectives rested on fundamentally different notions of the forest — on radically different systems of meaning. The ideology of 'scientific' forestry proclaimed that the imposition of state control was a logical corollary of the lack of 'scientific' management practices among the human populations that lived in and around forests. [chapter 4]

A recognition of the underlying cause of these differences is crucial if we are to succeed in addressing the large-scale environmental disaster which looms before us.

Notes

1.   See, e.g., chapter 1 of the report of the World Commission on Environment and Development 1987 (henceforth, the Brundtland Report). Other useful sources are Redclift 1984, Glaeser 1987, Center for Science and Environment (CSE) 1982 and 1985, Runnals 1986, and Worldwatch Institute 1986.

2.   Such ideas are expressed in many recent writings. In addition to the Brundtland Report 1987, prominent examples include CSE 1982, 1985, Ekins 1986, Glaeser 1987, Max-Neef 1982, Redclift 1984, Worldwatch Institute 1986, among many others.

3. For example, M. Nicholson writes in some bewilderment in his book, *The Environmental Revolution* (Penguin, 1972), 'certain quite primitive cultures somehow acquired and acted upon a better understanding of some of the essentials of conservation than is yet widely shared by modern Western man' (cited in Guha 1985: 18). See also Goldsmith and Hildyard 1984: 316–29.

4. On this issue see Marglin 1990: 217–82.

5. In the academic world, warnings about specific problems, such as the ozone hole or the 'greenhouse' warming of the planet, had begun to appear as early as the 1950s, and in the case of other problems even earlier. Popular movements containing a conservationist plank have marked social history in the South as well as the North for quite some time.

6. However, although governments and international bodies responded to these concerns through normal bureaucratic methods, the net result was, until very recently, quite limited: of the 26 resolutions and 109 recommendations of the 1972 report, none had been implemented by the time of the Nairobi conference of 1982. See Redclift 1984. Also, see Runnals 1986 for a review of initiatives and actions.

7. For example, the UN Report on Development and the Environment stated on the eve of the Stockholm conference, 'As we have repeatedly stressed, the problems of environmental disruption are still a relatively small part of the development concern of the developing countries, and it may be premature for many of them to divert their energies to the establishment of new institutions or machineries.' Cited in Redclift 1984: 48.

8. See CSE 1982: 33–5, 85–90; CSE 1985: 49–98; Redclift 1984: 25–30. Brundtland Report 1987: 147–67. Meadows et al. 1972. Interesting recent discussions are in Redclift 1984: 20–38; Brundtland Report 1987: 169–74; Ekins 1986: 12–14.

9. See Brundtland Report 1987: 174–80, 184–7; Brasseur 1987. This is generally attributed to the release into the atmosphere of chemical fluorocarbons (CFCs) which are used in aerosol containers and refrigerators.

10. Brundtland Report 1987: 184–5. The most spectacular cases have become household words: Three Mile Island, Chernobyl, Bhopal, Rhine River.

11. Fears associated with expanded pesticide use have been expressed in several recent news articles. See, e.g., Todd 1988, Perera 1988.

12. Waterlogging, salinity, soil erosion and silting, health problems (e.g. malaria epidemics) and climate and rainfall changes of an adverse nature. See, e.g., Goldsmith and Hildyard 1984, particularly part III.

13. We focus on timber demand to bring out the relative effects of local and indigenous use versus distant and instrumental use. Other causes, such as planned agriculture and fuel cutting, while technically 'local' in character, also represent the instrumentalist attitude towards nature.

14. CSE 1982: 39. The chir pine forests of the Western Himalayas have undergone the most massive deforestation. Below 2,000 metres there are no forests left; in the middle range, up to 3,000 metres, the forest cover has been reduced from a third of the total area to only 6–8 per cent. At least half of the forest land in Uttarakhand is degraded and of poor density. See CSE 1982: 35–6.

15.   CSE 1985: 86. Bastar District lies in Madhya Pradesh province, which has the largest forest in India, covering 35 per cent of the total land area according to government statistics. See CSE 1982: 34.

16.   The next five paragraphs rely heavily on the evidence provided in chapter 4.

17.   See CSE 1982:19. See also Shiva 1989.

18.   *Guardian* correspondent Walter Schwartz reports in a recent article that within a single decade flood-affected land has doubled from 20 to 40 million hectares. In 1970, an unprecedented flood washed away an entire village, several busloads of tourists and hundreds of head of cattle, and destroyed millions of rupees' worth of property along a 400 kilometre area. Following another flood in 1971, Chipko volunteers began collecting data on deaths of animals from floods and landslides every year. See CSE 1982: 39.

19.   *British Parliamentary Papers*, vol. 59 (1890–92). Cited in chapter 4, p.83 The rapid rate of deforestation was not, however, restricted to the Uttarakhand area.

20.   For an excellent historical documentation of the role of women in the Chipko Movement see Shiva 1989

21.   Shifting cultivation died out in most of Madhya Pradesh in the first half of this century, because of the active opposition of the colonial government's forestry department. Abujhmarh is the only area where it is still being practised on a significant scale, but here too, as chapter 3 shows, it is under retreat. See CSE 1985: 86–93 for a discussion of the condition of forests in Bastar District.

22.   The bias against shifting cultivation seems to be a deeply rooted one, despite a great deal of recent evidence in scientific writings that it helps sustain forests rather than destroy them. For example, satellite data released in mid-1984 by the Indian National Remote Sensing Agency (NRSA) show that forest cover in all Indian states except Tripura, Manipur, Meghalaya and Mizoram is below the official figures reported in government documents. Quite significantly, says the NRSA report, shifting cultivation is practised in all the exceptional states. Cited in CSE 1985: 80. For a review of debate on shifting cultivation, see Myers 1980, NAS 1982.

23.   CSE 1982: 38. This document cites a report from the *Times of India* which says that, given the observed rate of deforestation, if the Forest Department's claim of planting 20 million saplings every year with a success rate of 25 per cent were correct, then it must be the case that at least 30 or 40 trees are cut down illegally for every tree that is cut legally!

24.   For a thorough ethnohistorical documentation of this process in New England see Merchant 1989.

25.   Besides deforestation, population pressures can also lead to such problems as soil depletion because of insufficient crop rotation, de-vegetation due to over-grazing by an expanding livestock population, and municipal air and water pollution, transport congestion, or inadequate water supply or sewerage facilities resulting from the government's inability to expand civic services in line with the growth of urban populations.

26.   Others who take this view are Paddock and Paddock (1967) who advocate the strategy of 'triage', according to which humane action should be directed

only to those countries which 'can be saved', and denied to those who cannot be saved.

27.   At an intellectual level, this perspective leads to Environmental Impact Assessment studies (see, e.g., Biswas and Geping 1987), which, by bringing hitherto excluded factors into the analysis, would 'complete' the existing 'incomplete' models of the economy.

28.   Even with the current high rate of population growth, it will take Bangladesh 300 years to accomplish this task.

29.   Similar distinctions between managerial and popular approaches have been made by many writers. See, e.g., Max-Neef 1982, Guha 1985, Sandbach 1980.

30.   For example, Ramachandra Guha notes in the case of India that 'It is the ceaseless endeavour of grassroots activists ... that are chiefly responsible for making ecology a "public issue". In many instances, scientists [and government functionaries], far from raising issues on their own, have been closely following the lead of popular movements.' See Guha 1985: 22.

31.   The immense complexity of ecological interaction, brought out in any textbook on elementary ecology, is highlighted by many critics of scientific forestry. For a useful and brief summary with particular application to India, the reader is referred to Chakraborty 1987.

32.   This paragraph draws on Raumolin 1986: 1–7. See the various chapters for a discussion of the introduction of scientific forestry in the particular contexts.

33.   It must be emphasised that *control* is not the same as *ownership*. Scientific forestry is perfectly consistent with individual ownership so long as regulation and management are in the hands of a long-lived entity, such as the state, or a perpetual corporation.

34.   Clear-cutting and a shift towards monocultural forestry was not only unaesthetic, but also rendered the forest subject to insect attacks, in addition to making it an unfavourable environment for many birds and other animals. See Raumolin 1986: 3.

35.   An eloquent expression of the American Indian world-view is in the classic statement of Chief Seattle made in 1834 in response to the American government's offer to buy a large area of Indian land. Among other places, it is reproduced in full in Brown 1986.

36.   For an ethnohistorical documentation and discussion of these events see Merchant 1989.

37.   Such praise often comes from the most unlikely sources. For example, the former conservative Senator, US presidential candidate and ultra-nationalist Barry Goldwater states in a recent interview to Burton Bernstein, '[The Indians] make more sense of nature than white men do. They accept it and use it, even if they can't explain it.... They don't respect the white man. There's nothing to respect, when you really get down to it.' *New Yorker*, 25 April 1988: 73.

Bibliography

Ahmed, Durre Sameen and Tariq Banuri (1989), 'Official nationalism, the politicisation of ethnicity, and collective violence', Helsinki: WIDER (mimeo).

Anderson, Dennis (1986), 'Declining tree stocks in African countries', *World Development*, vol. 14 no. 7: 853–63

Apffel Marglin, Frédérique (1987), 'Smallpox in two systems of knowledge', in Apffel Marglin and Marglin 1990.

Apffel Marglin, Frédérique and Stephen A. Marglin (eds) (1990), *Dominating Knowledge: Development, Culture and Resistance*, Oxford: Clarendon Press.

Bahro, Rudolph (1986), *Building the Green Movement*, Philadelphia: New Society Publishers.

Banuri, Tariq (1990a), 'Development and the politics of knowledge', in Apffel Marglin and Marglin 1990.

Banuri, Tariq (1990b), 'Modernisation and its discontents', in Apffel Marglin and Marglin 1990.

Bellah, Robert et al. (1985), *Habits of the Heart: Individualism and Commitment in American Life*, New York: Harper & Row.

Berger, Peter (1974), *Pyramids of Sacrifice: Political Ethics and Social Change*, New York: Anchor Books.

Bernstein, Herbert J. (1987), 'Idols of modern science and the reconstruction of knowledge', in Marcus J. Raskin and Herbert J. Bernstein (eds), *New Ways of Knowing: the Sciences, Society, and Reconstructive Knowing*, Totowa, NJ: Rowman & Littlefield.

Biswas, Asit K. and Qu Geping (eds) (1987), *Environmental Impact Assessment for Developing Countries*, London: Tycooly Publishing.

Brasseur, G. (1987), 'The endangered ozone layer: new theories on ozone depletion', *Environment*, vol: 29, no. 1.

Brundtland Report (1987). See World Commission on Environment and Development.

Brown, Aggrey (1986), 'Communication technology and development: ideological and technical imperative', paper presented at the XVth International Association for Mass Communication Research, General Assembly and Conference, New Delhi.

CSE (Center for Science and Environment) (1982), *The State of India's Environment: the First Citizens' Report*, New Delhi.

———— (1985) *The State of India's Environment 1984–85: the Second Citizens' Report*, New Delhi.

Chakraborty, Satyesh C. (1987), 'Issues concerning management of ecosystem within the Indian reality', Calcutta: Indian Institute of Management, mimeo.

Commoner, Barry (1971), *The Closing Circle*, New York: Alfred Knopf.

Daly, Herman (1977), *Steady state Economics*, San Francisco, CA.: F. H. Freeman.

Dyson-Hudson, Neville (1985), 'Pastoral production systems and livestock development projects: an East African perspective,' in Michael M. Cernea (ed.), *Putting People First: Sociological Variables in Rural Development*, New York: Oxford University Press.

Farvar, M. Targhi and John P. Milton (eds) (1972), *The Careless Technology: Ecology and International Development*, New York: Natural History Press.

Finland in figures 1987 (1987), CSO, Finland.

Georgescu-Roegen, Nicholas (1971), *The Entropy Law and the Economic Process*, Cambridge, MA: Harvard University Press.

Glaeser, Bernhard (ed.) (1987), *The Green Revolution Revisited*, London: Allen & Unwin.

Goldsmith, Edward and Nicholas Hildyard (1984), *The Social and Environmental Effects of Large Dams*, San Francisco, CA: Sierra Club Books.

Guha, Ramachandra (1985), 'Eco-development debate: a critical review', *South Asian Anthropologist*, 15–24.

——— (1990), *The Unquiet Woods*, Delhi: Oxford University Press.

Hardin, Garrett (1968), 'The tragedy of the commons', *Science*, 162 (13 December): 12438.

Hartmann, Betsy (1987), *Reproductive Rights and Wrongs: the Global Politics of Population Control and Contraceptive Choice*, New York: Harper & Row.

Hillman, James (1975), *Re-visioning Psychology*, New York: Harper & Row.

Mamdani, Mahmood (1972), *The Myth of Population Control*, New York: Monthly Review Press.

Marglin, Stephen A. (1990), 'Losing touch: the cultural conditions of worker accommodation and resistance', in Apffel Marglin and Marglin 1990.

Max-Neef, Manfred A. (1982), *From the Outside Looking In: Experiences in 'Barefoot Economics'*, Uppsala: The Dag Hammarskjöld Foundation.

Meadows, Donnella H., Dennis L. Meadows, Jorgen Randers and William W. Behrens III (1972), *Limits to Growth*, New York: Universe Books.

Merchant, Carolyn (1983), *The Death of Nature*, Harper & Row.

——— (1989), *Ecological Revolutions: Nature, Gender, and Science in New England*, University of North Carolina Press.

Myers, N. (1980), *Conversion of Tropical Moist Forests*, Washington DC: NAS.

NAS (National Academy of Sciences)(1982), *Ecological Aspects of Development in the Humid Tropics*, Washington DC: NAS

Odum, Eugene P. (1953), *Fundamentals of Ecology*, Philadelphia, PA: Saunders.

Paddock, William and Paul Paddock, (1967), *Famine — 1975! America's Decisions: Who Will Survive*, Boston: Little, Brown.

Perera, Judith (1988), 'Nature's way out of the pesticide trap', *South*, May: 109–13.

Prigogine, Ilya and Isabelle Stengers (1984), *Order Out of Chaos: Man's New Dialogue With Nature*, New York: Bantam Books.

Raumolin, Jussi (1986), 'The impact of technological change on rural and regional forestry in Finland', Helsinki: WIDER, mimeo.

Redclift, Michael (1984), *Development and the Environmental Crisis: Red or Green Alternatives?*, New York: Methuen.

Runnals, David (1986), 'Environment and development: a critical stocktaking', Briefing Paper No. 16, Ottawa: North South Institute.

Shiva, Vandana (1989), *Staying Alive: Women, Ecology and Development in India*, London: Zed Books.

Todd, Halinah (1988), 'When pesticides help pests and harm people', *International Herald Tribune*, 16 June.

Turner, R. Kerry (ed.) (1988), *Sustainable Environmental Management: Principles and Practice*, Boulder, CO: Westview Press.

UNEP (1986), *The State of the Environment 1986: Environment and Health*, Nairobi: UNEP.

Vail, David (1989), 'The meanings of mechanisation: technological transformation of logging systems in Sweden and Maine, USA', Helsinki: WIDER, mimeo.

White, Lynn (1972), 'Technology and social change', in Robert Nisbet (ed.), *Social Change*, New York: Harper & Row.

White, Lynn, Jr (1975), 'The historical roots of our ecological crisis', in Robin Clarke (ed.), *Notes For The Future: an Alternative History of the Past Decade*, New York: Universe Books.

World Bank (1987), 'Environment, growth, and development', paper prepared by the World Bank staff for consideration by the Development Committee at its April 1987 meeting, Washington DC: World Bank, mimeo.

World Commission on Environment and Development (the Brundtland Commission) (1987), *Our Common Future*, Oxford: Oxford University Press.

Worldwatch Institute (1986), *State of the World 1986: a Worldwatch Institute Report on Progress Towards a Sustainable Society*, New York: W. W. Norton.

3. An alternative system of knowledge: fields and forests in Abujhmarh

Dr Savyasaachi

Introduction

The northern Abujhmarh in Narayanpur Tehsil in the Bastar District contains three distinct groups of people, each with a unique relationship to a common forest environment. Many differences separate these groups including differing modes of cultivation and unrelated languages. A widespread belief that it is not possible to live in a forest environment is held primarily by government officials. This led to a debate regarding the future of the forest environment. The two contending positions, the environmentalist view and the developmentalist view, both support the assumption that the forest is not fit for human habitation. Thus the objective of development programmes is to transform the forest into areas for commercial use, displacing the inhabitants.

Each of the three groups affected by development programmes scheduled for Abujhmarh not only speaks a different language, but also relates to the forest environment in ways specific to it. The differences in both language and relationship to the forest environment lie at the core of the current forest debates. The environmentalist view considers animals and trees more important than humans. As a result tribals are thrown out of the forests when the forest areas are declared national parks or wildlife sanctuaries. Tribals are considered to have no rights to their forest environment, in the environmentalist view, even though villages are located in the forest areas. Developmentalists seek to deprive tribals of the means of shifting cultivation in which the life-support of the communities is grounded. Records and survey reports, when kept at all, are used to support each point of view — a belief that a forest environment is detrimental for human life and livelihood. These records are both unreliable and bear no relation to the conditions in which the Hill Maria live.

The debate assumes one way of relating to and knowing nature and wrongly identifies the problem as one of preserving either human beings or the forests. It does not recognise the possibility that humans and their forest environment constitute a single habitat. Tribals, though, recognise precisely this possibility, but tribal knowledge is viewed, at best, as based on an inferior form of knowledge, and at worst as the negative 'other', which cannot be allowed to exist simultaneously with the universal form of knowing represented by scientific development. Scientific development, due to the necessity of its laws, destroys other ways of knowing in other ways of life on the grounds that they are illogical and non-rational. However, historically the destruction and loss of the plurality and multiplicity in nature and in social-cultural life by scientific development itself, have raised the problem of survival.

The above debate can be located in the relationship between the three groups of people examined. The following description will seek to identify the position of the Hill Maria in terms of the languages available to them in order to comprehend and articulate the changing relationship between forests and shifting cultivation.

It is argued that a multiplicity of languages are made available to the Hill Maria from outside their natural and social environment. These languages do not recognise the Marhia dialect as a language of discourse. On the contrary, the Marhia dialect is used only as an instrument to communicate to the Hill Maria their condition, understood from the outside, as that of the oppressed and the defeated. Marhia dialect as a valid language of discourse is denied a voice through its transformation into mere form, devoid of 'intellectual' content. This view from the outside can be stated to have been derived from three positions, namely: (1) the Hill Maria should be absorbed under the general category of 'tribes', (2) they should be left alone, and (3) they should be transformed in accordance with the principles of a positivist science of development. The Hill Maria cannot, however, locate themselves in any of these positions. For the Hill Maria the languages of the 'outside' are those of the government officials, migrants, anthropologists and traders.[1] They describe Hill Maria with reference to a specific geographical area on a map. This cartographic representation is a projection used by the outsiders to establish contact with the Hill Maria and for purposes such as development.

In fact, it is the outsider who has classified the tribes described in this paper by the term 'Hill Maria'. In reality, the Hill Maria call themselves *koitors* and do not know the existence of the term 'Hill Maria'. We use the inappropriate term Hill Maria only because it has been used in earlier academic studies and by the government. It will be clear from the arguments to be presented that 'Hill Maria' is not a name, but a classification, and that such classifications lead only to a particular understanding of the tribes. The use of other terms such as 'tribes', 'cultivation', 'environment', 'ecology', 'society' and 'culture', should be also understood the same way.

This study is divided into three sections. The first describes modes of relationship to the environment; the second focuses on dialects and social relationships; and the third focuses on the social structure of the three groups of people.

Modes of relationship to the environment

Abujhmarh: a developmentalist world-view

Abujhmarh in Narayanpur Tehsil constitutes a block — the smallest administrative unit. The block development office is located in the village Orcha. Narayanpur Marh begins from the villages of Orcha, Kokameta and Sonepur. The latter two are close to each other but far away from Orcha (see figure 3.1). Narayanpur Marh includes Orcha Marh as well as Sonepur and Kokameta Marh. Sonepur, however, though it is in the centre for the geographical area covered by Abujhmarh, is a revenue village and therefore does not belong to the category of Abujhmarh.

The very name of Abujhmarh reveals that this hilly forest country has not been surveyed: *abujh* means unknown, and *marh* means hill. Though mapped, as a part of cartographic space, the map does not show either shifting cultivation or settlements formed through the physical activity of the area's inhabitants. Neither does the map show any reserved forest or surveyed agricultural land, and the area has consequently been identified as 'primitive'. According to government officials, only the Hill Maria can stay in Abujhmarh; other tribes or groups of cultivators cannot occupy the area without the permission of the government. In contrast with Abujhmarh, the neighbouring area of rice cultivation is surveyed. This lies outside Abujhmarh, and therefore the Hill Maria constitute it as the 'outside'.

From Narayanpur town, a forest road leads to the three villages. The road to Sonepur divides Abujhmarh into two parts, and then continues to Maroda in Maharashtra via Konge — the last village in Abujhmarh on this road. Villages in the two areas of Sonepur and Kokameta Marh differ according to (a) the composition of the population, (b) the method of cultivation and (c) the mode of relationship with development programmes run by government agencies. The road continues from Narayanpur to Kokameta and then branches off at Kundla terminating at Kokameta. The area studied in this chapter adjoins the road going from Kokameta to Kundla to Sonepur.

Villages with heterogeneous populations either lie alongside the forest road or are in close proximity to it. The population in these villages consists of Hill Maria — the original residents, and the migrants (Halbas, Kopas, Bairagis, Pankas, Gurus, Chattisgarhis). There is at least one Hill Maria household in each village which conducts rituals and ceremonies associated with the village space. These rituals and ceremonies are considered essential for the cultivation process and for the well-being of the villagers.

The Hill Maria in these villages practise both shifting millet cultivation and settled rice cultivation. In contrast, the migrants practise settled rice cultivation only. However, the distribution of the two types of cultivation

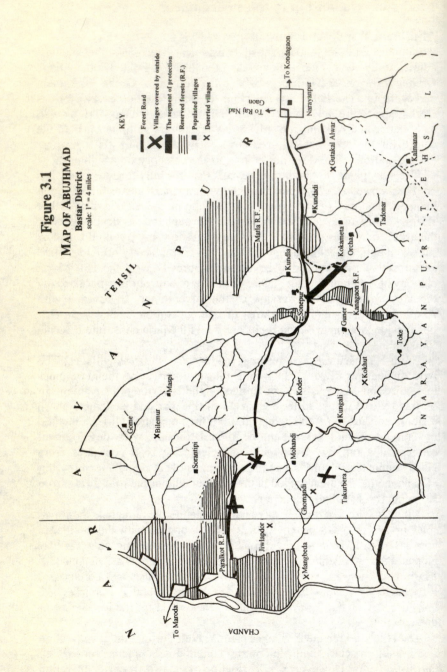

Figure 3.1
MAP OF ABUJHMAD
Bastar District
scale: 1" = 4 miles

KEY

- ⟋ Forest Road
- ✗ Villages covered by outside
- ▬ The segment of protection
- ▥ Reserved forests (R.F.)
- ■ Populated villages
- ✗ Deserted villages

in the villages varies. For example, Hill Maria in the villages close to the forest road have access to flat land and forested hills which enable them to practise both shifting millet cultivation and rice cultivation, although not all households do so. Hill Maria in villages directly alongside the forest road, in contrast, practise rice cultivation only. These villages which lie on the edge of or close to the forest road are targets of development programmes. These programmes are the primary source of representation regarding the 'outside' for the village residents, although this varies.

Not only do cultivation practices in the three villages vary, but the dialects spoken in these villages are also diverse. Marhia, Halbi, Chattisgarhi and spoken/colloquial Hindi belong to two different linguistic families: Marhia belongs to the Dravidian family and Halbi, Chattisgarhi and Hindi belong to the Indo-Aryan family. Of these dialects only Hindi has a script.

In terms of their spatial location, these villages are concentrated between Sonepur and Kokameta. It is possible to have direct access to the villages lying alongside the road which links Sonepur and Kokameta. But to reach villages away from the road, one has to go either from Sonepur or from Kokameta. These villages constitute a segment of the space between the two nodal points marked by Sonepur and Kokameta.

The Hill Maria world-view

The Hill Maria refer to their world as Shringar Bhum, which is viewed as distinct from Abujhmarh. Abujhmarh is a definite territorial unit; it has a shape on the map with a specific boundary, but for the Hill Maria, Shringar Bhum is not a point on a map, nor a territorial unit of a known shape. It is the universe of plants, animals, trees and human beings. It is a space for the Hill Maria which cannot be accurately represented (from the Hill Maria point of view) as a cartographic space on a geographical map — of which Shringar Bhum is only a part.

As space, it constitutes memory, myths, stories, songs and the daily life of the Hill Maria. It is not known as a place, as it is not located with reference to other places on a map. The term used for place is *jagha bhum*, which refers to the location(s) of social activities and is relative to other known places. For example, a village is also known as *jagha bhum*, because it is a place with reference to other villages. This is the 'place of village settlement'. Viewed from within, *jagha bhum*, the place of village settlement, is constituted by social activity and relationships. Together they constitute the space of the village. In other words, it is a place in relation to other villages. But viewed from within, it constitutes a living space for its resident members.

Thus, for the Hill Maria, Shringar Bhum is differentiated into several *jagha bhums*, including the 'space of the village' or village space; and within this space, there is *nage*, the place of village settlement, and *gera*, the remaining space covered by the forest. The physical place of village settlement is the single unit of the village space. Internally it is differentiated into several places and spots.

A village is known by the clan name of the village headman (the *kasar-gayta*), who performs sacrifices at the altar of Talurmuttee, mother of the *jagha bhum*. He is the caretaker of the *jagha bhum* on behalf of Talurmuttee and as such has the discretion to allow or disallow the settlement of new households in the *jagha bhum*. The households in the village are related to the clan of the village headman by either affinity or consanguinity. Although the headman has control over who settles in the village, he does not have control over the work rhythms of the households in the village.

In the internal space of the village, forests and the village settlement are contiguous. There are no fences to mark one from the other. However, cultivation plots are normally fenced to protect crops from animals. There is a difference between forests and fields. The forest undergoes seasonal changes, but fields change on account of the work done by Hill Maria. The distinction between the forests and the fields, on the one hand, and the contiguity between the forests and the village settlements, on the other, marks a third space — that of the fields. This space is separate from the space of the *gera* (forests) and the *nage* (place of the village settlement).

The field is viewed as a natural part of the forest landscape — a clearing in the forest — but also mediates the relationship between the forests and the village or between the natural environment and social structure. It is the place of work and is distinguished by the crop cultivated there. The field becomes a forest again through four stages. It changes in form when cultivation plots are prepared. Later, when crops are ready for harvest, the field is distinguished from the forest with reference to the difference between the forest vegetation and the cultivated crop. After harvest, the field is left fallow and it reverts to a 'clearing'. Finally, it transforms itself from fallow land into forest. Over the cultivation cycle, the field is a part of the social cultural life in the *nage* (during the first two steps) and that of the natural forest environment of *gera* (during the second two steps). It is in this way that the field is the third element, a mediation, establishing the differences and relationships between *gera* and *nage*. On the basis of these details the spatial arrangements and their social structures in the *jagha bhum* can be described with reference to a division between (a) the fields (b) *gera* and *nage*.

The households in the village are distributed over *paras* (neighbourhoods). The locations of the neighbourhoods constitute a centrally concentrated village settlement. The fields surround the village settlement and are differentiated according to their relationship to the specific mother goddesses of the various *jagha*. Nate Tali is mother goddess of the village settlement and all other goddesses relate to *buto* (work). Members of a neighbourhood go to work on fields associated with their respective mother goddesses. Several fields belonging to different households could be contiguous and the households who have contiguous fields may not be concentrated all within a neighbourhood. However, on account of the contiguity of the fields, they constitute a work group.

There is a space in the village centre for collective meetings to discuss village matters. In this space there is a large hut made of bamboo, wood and mud, enclosed on three sides, the *ghotul*. The *ghotul* members constitute an age-set consisting of unmarried boys and girls who are old enough to work. After singing and dancing at night, the boys sleep in the *ghotul* and girls return home.

The space immediately surrounding the *ghotul* is constituted by homes. Each house is divided into two or three rooms and the innermost room is used to store grain. Along a wall at the rear of the house is a small hut for women — the menstrual hut. It lies outside the space of the house. During menstruation women stay in and around it; they do not participate in the social activities of the household.

Surrounding the house (including the menstrual hut) are small fields where two secondary crops, maize and mustard, are cultivated. These fields are called *varum* and they are distinguished from the fields in the forest (*pendas*). The former constitutes a compound which is fenced in before the rains. After the harvest, the wood used for building these fences is used as firewood.

On the basis of this brief description of the layout of Shringar Bhum I will describe the comparative features of shifting and rice cultivation cycles practised in the Hill Maria villages.

Shifting *kosra* cultivation

The rhythm of social-cultural activity of a Hill Maria village is set in relation to the cultivation of *kosra*[2] (millet), the staple food crop. Two secondary crops, *jondra* (maize) and *harso* (mustard), are grown in small quantities. Mustard is the cash crop and although maize is not a cash crop, it is used to cook a gruel consumed in large quantities during work in summer and in lesser quantities during the winter and the monsoons. The demand for maize is less than that for millet and more than that for mustard.

Plots of land on steep hill slopes, called *pendas*, are prepared for the cultivation of millet. Plots of land on shallow slopes at the foot of the hills are used for the cultivation of an early variety of millet, called *deepa*. Every household has a minimum of nine *pendas* located in the forests. Each of these plots is prepared, using the axe, knife and *kaver* (made of two bamboo baskets slung at the ends of a bamboo pole to carry foodgrain on the shoulders), once in every eight cultivation cycles. Work for the preparation of *pendas* begins in the month of Dogar (February–March), which marks the beginning of the summer (*adhe*). This work is done by the members of a household, who begin by clearing the forests on their plots. By the end of the month of Chait (March–April) the cutting operations are over and the wood is left to dry in the sun. By the month of Baisakh (April–May) it is time to burn the dried wood, shrubs and other vegetation lying on the plots. On an appointed day all the plots are set on fire at the same time. After the fire dies out, each household surveys its plot to collect the unburnt wood and again sets it ablaze. The plot is then ready for the rains.

Sowing begins with the first rain in the month of Burbar (May–June) after the ashes have had a chance to mix well within the soil. A variety of seeds are mixed in one basket and sown in each plot. Ten varieties of seeds can be sown along with millet; but every household need not have all the varieties.

Heavy rains, leading to an excessive flow of water down the *penda* slope, can lead to crop damage. This is prevented during the first stage of crop growth because the crop is allowed to grow along with the forest vegetation. This also prevents excessive soil erosion. Towards the end of the monsoons, the forest vegetation is removed in order to allow the crop to ripen independently. As the crops ripen during the period from the month of Bija (July–August) to the month of Dushera (October–November), members of the household take turns to protect the crop from birds and animals living in the forest. When the early millet crop begins to ripen in the month of Dushera (October–November), Nua Polowa, a festival which marks the beginning of harvest, is celebrated. In the month of Pus (December–January), threshing is undertaken after all households have finished harvesting. Finally, the crop is carried home. The tasks of threshing and carrying home the crop are carried out collectively by the village. It is only after threshing that *kosra* (millet) becomes *nuka* (foodgrain). Marking the end of the year, the last festival, Koding, is celebrated in the month of Mah (January–February).

Through a combination of technology, work rhythm and social relationships the process of millet cultivation is set in motion. The process attains completion in two lunar years, the period of one cultivation cycle. All the activities connected with cultivation commence in the village collectively. There is no specified time limit to finish a particular cultivation activity nor do all households finish cultivation activities at the same time, since each household devotes various durations of time to these activities. The work rhythm of each household is determined by at least three factors — number of working hands available, demands at home and illness. The households that finish their work first often assist those who have not been able to finish it.

Until the month of Burbar (May–June), work is planned keeping in mind the time of the first rains. The work rhythm during this period is set in relation to the totality of work to be done in the household and in the fields. At home, preparations are made for the rains and in the fields *penda* plots are prepared for cultivation. It is not possible, the Hill Maria point out, to concentrate on one at the expense of the other. Preparation of *pendas* begins early, around the month of Dogar (February–March) and less and less work is done at home as the work on the *penda* plot increases. Every adult goes to work during the day while the children stay in the village.

Fields are ready by the beginning of the month of Baisakh (April–May) and in the month of Burbar (May–June), when the monsoon sets in, more attention is once again given to the work at home. During this period only seeds are sown.

The month of Bija, or seed, is named for the end of sowing which is marked by the first festival of the cultivation cycle, Bija Polowa. After this period, nature's rhythms determine the work rhythms of the Hill Maria villages until the month of Dushera (October–November). At this time when the monsoons have stopped and harvesting begins, the natural climate no longer plays a significant role in determining the work rhythm. Slowly over a period of three to four months until Pus (December–January), the crop is harvested and threshed.

After Pus, in the months of Mah, Dogar, Chait and Baisakh, the outside world is open to the Hill Maria: they visit markets at various places, they have their religious festivals, they renovate old houses and build new ones for the monsoons. In addition, every alternate year they begin the work of preparing new *pendas* in Dogar (February–March). The Hill Maria normally cannot attend equally to all these activities every year, as the festivals continue until Chait–Baisakh and cut into the time, from Dogar onwards, when *penda* preparation is undertaken.

The *penda* plots are not cultivated for two consecutive years, though, in some cases, a small portion could be reused for a small crop in the succeeding year. As already stated, it is a two-year cycle, namely a new *penda* is prepared every alternate year. After all the nine *pendas* belonging to a household have been used, then the first plot is again cultivated. That is, all *pendas* lie fallow until they are cultivated again.

The two-year cycle can be explained in the following way. Two equally important sets of activities take place simultaneously in the period before sowing and after harvest — between Mah (January–February) and Bija (May–June). These activities can be performed either sequentially over a period of time or simultaneously through their allocation to different people at a given point of time. Given that on average the strength of a household is not more than six to seven members covering three generations — the elders, the married couple and the children — the second possibility cannot be pursued.

The first possibility, which involves a sequential distribution of activities, is worked out in the following way: instead of using the year as a unit of time and then squeezing all the activities in the time available, the time cycle is extended over two lunar years, until all the activities have been completed. In one year the crop is cultivated and in the following year there is participation in the social and cultural activities mentioned above. The unit of time described above begins with the availability of foodgrains in Pus–Mah and it ends in Pus–Mah two years later. This is the duration of a moment of time. It must be pointed out, however, that the performance of one set of activities in one year does not mean the total exclusion of the other set of activities. Here it is referred to as the period of 'no cultivation'.

The cultivation cycle is related to the abundance and variety of food available in the forest. The period of 'no-cultivation', or when *pendas* lie fallow, is the period of seasonal hunger known by the term *kagaveku*. It is in relation to this period that the shifting cultivation cycle becomes defined.

Agricultural activities are sequentially arranged in relation to lunar calendar months. The annual cycle defines the wet months (the time of sowing), the dry months (the time for the preparation of the *penda*) and the cold months (the time for the ripening and harvesting of crops), associated respectively with wetness, dryness and coldness of the earth. According to the Hill Maria, the productivity of land and the wetness of the monsoons varies directly with the hotness and dryness of the summer months. During the hot months of the fallow period land recuperates its fertility. The heat helps the land to retain and enhance its fertility. Forests regenerate on fallow land before the land is again ready for cultivation.

The time period required for the regeneration of the forest on fallow land constitutes a larger cycle, which is not a crop cultivation cycle but the cycle of recuperation of fertility of fallow plots. It is within this cycle that the smaller crop cultivation cycle is placed. *Pendas*, it is said, will not yield good crops without the regeneration of forests in fallow plots over a period of nine cultivation cycles.

Fallow period, cultivation and social relations
The social-cultural activities performed in the village during the fallow period underline the principles of social structure and continuity and point to the significance of this period. In years when new *pendas* are not prepared, two sets of activities occur simultaneously in two different spaces: (1) in the field the self-regeneration of forests takes place on the fallow *penda* plots; (2) in the village social-cultural activities are

performed — such as visits to affines, marriages, building new houses or repairing old ones, collective hunting, clan festivals and visits to weekly markets. The language of cultivation is understood in terms of these social-cultural activities which then define the notions of fertility and fallowness in the *pendas*.

Each of the two sets of activity becomes a meaningful context for the other. The social-cultural activities in the village space provide meaning to the fallowness of the *penda* plots, while the regeneration of forest vegetation on fallow land becomes the context for the meanings of social and cultural activities in the villages. These relationships and their meanings emerge when forests, fields and the social structures are not related through the cultivation process, i.e. through work. During the fallow period land regenerates itself into forests without the use of technology and techniques. This period of self-regeneration in the *pendas* corresponds to social reproduction through social-cultural activities in the village. When no work is done on land, vegetation in the fields and social life in the village regenerate and are reproduced simultaneously. Natural regeneration and social and cultural production and reproduction overlap during this period. The relationship becomes clearer when we recognise that the *koitors* are not aware, either from memory or from any other representation of the past, that land may lose its fertility to such an extent that forests will no longer exist.

Similarities and differences in the two domains — the fields and the forests on one hand, and the village social structure on the other — are here manifest during the fallow periods. There is similarity between the rules of social structure and crop cultivation: they are grounded in the regeneration of forest vegetation. While the forest is regenerating itself in the fallow plot, a crop is being produced on a freshly prepared *penda*. There is simultaneity of crop cultivation and forest regeneration in the year of cultivation across *pendas* and there is sequentiality of cultivation and afforestation during two successive years in the same *penda*.

These in turn constitute parts of a larger cycle. While one plot of land is used for crop cultivation, the other plots of fallow land regenerate. To produce one crop in one cultivation cycle, each of the other plots must regenerate themselves. In other words, the same plot of *penda* has nine cultivation cycles as fallow periods and one cultivation cycle for forest clearing and crop cultivation. This explains why each household has a minimum of nine *pendas*.

The regeneration of natural vegetation, the cultivation of crop on *pendas* and the social structure form parts of one large structure, namely the structure of the *jagha bhum*. Natural vegetation and the *pendas* are located in the *gera* (the forest space) and the social structure is located in *nage* (the village space) — the two parts of *jagha bhum* described at the beginning of this chapter. Evidently, 'nature' or 'ecology' or 'environment' is not a separate category in Hill Maria social-cultural life. For the Hill Maria, since the time the world was 'first' created, the world of plants and animals has coexisted with human social structures. A village elder once told me:

> The sun, the moon, the air, the trees are signs of my continuity [the continuity of the self is only the way in which continuity of social structure is understood]. Social life will continue as long as these continue to live. I was born a part of the Bhum. I will die when this Bhum dies.

He added:

> I was born with all others in this Bhum; I go with them. That which has created us all will give us food. If there is so much variety and abundance in Bhum, there is no reason for me to worry about food and continuity.

Self-regeneration of nature: the cultivation cycle and the menstrual cycle

A second meaning of fallowness and of the year of 'no cultivation' is established by the correspondence between the menstrual cycle of a woman, the fallow land and forest regeneration. A woman is marriageable after her menstrual cycle starts; prior to it, she is not given away in marriage. An unmarried daughter is the responsibility of her parents. Since marriage is irreversible, if it breaks up or fails, a woman cannot return to her paternal home as a daughter. She is then known as a *rande*. She can take shelter in her paternal home; however there is a preference to settle near it. She is expected to find a man with whom she will live, but to whom she cannot get married. When she visits her paternal home she has to stay away from the *annal arka* (the earthen pot which symbolises the ancestral gods).

As we have already pointed out, women in menstruation stay outside the home in menstrual huts (*kurma*), and sometimes in menstrual huts outside the village. In some villages even visual contact with men by a menstruating woman is forbidden. She cooks her own food and stays away from all social and cultural activities. At the end of the menstrual period she takes a bath, returns home and resumes work.

The menstrual cycle determines the rhythm of household routines. When women of the house menstruate, the home looks barren, since during this period women do not perform any household function. Other women agnates and/or affines then assist in the maintenance of the house. Thus menstruation (like the fallow period) in one sense signifies fertility, and, in another, a condition of barrenness.

The rhythms of the household routines are set with reference to menstruation. This is similar to the way rhythms of cultivation work cycles are set with reference to the fallow periods. Both menstruation and 'fallowness' signify recuperation of fertility, although both create an illusion of barrenness (no crop from the fallow land and no activity on the part of the menstruating woman). But the illusion, in fact, confirms what it negates, i.e. fertility and reproductivity.

Another similarity comes from the crop cycle. In a forest the dry seasons are barren and the wet seasons are fertile. However, the dry season is necessary for clearing the forest and for the ripening of the crop, just as menstruation is necessary for the regeneration of fertility. Abnormal menstruation (in terms of the number of days of the period) is as much a condition of unproductiveness as is lack of menstruation. This is comparable to the situation in *pendas* when there is no crop because of lack or excess of rains. (See Figure 3.2.)

Rice cultivation in Hill Maria villages

In my analysis so far the shifting cultivation cycle has been understood in relation to the fallow period. This has made available a notion of time and continuity. Now it is essential to see how these notions emerge in relation to the rice cultivation process, as it is practised by the migrants.

Rice cultivation in its present form has been introduced from outside. The most significant differences between millet and rice cultivations lie in the method of cultivation.

Briefly, the method of rice cultivation, practised by the migrants, involves the following activities. rice fields are prepared after cutting down the forests on flat land wherever available. Since rice needs lots of water, the plot is bunded up on all four sides to prevent the water from flowing out of the fields. Ploughing begins after the first few monsoon showers in the months of Burbar (May–June) and Jeth (June–July). This is followed by sowing. After the harvest, threshing is done in the month of Dushera (October–November) and Divali (November–December) with the help of cattle.

Unlike the millet cultivation cycle, the cultivation cycle of rice is complete in one year. A fresh crop is harvested every year on the same field. Further, only one kind of crop is grown at a time on a rice field. After harvest, land lies fallow until the first rains in the following year. During this period only grass grows on the rice fields. Unlike the case of the pendas, the forests and the rice fields remain spatially dissociated from one another on a permanent basis and the quality of land gets radically transformed in the process of preparation of the rice fields. After two rice harvests the forest stops regenerating on the rice field.

Figure 3.2 Agricultural calendar.

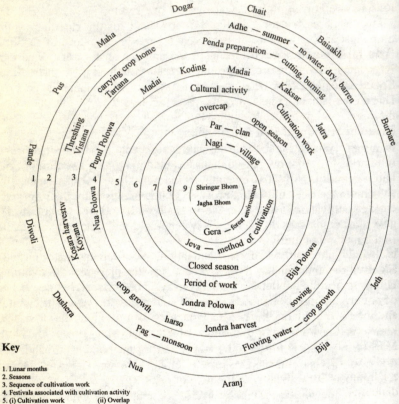

Key

1. Lunar months
2. Seasons
3. Sequence of cultivation work
4. Festivals associated with cultivation activity
5. (i) Cultivation work   (ii) Overlap
6. (i) Closed period   (ii) Open period
7. (i) Par – clan   (ii) Jiva – food cultivation
8. (i) Nagè – social structure   (ii) Gera – natural environment

One more consequence of rice-cultivation is that there is a change in village settlement patterns. Millet-cultivating village settlements are 'concentrated', in contrast to the 'dispersed' village settlements associated with rice cultivation. In a village, the desirable place of residence is near one's rice fields. As a result, rice cultivating households have been moving closer to their fields over a period of time. Through these changes dispersed settlements come to be a part of the shape of Hill Maria villages. In these settlements *paras* or neighbourhoods are formed with reference to the location of fields.

The Hill Maria and the migrants

Social relations

Due to the isolation and laws protecting the Hill Maria from outsiders, the rate of migration in Abujhmarh is low. Nevertheless, in the forest environment (as a shared living space), the difference in the knowledge of dialect and the differences in the method of cultivation, when represented by two groups of unequal population strength, namely the Hill Maria and the migrants, constitute non-antagonistic differences. The stratification of these differences, as will be shown in the next section, emerges in the relationship of these two groups to the third group, the government officials.

The social relationship between the Hill Maria and the migrant outsider is based on the differences in the knowledge of each other's dialect, acquired in the interaction over time. Marhia, the dialect of the majority Hill Maria, and Halbi and Chattisgarhi, those of the minority migrants, do not resemble each other; the former is the language of millet cultivation and the latter is of rice cultivation. Furthermore, only a few Hill Maria know the dialects of the migrants, whereas almost all migrants know Marhia. They learnt Marhia in order to familiarise themselves with their new social and cultural environment, which for them means *parades* — a land away from home. Differences in the knowledge of each others' dialects does not lead to their instrumental use as means of acquiring wealth.

At the time of the first migrations the rate at which people came into Abujhmarh was low. The forbidding forest environment, the differences of dialects and their different cultivation activities prevented large populations from migrating. The migrants were not in search of a promised land, and their arrival was accidental and contingent. The natural forest environment regulated the movement of migrants. Those in real need came, others did not. Some Hindus, therefore, describe this place as a *tirath*, that is, place of pilgrimage.

From the point of view of the Hill Maria, the relationship to migrants is based on the mode of the latter's arrival in Abujhmarh. Some came to graze cattle, some to distribute salt and some fled from nearby areas to seek shelter for short periods. Their visits were erratic to begin with. In the course of several visits they acclimatised themselves to the place, the people and the environment. The Hindus presented themselves to the headman of the village, and only after getting his consent did they settle in the village. The headman made available to them land for cultivation. The process for introduction to the headman and to the villagers and the final incorporation lasted over long periods of exposure and interaction.

Initial perceptions were focused on external characteristics. For example, the Hindus, like the Hill Maria, are barefoot, bare-bodied and wear a loin cloth. Unlike Hill Maria, on ceremonial occasions they wear a *dhoti* above the knee. Their feet are hard and calloused. Their belongings when they travel are few and select: some rice, a sheet of cloth to cover themselves and a loin cloth to wear. The government officials, unlike the Hill Maria and migrants, are very 'soft', say the Hill Maria; their feet are soft and their hands are even softer.

There are several features that are common to the Hill Maria and the migrants. They recognise similar sets of necessities. Their dialects use different names for several objects of daily use such as firewood for cooking, mud for making houses, air, water and land. However, they differ in their lifecycle rituals and in their remembered past.

More importantly, while their dialects differ from each other, both communities as cultivators recognise the language of food also known as *jiva*, (the life force; this is a qualitative description) common to both methods of cultivation. Despite the partial isolation created by the limited access to each other's dialect, the migrants and Hill Maria can continue to produce their respective food crops in the same village, because they share a common understanding of the relationship between work and food.

This shared understanding between the two groups is reflected or represented in their relationship to the village (*jagha bhum*). Together with the Hill Maria, the migrants follow and participate in all rituals and festivals in the cultivation cycle which are associated with the *jagha bhum* and with the process of cultivation in the calendar. The acceptance of the Hill Maria calendar by the Hindus reflects a similarity in the relationship between people and the village; between the cultivator and the cultivated crop. Within the framework of village social life the differences in the modes of cultivation are mediated by work within a common calendar. The Hill Maria have accepted the difference in cultivation methods because the cultivation of rice is done in relation to the Hill Maria agricultural calendar within the framework of the rituals and ceremonies of *jagha bhum*.

The differences are based on lifecycle rituals and methods of cultivation and the similarities are based on *jiva* (food; the life force). They are represented by the Hindus in terms of the five senses and the stomach respectively. It is *karma* (work) associated with the five senses that define the caste (*jati*). The stomach 'speaks' the language of hunger and food irrespective of caste. This is the language of *jiva*. The similarities define the two different ways of cultivating *jiva*.

The migrants and the Hill Maria, like members of a family, are related through complementarity as well as supplementarity, the former based on differences in quality and the latter on differences in quantity. This can be best described in terms of an analogy with allocation of responsibilities between two brothers in a household. As brothers they complement each other, while as cultivators they supplement each other. For example, after a quarrel with his elder brother, a boy once said:

Just because he is elder, he asks me to work in his fields, while he himself keeps sitting and walking around aimlessly. This is unfair. It is true that a person is elder or younger by birth which defines his social responsibilities. However, a person old or young must earn for his *jiva*. I can only assist him.

Similarly, as migrants or Hill Maria, the two groups complement each other; as cultivators, they supplement each other. This belief is shared by both groups, and makes it possible for them to practise two different modes of cultivation alongside.

There are other similarities also. The propitiation of Thakur Dei by Hindus is similar to the propitiation of Talurmuttee by Hill Maria. On account of this, they recognise both Talurmuttee and Thakur Dei as mothers of the *jagha bhum*. For the Hindus Thakur Dei is Niranjani (the earth goddess) — the literal meaning of the word is 'not prejudiced towards any form'. The term for soil as Niranjani is *mati* (the earth) — the universal giver of life to all forms.

The Hindu deity Shiva has the same symbol as Rau, one of the *darma* worshipped by Hill Maria, namely the cobra snake. It is said that when Rau is angered he sends the cobra which is his gun (*topak*). The tiger is Rau's dog (Kurur). The tiger is also related to the Talurmuttee. When she is angry there is tiger menace. For the Hindus, the tiger is the vehicle of the great goddess Durga.

Both Hill Maria and the Hindu migrants assign the same value to menstruation. Women in both social structures stay away from the hearth. Both groups have similar 'possession' ceremonies, they use earthen pots for the propitiation of ancestral gods and believe in the magical and the healing quality of the 'blown breath'. They recognise their bodies as similar to, but different from, those of the government officials. They follow similar treatments for illness.

Finally, they believe that life would not be possible without air, water and land. Their notion of time and continuity derive from the continuity of the relationship between the three elements. Along with other things, for both of them these determine the three seasons within which cultivation is possible.

The influence of Hindus cannot account for the above similarities. On the basis of these similarities, however, the Hindus have adapted and changed as much as the Hill Maria have. This is the ground on which two to three generations of Hindu migrants have stayed together with Hill Maria in Abujhmarh.

Marriage systems

In terms of marriage systems, both groups marry cross-cousins. While the immigrant Hindus marry classificatory cross-cousins, the Hill Maria prefer to marry their actual mother's brother's daughter or their father's sister's son.

To the Hill Maria the Hindus are consanguines and affines. Though kinship and affinal terminology is used to address them, intermarriage is neither prescribed nor preferred. Such marriages go against the principle of ancestry which according to the Maria is passed down through men but is protected by the women. The restriction is aimed at the generalisation of symbolic capital (Bourdieu 1977).

Intermarriage between Hindus and Hill Maria, if it became the norm, would be a threat to the social structure. It would weaken the Hill Maria. It would either break or threaten the continuity of ancestry — a fundamental principle of the Hill Maria social structure.

Marriages between Hindus and the Hill Maria, when they do take place, are tolerated but generally discouraged. The new household is neither of the *jati parade*, of the man nor of the clan of the woman because both of them are excommunicated. Though a mixed household continues to be defined in relation to the social structure, it is outside the social structure because the marriage is not given legitimacy, and the married couple cannot participate in the sacred rituals and ceremonies. A fine is levied on the families of the girl and the boy; the boy and the girl are socially ostracised. While the ostracised couple cannot partake of the sacred food of the *annal* (ancestral gods) or the *pane* (clan gods), the exchange of foodgrains, work, friendship and enterprises are not forbidden.

The *koska* and the Marhia dialect[3]

The government officials

The government officials, known as *koska* to Hill Maria, wear either trousers or *dhotis* (down to their ankles) on the lower half of their body, and shirts on the upper half. Unlike the Hill Maria, they are not barefoot; they can read and write; they speak Hindi and some of them can even speak the dialects of the migrants, namely Halbi and Chattisgarhi. When they travel, their belongings weigh more than what they can carry themselves. They are neither permanent nor long-duration residents of Abujhmarh. Hill Maria point out that they live in Tehsil headquarters at Narayanpur. On being transferred they leave and never come back.

It is the opinion of the *koska* that to live in Abujhmarh for long periods is to accept an invitation to death. According to them, there are neither proper conditions nor adequate means for maintaining good health, nor the facilities for procuring the right kind of food, shelter and clothing. They fear stomach disorders. For them the water of the rivers is unclean. They fear cerebral malaria, for there are mosquitoes in the air. Also feared is the wilderness of the dark forests, which for them is the home of wild animals. As outsiders, the *koska* view the forest and the climate of Abujhmarh as 'environment' or 'ecology' or as 'jungle' or 'wilderness' — separate from the village and home. It is for these reasons that the development programmes are implemented by *koska*, from outside Abujhmarh, and their posting to Abujhmarh is considered by them as punishment.

According to Hill Maria, two generations ago a *koska* was feared. The sight of him or the sound of his jeep sent the villagers running into the forest. Today they walk into a village for the business of development.

The *koska* are in active contact with Hill Maria during the summer and winter months, when development programmes are executed and weekly markets are held in various places in and around Abujhmarh. With the coming of the monsoons, they suspend their visits to Abujhmarh.

To the Hill Maria, the government is associated with the written word, numbers and quantities. For instance, the census operations are understood by the Hill Maria as an exercise in writing names. This has created what is popularly called 'population mixtures'. It is said, 'ever since our names have been written down, the distinction in respect of *parade* [clan] has become insignificant'.

In the remembered past of the Hill Maria the *koska* initially came with a rupee to buy grain. The villagers, not knowing the value of a rupee, contributed one measure (*soli*) of grains per household. The total quantity of grains collected was more than the *koska* could carry. The rupee was also returned to the *koska*. The *koska*, therefore, took away both the grains as well as the rupee. But today the *koska* gives the Hill Maria 8.50

rupees as daily wages to work for road construction, and takes away everything, i.e. forests, grain, women, men, children. As one villager put it: 'When *koska* came first, they were one or two in number — there was one forest guard for the whole area. Today it is difficult to keep count of them.'

Encouragement of rice cultivation

The agricultural and the forest departments discourage shifting cultivation and encourage rice cultivation. The banks and the weekly markets encourage the use of money. Loans given to prepare rice fields are used to hire wage labour. Rice has to be produced and sold to earn money, to repay the government loans. Over the years a section of the tribal population in the villages near the Tehsil town of Narayanpur has become permanent wage labourers. They do not work in their own rice fields. This is one of the prospects projected for the Hill Maria.

There is, however, another contradiction. Officially the outsiders consider millet inferior to rice. Government officials do not eat it. They believe its cultivation destroys forests. Moreover, rice fetches a better price in the market. Those who eat rice are preferred by government officials to those who eat millet. It is also for reasons of taste that millet is seen as inferior to rice. But unofficially millet is rated higher than rice by government extension workers for its intrinsic food value. It is accepted that 'millet is good for hard work and it tastes better after hard work. But rice gets digested soon and does not sustain people through long periods of hard work.'

The value differences between rice and millet are based on the distinction between the two as foodstuff and as the products of an economy. The food values of rice and millet are generated internally; their values as products of an economy are generated externally. As food items, rice and millet are defined as *buto kamai*, that is, constituted by the blood and sweat that goes into their cultivation. In contrast, as a product of the economy, rice is defined in terms of the loans given by the government to prepare and plough the rice fields and millet is defined in terms of the destruction of the forests by shifting cultivation. Lunar months become coterminous with the production year. Consequently, food production steps out of the discourse of Shringar Bhum.

With the increasing flow of finances from the government, money rather than forest emerges as the major factor in social production and reproduction. Rice production depends on the money that can buy the cattle, new varieties of seeds, fertilisers, and knowledge of better bunding and cultivation techniques. Consequently, the rituals and ceremonies of the cultivation cycle become separated from the technology and techniques of cultivation.

The cultivation cycle is then constituted of two unrelated elements: the 'real' factors of production and the 'belief' systems. The government-supplied inputs constitute the real factors of production, and the world-view of the Hill Maria constitutes the 'belief' system.

In early 1987 a few film-makers entered the interior of one part of Abujhmarh. When the government officials learned about this intrusion they were ordered to leave and their films were confiscated. Later the *koska* undertook to throw out all migrant residents in Abujhmarh. For reasons not known to the Hill Maria, this project was abandoned.

This event led to two consequences. In the minds of the migrants on the one hand, there was uncertainty about their position vis-à-vis the government. This led to an increase in cooperation and exchange with the Hill Maria. In the minds of the Hill Maria, on the other hand, it was a confirmation that the method of rice cultivation was going to be promoted.

Today both Hill Maria and migrants realise that there is a scarcity of land for the coming generation. In the area, flat forested land is not available in large quantities for settled cultivation.

Dialects and power

Rice cultivation and the dialect of the migrants acquire a new significance in their relationship to the government. Government officials do not know the Marhia dialect, but they speak the dialect of the migrants. The success of the development programmes thus depends on setting up successful demonstration models with the help of the migrants.

The Hill Maria are not familiar with the dialects of the migrants. Since they are unable to communicate in the language of government officials, they suffer losses in market transactions. Differences in dialect represent to the government differences in the ability to benefit from the development programmes.

In the mind of the Hill Maria dialects are now hierarchically ordered according to the benefits they can get. In descending order the dialects are arranged as follows: Halbi, Chattisgarhi and Marhia. However, this order is reversed in terms of the subsidies given by the government to the various groups. The Hill Maria get 80 per cent subsidy; the migrants, Halbas and Chattisgarhis get 50 per cent. The Hindi-speaking Hindu population do not get subsidy; they earn salaries or income through service. The hierarchy of dialects articulates their instrumental value. In the mind of the Hill Maria and the migrants, dialect and wealth are correlated. As a result, now the Hill Maria are more keen to learn Halbi and Chattisgarhi. On the other hand, even though economically poor, the Hill Maria are regarded as the privileged ones by the migrants and the government officials. The migrants, though less privileged, have in the process become, for the Hill Maria, models to be emulated.

To understand the significance of Marhia dialect as a language of discourse it is important to find out what would be left of it (that is, of the dialect and the language) after forests and shifting cultivation cease to constitute the social-cultural landscape of the Hill Maria.

Is it possible to know or see what is being lost on account of the implementation of development programmes from outside? Is it possible to study the shadows left behind by the methods and programmes of development and progress?

The forests

To the *koska*, Abujhmarh is a repository of mineral and forest resources which contribute to national wealth. In the opinion of the *koska*, shifting cultivation destroys the forests. Consequently, settled rice cultivation is encouraged and shifting millet cultivation is discouraged.

The *koska* introduced a new classification of the forest, namely 'reserved' forests and 'unreserved' forests. In the reserved forests, which belong to the *koska*, no human settlement is permitted. A large portion of the Abujhmarh forest is not yet classified as reserved forests because the Hill Maria stay there.

Reserved forests are rich in resources. The rights to use them are controlled by the Forest Department. The reserved forests and the Hill Maria villages are separate and not contiguous. The relationship between the Hill Maria and the reserved forests, the *koska* believes, is antagonistic because of the practice of shifting cultivation. In the villages which lie in proximity to the reserved forests, settled rice cultivation is practised. Some rights have been given to the villagers in these reserved forests. For example, they can collect firewood, a specified number of bamboos and a specified quantity of wood for the construction of houses and fences and for making baskets and other such things needed for the household.

In contrast, the Hill Maria practise shifting cultivation in the unreserved forests. There is no restriction, in principle, on the use of the unreserved forests by the residents. However, since the classification of the forests can be changed from 'unreserved' to 'reserved', the Hill Maria live under the constant fear of having to give up their forests and stop shifting cultivation.

The development perspective

Thus, the main features of the emerging social structure which the government officials represent are that (a) rice is better than millet; (b) loans and money are the factors of production and reproduction; and (c) dialects do not represent differences in culture but they are the means of getting benefits under the development schemes.

Broadly, the space between Sonepur and Kokameta (see Figure 3.1) represents the zone of transition which is influenced by the government development programme. Villages in this area, the state officials point out, serve as examples for villages in the interior beyond the zone of transition. This does not mean that all the villages in this transition zone or in the interior will become like either Kokameta or Sonepur. They may or they may not. To the Hill Maria staying in the interior, it is important that there is talk about whether the government is going to stop shifting cultivation or not, because they know that in their environment there is no flat land available for rice fields.

Sonepur and Kokameta, which are being presented as model villages for the Hill Maria who stay in the interior, project the various possible results of government development programmes to the Hill Maria. Villages which lie in between can be differentiated with reference to the scale and depth of the projection of these models. The scale and the depth, in turn, are determined by the distribution of the things offered by the development programmes.

The schools and participation-in-development programmes, both symbols of *koska* culture, emphasise status acquired through the use of the written word. This is in contrast and opposition to ascribed status, inherited by being born a member of a household, a lineage, a clan and a village. Further, while the written word records an achievement, the spoken word expresses an oral tradition constituted by memory and forgetting, both associated with names, places, events, things and social relationships.

In the mode of learning in a school there is a separation between the home, the place of work, and the place of learning. To know how to read and write in the school enables a Hill Maria to sign a document on the basis of which a *koska* sanctions loans. The ability to sign one's name is considered by *koska* a good enough criterion to decide that the loan would be used better by the Hill Maria who can sign than by the Hill Maria who cannot.

The health centres dispense medicine to those who come to ask for it. More significant is the work of the malaria worker in this area infested with the cerebral malaria parasite. It is the duty of the malaria worker to collect blood samples. But for the Hill Maria this task is representative of the loss of blood, which they fear.

An alternative perspective

The above description of the depth and scale of the social context in which the Hill Maria and the government officials are located has three dimensions. First, from the 'outside', the Hill Maria constitute a specific type of social system. It is part of the plurality and multiplicity of culture. This includes traditional cultures as much as it includes modern scientific social structures. This plurality and multiplicity describe the problems created by other languages for the Hill Maria. The condition of the Hill

Maria today is articulated, not as their own history, but as part of the 'history of the outside'.

Second, from the position of the Hill Maria, the 'history of the outside' and its languages are not available to them. In the language of the 'outside' the Hill Maria are constituted in a historical moment, which is defined by three parameters: it comes in a chronology of events; everyone in it is affected by historical events; and any act at the moment can lead to a historical event which can change history. The Hill Maria speak the Marhia dialect. This language of their social-cultural life does not have a representation of the historical moment either as a fact or as an event or as a record. However, they have a notion of time and continuity against which they understand the emerging landscape of rice fields, brick constructions, loss of forest, money and the increasing heterogeneity of the outsiders. The historical moment and time, in the sense we use it here, is a construct of the 'outside', it is a stage in the linear progress of primitive cultures.

The Hill Maria do not share this historical past of the 'outside'. Grigson (1938) gives us an account of the isolation of Abujhmarh from the outside world. He, as the British administrator, for the first time went into Abujhmarh. However, the Hill Maria environment today includes the 'outside' in its various representations. This environment is constituted of (a) the ecological space of the forests, (b) the social environment, including the government officials, the migrant rice cultivator and fellow Hill Maria, and (c) the anthropologists.

The rice fields, money, schools and the other representations of the outside described above were not known to the Hill Maria in 'their past'. To be able to talk about or describe their environment as a here-and-now, the Hill Maria have no language available, other than the dialect of the outsider, namely, Halbi, Chattisgarhi and Hindi. Their own dialect cannot be used because no written transaction or discourse between the government and the Hill Maria is conducted in Marhia dialect. There is thus a disjunction, both within Hill Maria life and between the Hill Maria and the outsider.

Third, the Hill Maria and the outsiders nevertheless share a contiguity in the physical landscape. In their consciousness and in their daily lives they have an awareness of each other.

Several questions arise in the minds of the elders of the Hill Maria. It has become quite evident to them that their way of life, cultural values and truths are going to be lost. The question they ask is, will these values and truths return to reassert themselves? The following salient points in the foregoing analysis are relevant to this question.

Shifting cultivation is discouraged and settled rice cultivation is encouraged in Abujhmarh. There is a total elimination of forest vegetation when the rice fields are left fallow. To the Hill Maria this indicates the death of the forest and with it the death of their life-world.

That shifting cultivation does not destroy forests needs no proof in Abujhmarh. The elders of the Hill Maria say that they have been living in these forests and practising shifting cultivation for several generations and that there has not been any sign of deforestation. They suggest that in order to understand the causes of this destruction, the factors which are responsible for the separation of the natural environment of forest from the agricultural processes of rice production and village life need to be examined.

This description is the basis of their oral history which recollects the losses incurred. In the span of one generation, since the time of their contact with the *koska*, the water table has dropped to 120 feet below the surface of the earth. There is only one monsoon nowadays, in contrast to two monsoons in the past. Such memories are a sign of their contemporaneity with the history of the *koska*, pointing towards the conditions of their environment, in which the Hill Maria and the succeeding generations will have to live.

Conclusion

It must be recognised that in place of the oral word in oral tradition, the written word is now available to Hill Maria through government schools to assist an understanding of the changes which have resulted from development programmes. Writing is a medium to represent the spoken word. On the one hand, for those living an oral tradition, the written word is also part of a technology of the 'outside'. On the other hand, for those living in the tradition of the written word, the use of the written word provides the infrastructure for building all discourse of which the final form is a written text. Without such a text no discourse built on the written word is valid. For it is the text which gives legitimacy to such a discourse.

Finally, the power of the written word lies in effecting a disjunction between the text and the author. It is available to anybody for use and application. For example, although it was not intentional on the part of those studying tribes, when the study of tribes began, concomitantly the process of their extinction also began. It is true that the texts are not used and applied directly to destroy a tribe or its life-support system, but the text can be used to ameliorate, or improve, the condition of the tribals. Nevertheless in some ways not yet understood, the text also gives legitimacy to the destruction of the name of the social-cultural place and space to which the tribals are born, for a text can lay down a procedure by which no place, whether known or unknown, is not the property of the state. In this case, the *koitors* are now identified as a classification known as Tribes and Hill Maria.

With these considerations in mind I have tried to introduce in this chapter a people whose name, i.e. the *koitors*, and whose cultural space, i.e. Shringar Bhum, are not recognised. Perhaps location of a people on a map of Abujhmarh and on a frequency distribution table may be enough to control them. However, if a people and their social-cultural space already had a name before the written word reached it, the possibility of another method of enquiry into its constitution must be explored.

Notes

This study was done at the Committee for Cultural Choices and Global Futures, Delhi, as a part of the research project on Development and Technological Transformation: Alternative Approaches sponsored by WIDER. It was first presented at a project meeting in Helsinki, in August 1986. I am grateful to Professor Chie Nakane, Stephen and Frédérique Marglin, Shiv Visvanathan, Arjun Appadurai and the other participants in the meeting for their comments.

I also wish to express my thanks to Professors J.P.S. Uberoi and Ashis Nandy for their help and guidance; to my friends Punam Zutshi, Deepak Mehta, Anil Misra, Dr. Shahid Amin, Madhu Ramnath, Felix Padel, Luis Esparza for their criticisms; and to my people in Delhi and in Bastar for their tolerance and faith.

1. To the Maria this 'outside' is best apprehended through the language of the migrant. By implication, the tribe constructs its outside, just as much as the outside constructs the Hill Maria. This suggests that this 'inside' and 'outside' contrast is something more than a polar opposition: they constitute elements of an inter-subjective discourse.

2. *Kosra* – millet; *Panicum miliaceum*. Other crops sown in a *penda* are: *Panicum frumentaceum*; *Panicum miliare*; *mandia* – *Elensia coracana*; *bajra* – *Penicillaraia spicata*; *pupul (urad)* – *phaseolus radiatus*; *arhar* – *Cajanus indicus*; *jata-sem-dolichos lablab*; *teriang*; *jeera*; *naing*. Seeds of these crops may not be available with all the households. In contrast only one crop (rice) can be sown at a time in rice fields.

3. The term *koska* derives from *kosé* — this is the unit used to measure distance between two or more places. *Koska* therefore refers to the distant ones.

Bibliography

Allan, W. (1965), *The African Husbandman*, Edinburgh: Oliver and Boyd.

Appadurai, Arjun (1981), 'The terminology of measurement in a peasant community in Maharashtra', unpublished paper.

Berlin, Brent, Dennis E. Breedlove and Peter H. Raven (1974), *Principles of Tzeltal Plant Classification: an Introduction to the Botanical Ethnography of a Mayan Speaking People of Highland Chiapas*, New York: Academic Press.

Boserup, E. (1965), *The Conditions of Agricultural Growth: the Economics of Agrarian Change Under Population Pressure*, Chicago: Aldine.

Bourdieu, P. (1964), 'Attitude of Algerian peasant towards time',in Julian Pill-Rivers (ed.), *Peasants in the Mediterranean*, The Hague: Mouton.

——— (1977), *Outline of a Theory of Practice*, Cambridge University Press.

Chapman, C.P. 'Folklore of the perceived environment in Bihar', unpublished paper.

Conklin, H.C. (1954), 'An ethnoecological approach to shifting cultivation', *Transactions of the New York Academy of Science*, series 2, vol. 17, no. 2, pp. 133–42.

Geertz, C. (1963), *Agricultural Involution*, Berkeley: University of California Press.

Grigson, W.V. (1938), *The Maria Gonds of Bastar*, Bombay: Oxford University Press.

Hunn, Evsenes (1977), *Tzeltal Folk Zoology: the Classification of Discontinuities in Nature*, New York: Academic Press.

Malinowski, B. (1935), *Coral Gardens and their Magic*, New York: Am Book, vols 1 and 2.

——— (1955), *Magic, Science, Religion,* New York: Doubleday.

Netting, Robert McC. (1968), *Hill Farmers of Nigeria: Cultural Ecology of Kotyar of the Jos Plateau,* Seattle: University of Washington Press.

——— (1974), 'Agrarian ecology', *Annual Review of Anthropology,* vol. 3.

Uberoi, Patricia (1976), 'Towards a new sociolinguistics: a memoir of P.B. Pandit', *Economic and Political Weekly,* Bombay, vol. 11, no. 7, pp. 637–743.

Wald, Benjii (1974), 'Bilingualism', *Annual Review of Anthropology,* vol. 3.

Whyte, Ann W.T. (1977), 'Guidelines for the field study of environment perception', Paris, NAP Technical Notes No. 5, mimeograph.

4. The malign encounter: the Chipko Movement and competing visions of nature

Ramachandra Guha

The blood of the villages is the cement with which the edifice of the cities is built. Mahatma Gandhi

Introduction

The Chipko ('hug the tree') Movement, a popular initiative to stem deforestation in the Uttarakhand Himalaya,[1] is possibly the best-known ecological movement in the world. As a grassroots movement it has an authenticity somewhat lacking in purely intellectual appraisals of the ecological implications of modern industrialisation. A token genuflection to Chipko has, as a consequence, become a ritual in both Indian and international debates on development alternatives.

In these circumstances the absence of detailed scholarly studies on the movement is noteworthy. The present chapter, distilled from a much longer dissertation on the subject (Guha 1985a), situates Chipko in its social and historical context and assesses its wider significance. It will continually shift between these two levels. Clearly, Chipko must be viewed as a constituent element of an overall history of peasant protest in Uttarakhand. At the same time, one can hardly underestimate the movement's significance in lending popular support to environmental critiques of the development process.

The sociological study of Chipko must grapple with three sets of issues. First, there is the understanding of the movement in its historical dimension. Chipko can best be understood in the context of a history of social movements — dating from the earliest days of state intervention — centring around the question of peasant access to forests and pasture. One must also examine the interconnections between Chipko and different aspects of state intervention, and scientific forestry in particular. In this manner, social participation in Chipko can be depicted in terms of the changing relationship between the state and the peasantry.

Second, the links between the specific forms taken by Chipko and its relationship to the social structure of Uttarakhand need to be spelled out. Here I shall emphasise commercial penetration and the gradual flow of raw materials and, more recently, cheap male labour out of the hills. Thus Chipko can be read as a response to the fragmentation of the village community in recent decades. Again, women have always played an important role in the agrarian economy and this structural constant may explain the widespread participation of women in contemporary social movements in the hills.

Finally, while Chipko lies in a direct path of continuity with an earlier history of social protest, simultaneously as an organised and sustained social movement it represents an expansion in the scale of both popular consciousness and mobilisation. This extension has two distinct aspects. On the one hand, the enduring nature and organisational development of Chipko has raised major questions: the nature of leadership, the ideological clashes between different subcultures of the movement and the redefinition of gender roles, which were absent from the earlier, largely 'unorganised' movements in Uttarakhand. On the other hand, notwithstanding its internal schisms, Chipko has made a significant effort to combat the growing social and ecological disintegration of hill society. Noteworthy here is the alternate model of an environmentally sustainable and socially just economic development articulated by Chipko, a model whose relevance is scarcely restricted to Uttarakhand.

These are some of the questions with which I hope to grapple in the present chapter. The chapter is divided into five sections. The first closes with a profile of Uttarakhand economy and society. The second juxtaposes two ecological critiques of colonialism: a popular critique, represented by peasant movements protesting against state control over natural resources, and an intellectual critique, put forward by ecologically conscious nationalists in the Gandhian tradition. The next section analyses the strategy of heavy industrialisation adopted by the Indian state and outlines its implications for the Himalayan forests. Fourthly, I present a sociological interpretation of Chipko, focusing on its social idiom, organisational base and strategies of mobilisation. I shall analyse the recent schism in the movement with reference to two distinct positions in the environmental debate in the concluding section and, finally, indicate the possibilities for a widening of the movement's horizons.

Uttarakhand society

A profile

The British acquired control over the northern hill districts of India early in the nineteenth century. During this period of their rule (*c.* 1815–1947), Uttarakhand was divided into two contiguous but distinct sociopolitical units, the nominally independent chiefdom of Tehri Garhwal and the British administered Kumaun Division. While caste distinctions have always been rather lax as compared to the 'great tradition' of Hinduism, the agrarian structure of Uttarakhand radically differs from the adjoining plains. With agriculture dominating economic activity in both Tehri and Kumaun, over 80 per cent of the total population farmed largely with the help of family labour. In this respect the social structure of Uttarakhand was far less differentiated than in most other parts of India, resembling the archetypal peasant community often used as an analytical contract by scholars.[2]

Whether carried out along the river valleys or on terraces cut out of the hillside, the successful practice of agriculture was clearly dependent on a healthy forest cover. Since animal husbandry was as important to the local economy as cultivation, the peasants depended on the forests for fuel, fodder, agricultural implements, building timber, medicines and, in times of dearth, food as well. In the period before state intervention, not only did the peasantry have full access to the forests, but their strong communal institutions fostered the prudent utilisation of forest produce (Guha 1985c: 1938–40). In the circumstances, not only were subsistence needs comfortably met, but there was often a surplus of grain for sale. Thus the hill peasantry was variously described as 'probably better off than any peasantry in India'[3] and again as 'more free from the res angustae domi' (i.e. straitened circumstances at home) than 'any peasantry in the world' (Pearson 1866: 300).

The picture I have briefly sketched refers to the period before India attained independence in 1947 and is at considerable variance with the situation as it exists today. Caught in the vortex of the market economy and faced with multiple environmental hazards, hill society is today in a state of 'continuing economic deterioration' (Gross 1982: 184). The past few decades have seen the transformation of Uttarakhand from a subsistence-oriented peasant economy to one dependent on outside remittances for survival. In this 'money order' economy agricultural production is no longer adequate for subsistence and the bulk of the family income is generated outside by migrant males, who remit a major portion of their earnings to the village.[4]

While this process had been set in motion during the colonial period, it has clearly been exacerbated since 1947 and following the onset of planned economic development. The emergence of the 'money order' economy is due to a complex set of interrelated factors, including population growth (currently around 2.3 per cent per annum) and the lack of employment opportunities outside agriculture. The most important factor is undeniably the deterioration of the ecosystem. In undermining the basis of the agrarian economy, environmental degradation has led to considerable social stress. Most notably, deforestation has placed an additional burden on women, forcing them to travel long distances for supplies of fuelwood and fodder. The forced absence of the male members of the household ensures that woman's lot is a miserable one — a lot portrayed vividly in the writings of local activists.

Ecological critiques of colonialism

Colonial forest management

The advent of British colonial rule marked an important watershed in the ecological history of India. The encounter with a technologically advanced and dynamic industrial power introduced profound dislocations at various levels of Indian society. From an ecological point of view, by far the most crucial of these changes was the take-over of woodland by the state. During the first century of British rule there was little interference with the traditional uses of the forest, but the period of railway expansion (*c.* 1855 onwards) led to a radical change in colonial policy. Faced with an acute shortage of the durable wood used under the railway tracks as sleepers, the colonial state hastily called in German experts to start a forest department.

However, the lack of state control over forests was regarded as a major impediment to the effective functioning of the new department. Key figures in the colonial bureaucracy stressed the need to enact legislation that would enable the forest department to commence commercial timber production. Thus in one fell swoop, through the Indian Forest Act of 1878, the state reasserted its rights of ownership and control over one-fifth of India's land area. In succeeding decades this vast forest estate was managed with the help of a sophisticated legal and bureaucratic infrastructure that closely monitored its use. The imperatives of colonial forest management were essentially strategic, i.e. to meet the critical imperial need for wood for railways and during the world wars, and commercial, i.e. to assure a steadily increasing revenue to the state. However, the abrupt extension of state control sharply conflicted with the customary use of the forest by rural populations all over India. This exclusion of agrarian society from the fruits of colonial forest management was, as contemporary critics observed, quite by design rather than by accident. As an agricultural chemist called in to advise the colonial government remarked, the main aim of the forest department was the preservation and development of large timber. In his view, the new department's objectives

> were in no sense agricultural, and its success was gauged mainly by fiscal considerations; the Department was to be a revenue-paying one. Indeed, we may go so far as to say that its interests were opposed to agriculture, and its intent was rather to exclude agriculture than to admit it to participation in the benefits. (Voelcker 1897: 135–36)

As the one source of coniferous timber in the subcontinent, the Himalayan forests attracted the attention of British forest officials early on. Dominated by magnificent deodar (*Cedrus deodara*) stands, the forests of Tehri Garhwal were leased by the colonial government as early as 1865. Preliminary surveys established beyond doubt that the property — acquired for the nominal fee of 10,000 rupees per annum — would 'yield a fine yearly revenue, besides supplying the wants both of the government and the Railways for timber'. (Pearson 1869: 121). At a time when the rate of forest denudation in peninsular India imperilled the consolidation of the railway network, the forests of Tehri Garhwal proved to be a strategically valuable resource for British colonialism. Over 6.5 million deodar sleepers were exported between 1869 and 1885 from the Yamuna valley alone (Hearle 1888: 1, 16).

The enormous commercial value of his forests thus made apparent, the king of Tehri did not renew the lease in 1925, preferring to work the forest with his own, newly created department. Under his management the revenue orientation became more marked, and over time the forests came to constitute the largest single item of revenue for the treasury. In 1935–36, for example, forests accounted for 0.73 million rupees out of a total of 1.79 million rupees that accrued to the exchequer on all heads.[5]

Chiefly on account of the varying species composition of the forests, commercial forestry began somewhat later in British-ruled Kumaun. The forests of Kumaun were dominated not by deodar but by the long-leaved chir pine (*Pinus roxburghii*). Less durable than deodar, chir's potential commercial value was determined by two scientific developments reported in the early years of this century — the successful chemical treatment of the wood for use as railway sleepers and the distillation of the chir extract known as oleo-resin, whose two chief by-products, rosin and turpentine, had a wide variety of industrial uses (Guha 1985c: 69–73). Shortly after these discoveries, the Kumaun forests were logged on a sustained basis for both timber and resin. Since India was the only source of resin within the British Empire, increased production enabled the substitution of American and French varieties that had hitherto ruled the market. By 1920 over 2 million resin channels were being tapped in Kumaun, with annual output of close to 4,000 tonnes (see Smythies 1914; 1925).

Simultaneously, the extraction of chir sleepers had been given a boost by World War One. Almost 400,000 sleepers were exported from Kumaun during 1916–18. In fact, operations were considerably stepped up during World War Two, when 'fellings and sawings were pushed into the remotest forests of the Himalayas' and in 1940–41, for example, 440,000 sleepers were supplied to the railways, mostly of chir pine (see Champion and Osmanston 1962: chapter IX).

The underlying commercial orientation was reflected both in the legal basis of colonial forest management and the technical strategies it used to achieve its ends.[6] The silvicultural agenda of colonial foresters working in the Himalayas was the transformation of mixed forests of conifers and broad-leaved species into pure stands of the commercially valuable conifers. The manipulation of a delicate and imperfectly understood ecosystem was further complicated by the competing demands exercised on the forest by the peasantry.

Faced with a set of constraints that were both ecological as well as social, British foresters arrived at two mutually reinforcing solutions. At an instrumental level, they carefully regulated peasant access by restricting it to areas of forest not deemed commercially profitable. While forbidden to enter areas under commercial working, peasants were by no means at liberty to use the rest of the forest at will. The detailed provisions of the 1878 Act sharply defined — and delimited — the amount of fuel, fodder etc. each family was allowed to take from the forest. At the same time, the punitive sanctions of the Act were a strong deterrent to its transgression. At a deeper epistemic level, the language of scientific forestry worked to justify the shift towards commercial working. The terms 'valuable' and 'desirable', for example, commonly used to describe certain species (especially conifers), were in every instance euphemisms for 'commercially valuable and profitable', while the prefix 'inferior' (used mainly to refer to oaks) bore no relation to the ecological and other functions the species thus described may have performed for the surrounding countryside. By a similar act of redefinition — one that rested on a prior usurpation of 'legal' rights of ownership by the state — the customary users of the forest were designated its enemies. Thus the management profile of each forest division, the so-called 'working plans', while indicating possible sources of injury to the forest crop, include 'men' in the same category as natural hazards and wild animals.

This manipulation of ecological systems and human beings was deemed necessary to maintain a permanent supply of marketable forest produce. Given its poor statistical base and scanty knowledge of the Himalayan ecosystem, 'scientific' forestry was not able to fulfil even its primary objective. Recent research by Indian ecologists — ironically enough, commissioned by the Forest Department — clearly demonstrated the yawning gulf between the ideology of 'sustained yield' — the *sine qua non* of scientific forestry — and the actual operations of timber harvesting, wherein the output of logged material often exceeds the increment to forest stock (Gadgil, Prasad and Ali 1983: 127–55). What is more relevant to our concerns, however, were the processes of social change that came in the wake of the commercialisation of the forest. By introducing a radical shift in the management priorities of the Himalayan ecosystem, commercial forestry came into sharp conflict with a system of management that predated it by several centuries and whose priorities could hardly have been more dissimilar. It is to this conflict, between the imperatives of scientific forestry and the economic and cultural values of the hill peasantry, that we must now turn.

Social protest movements

The operations of commercial forestry, by drastically curtailing peasant access to forest produce, had far-reaching consequences in Uttarakhand. There were several protest movements in Tehri Garhwal that centred around the new system of forest management. These protests took the form of organised attacks on forest officials, occasionally accompanied by a call to the monarch to rescind the new regulations. Thus in 1904 opposition to forest settlement operations in the *patti*[7] of Khujni culminated in attacks on the staff of the Conservator of Forests (Pathak 1980: 461–2). Two years later, similar operations in the *patti* of Khas provoked a direct confrontation with the Conservator conducting the forest settlement. Attacked by the villagers, who branded his face with a cattle iron, the official was forced to flee to Tehri town.[8]

The most celebrated of the movements against forest management, however, occurred in Rawain in 1930. This was a consequence of the revision of the forest settlement under which the allotment of forest produce to the villagers was considerably reduced. Refusing to submit to the new rules, the peasants drove out state officials from the area, and proclaimed their own '*sarkar*' (government). The administration responded by sending an armed force to Rawain under the command of the chief minister. This force quelled the revolt by firing on an unarmed gathering of peasants, killing many.[9] Fifteen years later forest grievances and the aftermath of the Rawain firing also played a part in a major peasant movement that engulfed most of the state. Sparked off by land settlement operations, this movement resulted in the merger of Tehri Garhwal with the Indian Union in 1949 (Guha 1985a: chapter 5).

Peasant opposition to the operations was, if anything, more intense in Kumaun. Here the wide-ranging impact of commercial forestry manifested itself directly in the form of restricted access to forest and pasture, and indirectly through the growing burdens imposed by touring officials. The latter emanated from the system of forced labour or *begar* whereby the peasantry had to provide, for state officials on tour, both labour services and provisions. These services increased dramatically with the advent of the Forest Department, when forest officials demanded *begar* as a matter of course.

Operation of the *sarkar* system, sporadic and localised in earlier years, assumed a new dimension with the reservation of the Kumaun forests. Villagers often refused to supply provisions to the Forest Department, whom they regarded as 'disagreeable interlopers to be thwarted if possible'.[10] Several strikes were reported in different parts of Kumaun. After the opposition had assumed an organised form, it crystallised into a widespread movement. A climax was reached during a well-attended religious fair in the temple town of Bageshwar during January 1921 culminating in several days of hectic activity, including labour strikes and massive processions. These actions finally forced the state to withdraw the *begar* system (Guha 1985b: 84–96).

Concurrently, opposition to forest management was expressed through the wholesale breach of forest law; the convictions obtained under the Forest Act in Kumaun far exceeded those in other parts of the province. Two major campaigns, conducted in 1916 and 1921, witnessed the systematic burning of forests controlled by the state. Constituting a direct challenge to the state to relax its control over the forests, these movements enjoyed an enormous popular support that made it virtually impossible for the administration to detect the persons responsible for the fires. The fires were almost always directed at areas where the state was at its most vulnerable, e.g. compact blocks of chir forest which were being worked for timber or resin. Significantly, there is no evidence that the large areas of broad-leaved forests, also under the control of the state, were at all affected. In other words, arson was hardly indiscriminate, sparing those species useful to the village economy (Guha 1985b).

As that careful student of peasant society, J.C. Scott, has observed, lower-class resistance to élite demands typically has both a utilitarian and a symbolic significance.[11] Faithfully reflecting disciplinal boundaries, anthropologists are prone to emphasise the latter, political economists the former. Peasant rebels' actions or ideology, however, are not themselves inclined strictly to separate economic and cultural realms. The characteristic interpenetration of utilitarian and symbolic elements in peasant revolt is clearly evident in the widespread opposition to scientific forest management in Uttarakhand. In its most elementary form, protest was aimed at the restrictions on customary patterns of use entailed by commercial forestry. The take-over of the hill forests and their subsequent management on commercial lines were at once a denial of the state's traditional obligations and a threat to the 'subsistence dilemma' of the peasantry (Scott 1976).

Peasant attacks on the new regulations most often made two claims. First, they unequivocally asserted the continuing rights of use and control. Thus in the Khaspatti movement of 1906 (described above) villagers objected to *any* state interference with forest over which they claimed *full* and *exclusive* rights. In the collective memory of the hill peasantry, this movement was, and remains, especially significant for the act of branding the Conservator's face with a hot iron — an act which symbolised a decisive triumph over the inimical powers of forest officials. In Kumaun the idiom of social protest similarly reflected the contending claims of villagers and the state. Arsonists chose as their target blocks of forest especially valuable to the state or official buildings that were the most visible symbol of alien rule.

Second, while asserting traditional claims to ownership and control, opposition to state management also contrasted the subsistence orientation of village use with the commercial orientation of the state. Gandhi, the Kumaun peasantry believed, had been sent by God 'in the form of [a] Bania to fight [the] Bania Government'. As the use of the stereotype 'Bania' (merchant) indicates, by emphasising commercial use, the colonial government had lost legitimacy — indeed, 'the Government that sells the forest produce is not liable to be called a real Government' (Guha 1985b: 88).

In this manner, protest brought to the fore, on the one hand, alternative conceptions of property and ownership, and on the other, conceptions of forest management and use.[12] This clash between scientific forestry and village management was not merely economic. The conflicting perspectives rested on fundamentally different notions of the forest — on radically different systems of meanings. The ideology of 'scientific' forestry proclaimed that the imposition of state control was a logical corollary of the lack of 'scientific' management practices among the human populations that lived in and around the forests (Stebbing 1922–27). Yet the fragmentary historical evidence that is available tells a different story: it reveals the existence of a highly sophisticated system of conservancy in pre-colonial Uttarakhand. Perhaps the most visible form was the designation of large areas of forest as 'sacred' areas where no villager was allowed to injure the vegetation in any way.[13] As the traditional form of forest preservation, sacred groves testified to the role played by folk religious beliefs in the conservation of nature. Simultaneously, informal management practices, both between and within village communities, carefully regulated the utilisation of forest produce. In many hill villages, while there existed no formal management, the protection and long-term use of common forests was secured by customary limitations on the amount of fuel, fodder and other forest produce available to each family.[14]

Through a mix of religion, folklore and tradition, the peasants of Uttarakhand had drawn a protective ring around the forest. As with other forest-dwelling communities, the continuity of their world rested upon a continuity in their relationship with the forest.[15] Scientific forestry threatened to rupture this continuity, first by denying villagers physical access, but perhaps more significantly by imposing an alien system of management on the forest. As one hillman bitterly reflected, 'the forests have belonged to us from time immemorial, our ancestors planted them and protected them; now that they have become of value, Government steps in and robs us of them'.[16]

The social idiom of agrarian protest strongly reflected the threat to traditional cultural and communal values that scientific forestry represented. Most strikingly, there was a close association of protest with folk religion: an association that was at once formal and informal, organisational and symbolic. The religious milieu of everyday peasant existence influenced forms of resistance taken by the peasants in two distinct ways. First, protesters sought a moral–religious sanction for their acts. This was accomplished either by involving priests and *sadhus* (ascetics), who enjoyed enormous prestige and influence locally, or in a more institutional form by using religious networks as means of communication. Thus, both temples and fairs frequently served as loci at which support was canvassed or from which activities were coordinated. Second, the ideology of peasant protest was heavily overlaid with religious symbolism. In the Kumaun movement of 1921, for example, peasants invoked symbols from the Hindu epics characterising the colonial government as evil and demonic (Rakshas Raj).[17]

While the participation of priests testified to the involvement of figures of spiritual authority in social movements, holders of temporal authority were also prominent in the communal resistance to forest management. Both the colonial state and the Tehri Garhwal Darbar tried without success to woo village leaders, especially headmen and retired soldiers. Almost without exception they rejected these overtures, and played a leading role in the mobilisation and organisation of the peasantry.[18] By choosing to cast their lot with their kinsmen, religious and community leaders were upholding their symbolic status as representative of social continuity. The use of a religious idiom and of primordial networks of community solidarity suggests that the culture of resistance in Uttarakhand was simultaneously instrumental and symbolic. For if, as I have argued, scientific forestry represented a threat to the economic as well as cultural survival of the village communities, opposition to its workings had necessarily to invoke an alternate system of use *and* meanings.

The nationalist critique

Although the movements in Uttarakhand were arguably the most sustained in the subcontinent, peasant resistance to colonial forest management was widespread. Major movements occurred in Bastar in 1910, in Gudem-Rampa in 1876–78 and 1922–23, in Midnapur in 1919–21, and in Adilabad in 1940; they were all closely related to forest grievances. Even where protest did not take a confrontational path, the peasantry made evident their dislike of state forest management in other ways. Thus in most parts of India the incidence of forest 'crime' — i.e. the breach of the new laws — followed a steadily escalating trend (Guha and Gadgil n.d.).

This incipient 'ecological' critique was an element of the wider national response to colonialism, even if it is not normally seen as such. The denial of peasant access to forests was but one of the many ways in which colonial rule profoundly affected agrarian social structure. As writers have argued for over a century, British land and legal policies worked towards the increasing differentiation of the peasantry and the decline of communal institutions. Losing autonomy, the peasant was forced out of production for use and into the vortex of the market economy. This forced commercialisation of agriculture led to new forms of dependence and strengthened existing ones — what one student of the peasantry called the dreaded triad of 'Sarkar, Sahukar, and Zamindar'.[19]

Early nationalist critiques — those of Dadabhai Naoroji, R.C. Dutt, and M.G. Ranade, for example, restricted themselves to delineating the 'drain of wealth' away from India. Far from their being unequivocal critics of colonialism, in the work of these writers 'criticism of specific policies [was] balanced by general admiration and even a belief in the providential nature of British rule' (Sarkar 1983: 91). However, the move of the premier nationalist organisation, the Congress, away from élite nationalism was conducted under the leadership of a man whose personal philosophy was quite antithetical to modern industry. Mahatma Gandhi had written in 1909 a slim tract that contained a massive indictment of Western civilisation. Rejecting modern industry in its totality, Gandhi pleaded for the revival of the organic village communities of the pre-colonial and pre-industrial past (Gandhi 1966).

As the political scientist Partha Chatterjee has pointed out, Gandhi's idealisation of the village community and the integration within it of craft production was central to the transformation from élite to mass nationalism (Chatterjee 1984). 'Hind Swaraj' can be read as essentially a *moral* statement, in which Gandhi deplores the limitless greed of modern industrial civilisation and of what he saw as its logical consequence, colonialism. In response to criticism, and in anticipation of Indian independence, Gandhi in his later writings formulated his critique in economic and political terms. In a labour-surplus country like India, he argued, the craze for modern machinery would throw millions out of work. Anticipating the terms of the 'alternative technology' debate, he believed that forms of industrialisation appropriate to a labour-short country like the USA were highly unsuited to India. He was prepared to allow for powerdriven machinery in certain key industries, with the caveat that these should be state controlled. These exceptions notwithstanding, he continued to give primacy to the revitalisation of the agrarian economy.[20]

The formal elaboration of a 'Gandhian' economic philosophy may be found in the writings of the Kumarappa brothers.[21] In these writings the plea for a 'village-centred economic order' in India was put forward through a critique of existing social systems. The Kumarappas' critique of capitalism closely mirrored Marxist analyses stressing the enslavement and alienation of the working class and the disjunction between individual profit maximisation and the social good. They diverged from Marxism in their relentless critique of industrial socialism. Notwithstanding its laudable ideals, socialism was considered unacceptable by the Kumarappas for its centralisation of power, the gulf between the party, state and the people, and the acceptance of the capitalist principle of the multiplication of wants. Economic policy in an independent India must, therefore, concentrate on agriculture and revive the integration of handicrafts with food production. The expansion of centralised industry was to be carefully controlled and must in no way compete with small-scale production. In general, the decentralisation of political and economic organisation, and local self-sufficiency were to be the defining features of this alternative mode of production. Termed 'villagism', this was nothing but 'socialism decentralised and freed from violence; for only thus, would it seem that the socialist's ideal of each for all and all for each can really be attained' (Kumarappa 1965: 115).

One is immediately struck by the remarkable congruence between the unhappily termed 'villagism' and the utopias of modern ecological visionaries — of a society adopting humanistic and ecologically wise technology, decentralised economy, and face-to-face democracy (Bookchin 1980). The Kumarappas explicitly incorporated ecological considerations into their analysis, arguing for example that 'the capitalist's only concern being to make as much profit as possible for himself, he cares little for the country or its future, and uses up its natural resources — forests, oil, coal, and other minerals — heedless of what will happen in the future when these limited resources are exhausted' (Kumarappa 1965: 19).

Arguably, such an awareness of the ecological 'limits to growth' can be traced to Gandhi's own writings. Drawing a link between industrialisation, militarisation and conquest, Gandhi believed that to 'industrialise India in the same sense as Europe was to attempt the impossible'. For industrialisation depended entirely on the capability to exploit the markets and resources of other nations. In this sense, the historical options available to non-Western countries were limited. As he observed in 1928:

> God forbid that India should ever take to industrialisation after the manner of the West. The economic imperialism of a single tiny island kingdom (England) is today keeping the world in chains. If an entire nation of 300 million took to similar economic exploitation, it would strip the world like locusts. (Gandhi 1966: 26, 28, 31–2)

Industrialisation and the Himalayan forests

The vision of the modernisers

The environmental and social critique of heavy industrialisation undertaken by Gandhi and his followers ran parallel to the widespread opposition to colonial rule in rural India. If peasant resistance constituted an 'immanent' critique of colonial forestry (and the wider processes of social change of which it was an integral element), the intellectual critique of the Gandhian economists rested on similar political and ecological underpinnings. Most Indian nationalists, however, drew a wholly different conclusion from the colonial experience, arguing that India's subjugation was a consequence of its intellectual and economic backwardness. In this perspective, as contrasted with the dynamic and progressive West, India was a once-great civilisation that had stagnated and atrophied under the dead weight of tradition. Its revitalisation could only come about through an emulation of the West, intellectually through the infusion of modern science, and materially through the adoption of large-scale industrialisation. The person most closely associated with this view was, of course, Jawaharlal Nehru, prime minister for nearly two decades after independence (Nehru 1946: 346-8).

As a nationalist leader who had spent many years in British prisons, Nehru was ambivalent in his attitude towards the West — his admiration for its industrial progress was coupled with a bitterness resulting from the colonial experience. Other leaders, however, more openly praised the West for awakening India out of its slumber.[22] An early and influential statement may be found in the work of the Mysore engineer and statesman Sir M. Visvesvaraya. As Visvesvaraya saw it, the choice before the Indian people was stark:

They have to choose whether they will be educated or remain ignorant; whether they will come into closer contact with the outer world and become responsive to its influences, or remain secluded and indifferent; whether they will be organised or disunited, bold or timid, enterprising or passive; an industrial or an agricultural nation; rich or poor; strong and respected, or weak and dominated by forward nations. The future is in their own hands. Action, not sentiment, will be the determining factor. (Visvesvaraya 1920: 273-4)

Operative here are the standard assumptions of modernisation theory, even if Visvesvaraya was writing several decades before that body of literature made its first appearance. Through rapid industrialisation and urbanisation, and the creation of a strong nation-state, India could 'catch up' with the West. As exemplars of radically compressed and state-induced industrialisation, Meiji Japan, Stalinist Russia and

Bismarckian Germany were variously held aloft as the beacon. Not surprisingly, this vision coincided with that of the rising Indian capitalist class. In the 'Bombay Plan' of 1944, leading industrialists agreed upon the importance of a strong and centralised state. This plan also stressed the need for government investment and control in heavy industry and public utilities, areas in which private investment would not easily be forthcoming.[23]

What Visvesvaraya termed the 'industrialise or perish' model of economic development was formally institutionalised in the Second Five Year Plan, for which underdevelopment was 'essentially a consequence of insufficient technological progress'.[24] Underlying a strategy of imitative industrialisation was the adoption of the most 'modern' technologies, with little regard for their social or ecological consequences. As a prominent Indian ecologist Madhav Gadgil has pointed out — admittedly, with a great deal of hindsight — even while accepting the imperative of industrialisation, there were many options available to the Indian state. Thus:

> The technologies adopted could be capital or labour intensive; they could be oriented towards satisfying the demand for the luxury goods or fulfilling the basic needs of the masses; they could be degradative of the environment or could be non-polluting; they could use energy intensively or sparingly; and they could use the country's endowment of natural resources in a sustainable fashion or liquidate them; and so on. On these critical choices of technology depended the future of the society and the land, the waters and the life of the country. (Gadgil 1985a: 30–1)

As Gadgil continues, in a sharply stratified society like India these choices were critically affected by three interest groups: capitalist merchants and industrialists, the technical and administrative bureaucracy, and rich farmers. The influence of the capitalists was reflected in the massive state investments in industrial infrastructure — e.g. power, minerals and metals, and communications, all provided at highly subsidised rates — and in the virtually free access to crucial raw materials such as forests and water. Large landowners, for their part, ensured that they had an adequate and cheap supply of water, power and fertiliser for commercial agriculture. Finally, the bureaucrat–politician nexus constructed an elaborate web of rules and regulations in order to maintain control over resource extraction and utilisation. In this manner, the coalescence of economic interests and the seductive ideology of modernisation worked to consolidate dominant social classes. This strategy willingly sacrificed the interests of the bulk of the rural population — landless labour, small and marginal farmers, artisans and various aboriginal communities — whose dependence on nature was far more direct (ibid.: 31–2).

The march of commercial forestry

The policy of rapid industrialisation would considerably hasten the process of commercialisation of the forest, initiated under colonial rule. However, as envisaged by the National Forest Policy of 1952, the state would retain control over forest working. The new policy reiterated, in the name of the 'national interest', the assertion of state monopoly. Thus 'the accident [sic] of a village being situated close to a forest does not prejudice the right of the country as a whole to receive the benefits of a national asset'.[25]

While the institutional framework for forest working remained intact, new demands were placed on the technical agency entrusted with the task of managing the forests. 'An expanding economy on the eve of modern industrialisation', an expert from the Food and Agriculture Organisation (FAO) warned the Indian government, requires 'the *highest* tonnage of production of organic raw material within the *shortest* possible period and at the *lowest* possible costs'. The changed circumstances, he added, required the Forest Department to discard its earlier 'conservative' policy in favour of a more 'dynamic' approach to timber production and harvesting (Von Monroy 1960: 8, emphasis added).

What were the implications of this new strategy of 'production' forestry for the Himalayan forest? To begin with, the increased pressure on the hill forests required the building of roads into hitherto inaccessible areas. Along with the communications network came the ubiquitous contractor whose job was to transport the forest produce to the processing industries in the plains. Since 1947, road building has proceeded at a rapid pace, especially since the creation of three border districts following the Chinese war of 1962. A 56 million rupees World Bank project was started in 1972, for the construction of 1,330 kilometres of new roads and 16 new bridges, and the renovation of 620 kilometres of existing roads, in Uttarakhand. The project was initiated on the grounds that past road construction represented but a 'nominal fraction of the total requirements for the full exploitation and proper development of these [hill] forests'.[26]

Table 4.1 gives some details of the increased pressure on the Forest Department. A dramatic expansion in resin tapping operations was also made possible by the new network of roads. Resin outturn, after reaching a peak of 41.8 million kilograms in 1974–75 (valued at 74.8 million rupees), was 13 million kilograms in 1978–79.[27] To meet the increased demand, important modifications were introduced in forest working. These included a reduction in the diameter at which resin tapping was commenced and the lowering of the age at which chir trees were cut. Silvicultural practices also continued a trend started in the colonial

Table 4.1 Outturn of selected species in Uttarakhand, 1931–79 (cubic metres of sawn wood)

Year	Deodar	Fir/spruce	Blue pine	Chir pine
1931	2,917	–	14,191	31,885
1935	4,333	–	–	30,299
1949	7,561	4,616	595	59,041
1951	9,542	10,987	5,135	87,415
1956	9,316	14,923	–	99,761
1961	9,571	39,502	5,380	1,07,435
1966	10,531	20,010	4,727	1,34,587
1971	11,621	39,766	5,166	2,00,030
1972	67,379	29,722	8,362	1,59,930
1973	48,623	60,106	5,162	2,06,645
1974	10,830	28,926	8,983	2,30,787
1975	15,464	37,463	9,742	1,86,114
1976	29,971	71,493	10,896	2,95,745
1977	14,712	37,980	5,632	2,67,458
1978	8,863	67,682	5,077	2,64,509
1979	7,965	84,954	6,023	3,19,081

Source: Uttar Pradesh Forest Statistics, 1978–79.

period — expanding the area under commercially valuable coniferous species at the expense of broad-leaved varieties more suited to the local economy (Singh 1967).

There has, therefore, been a marked continuity in the operations of forest management between the colonial and post-colonial periods. While the pressure of the commercial and industrial bourgeois

> may have replaced strategic imperial needs as the cornerstone of state forestry practices, in both periods 'successful' implementation has been at the expense of the hill peasantry and their life support systems. The use of legal and scientific techniques designed to limit and regulate the access of the surrounding population to the forest, have been remarkably invariant during this time span. (Guha 1985c)

Finally, the Forest Department, assigned the role of a revenue-generating organ by both the colonial state and the Tehri Darbar, has continued to be a veritable money spinner for the government of Uttar Pradesh. Between 1967–68 and 1978–79, forest revenue from the hill districts increased from 96 to 202 million rupees (*Uttar Pradesh Forest Statistics, 1978–79*).

While largely oriented towards industrial needs, state forestry was also unable to involve the local population adequately in the commercial working of the forest. As we shall see below, this neglect would provide a major impetus to the Chipko Andolan 'Movement'.

Commercial timber operations were given a boost when laboratory trials at the Forest Research Institute (FRI) showed that the utilisation of chir waste (i.e. the material left after the conversion of logs to railway sleepers) for paper making was a viable proposition. Selling the waste and utilising the considerable areas of chir affected by twist (and hence unsuitable for sleepers), the Forest Department entered into a contract with a large paper manufacturer, the Star Paper Mills of Saharanpur. From 1961 to 1981, under the terms of the agreement, the mill would be sold waste timber and twisted chir trees at highly subsidised prices. Approximately 15 to 20 thousand tonnes of pulpwood were supplied annually to the mill. When further research at the FRI established that ash and hornbeam could be used for the manufacture of sports goods, the Symonds Company of Allahabad was granted access to the hitherto unexploited broad-leaved forests.

The state's eagerness to further commercial working inevitably involved greater restrictions on village use. In a bid to tighten control, the government had given the Forest Department extensive powers in the management of forest *panchayats* — i.e. forests nominally controlled by the villagers. Under the new rules, *panchayats* could only fell trees marked by the department. Local sale of slates and stones (used in the construction of houses) and export of resin were allowed only with the permission of senior forest officials, who also directed the quantum of exploitation and its destination. Finally, *panchayats* could retain only a fixed share (40 per cent) of any royalty on the sale on produce from their forests.[28]

More crucial, however, was the almost wilful neglect of the local population in the extraction and processing of forest produce. Initial hopes that road building would lead to the setting up of local industry were belied by government policy that consistently favoured the export of raw materials to large industries in the plains. A sizeable proportion of the resin extracted — estimated at 85–90 per cent of total output — was dispatched to the Indian Turpentine and Rosin Company (ITR) in which the government had a majority shareholding. Of the remainder, portions were allotted to local cooperatives and the rest was sold by open auction. Initially ITR and cooperatives were sold resin at the same rates. This policy was changed in the early 1970s with ITR being sold resin at earlier subsidised rates, while cooperatives had to buy resin at open auctions. The cooperatives were often allotted inaccessible forest where tapping was not economically feasible. As a result of such discrimination, they rarely operated at more than 50 per cent capacity (Verma 1981).

Discrimination against small units by the government was matched by its refusal to end the contractor system of forest working. While policy documents recognised the need to do away with these intermediaries who, it was admitted, exploited both their labour and the forests, in practice the system continued to be viewed favourably. Under the initiative of Sarvodaya (Gandhian) workers, forest labour cooperatives (hereafter FLCs) were started in different parts of Garhwal and Kumaun. Repeated pleas to the government to allot them blocks at concessional rates were not heeded. In fact, the Chief Conservator of Forests (the province's senior forest official) had himself suggested at one stage that the department actively promote the working of FLCs in the hills. He was, however, tersely informed by the Governor that 'since the Forest Department is a sort of commercial department, it cannot be expected to extend concessions transaction of its business, even to cooperative societies'. One is reminded of the experience of Bombay state, where such a scheme had cost the government quite dearly and considerable amounts were lost to the exchequer.[29] Apparently the role played by contractors as political patrons and the neo-colonial treatment of the Forest Department as a revenue-generating organ stood in the way of the implementation of stated policy objectives.

Chipko: a sociological interpretation

The origins and spread of the movement
Not surprisingly, the continuation of forest policies inimical to village interest provoked a sharp response. In 1958, a committee was formed to investigate the 'grievances of the people of Uttarakhand concerning forest management'. It deplored the situation where, even after the attainment of Indian independence, in the hill tracts 'not only great discontent against the Forest Department prevails at several places, but it is also looked upon with extreme suspicion and distrust'. While recognising the need to develop the resources of the hills locally, the committee regarded as inevitable the continuance of restrictions viewed by the people as a forfeiture of 'their hereditary natural rights'.[30] Local legislators warned that in the absence of concrete programmes there was every chance of a popular upsurge in the tradition of movements against the British and the Tehri Darbar. Great resentment continued to be expressed against the sale of large blocks of forest to outside contractors. Forest officials were also believed to be in connivance with timber thieves. In protest at their continuing exclusion from the benefits of forest management, villagers refused to help forest staff extinguish fires, as they were bound to do under the Forest Act.[31]

The undercurrent of protest against forest management was combined with opposition to other facets of commercialisation and the continuing underdevelopment of the hills. An important movement was organised by Sarvodaya activists in the 1960s, when thousands of villagers (mostly women) opposed the widespread sale and distillation of liquor. The movement was marked by vigorous demonstrations. Several fasts were undertaken by the movement's leader, the prominent Sarvodaya worker Sunderlal Bahuguna. These protests led several years later to the demand for a separate hill province, a demand which gathered momentum and focused on the export of natural resources and the growing unemployment in the region. Students played an important part, organising several *hartals*, or general strikes, in the towns.

The unusually heavy monsoon of 1970[32] precipitated the most devastating flood in living memory. In the Alakananda Valley water inundated 100 square kilometres of land, washed away six metal bridges and 10 kilometres of roads and many vehicles. Loss of human and bovine life and standing crops was considerable. The damage was not restricted to the hills though. Due to the blockage of the Ganga canal, 9.5 million acres of land in eastern Uttar Pradesh went without irrigation (Bhatt 1980: 11–13).

The 1970 flood marks a turning point in the ecological history of the region. Villagers, who bore the brunt of the damage, were beginning to perceive the links between deforestation, landslides and floods. It was observed that some of the villages most affected by landslides lay directly below forests where felling operations had taken place. Preceding official initiative, 'folk sense was the only body that surveyed the grim scene and drew conclusions. The causal relationship between increasing erosivity and floods on the one hand, and mass-scale felling of trees on the other, was recognised.'[33]

On behalf of the villagers, the cudgels were taken up by the Dashauli Gram Swarajya Sangh (DGSS), a cooperative organisation based in Chamoli district in the upper Alakananda valley. Organised in the mid-1960s, the DGSS had as its major objective the generation of local employment. Despite serious obstacles, it operated a small resin and turpentine unit, manufactured agricultural implements and organised the collection and sale of medicinal herbs. In the aftermath of the 1970 flood, DGSS organised several demonstrations asking for priority in the local use of forests. Arguing that they had nurtured forest growth themselves, villagers demanded that the contractor system be abolished and local units given preference in the allocation of raw material (*Yugvani*, 31.10.1970).

Chipko originated in 1973 in the village of Mandal in the upper Alakananda valley. Here, the DGSS was refused permission to fell ash trees to be converted into agricultural implements. Instead, the Forest Department allotted the same patch of forest to a sports goods manufacturing firm, Symonds of Allahabad. This blatant injustice inspired the DGSS to organise resistance to the felling. Two alternatives presented themselves: (1) to lie down in front of the company's trucks; (2) to burn resin and timber depots. When Sarvodaya workers found both methods unsatisfactory, a leading activist of the DGSS, Chandi Prasad Bhatt, suddenly thought of embracing the trees. Thus, Chipko ('to hug') was born.

The early opposition was coordinated by the DGSS in the Alakananda Valley, but in the following years forest felling was successfully opposed in other parts of Garhwal and Kumaun. The government responded by setting up an autonomous Forest Corporation to coordinate felling operations. When this failed to encourage FLCs or stop the contractor system of forest working, the Sarvodaya leader Sunderlal Bahuguna was instrumental in initiating Chipko mobilisations in the Bhageerathi valley of the erstwhile Tehri Garhwal state. The latter part of the decade also witnessed the spread of Chipko to the districts of Almora and Pithoragarh in Kumaun, where student activists of the Uttarakhand Sangharsh Vahini played a prominent part.

In all, about a dozen Chipko agitations have been organised in different parts of Garhwal and Kumaun since the inception of the movement in 1973, and in 1980 a hunger fast by Bahuguna led to a moratorium on the felling of green trees in Uttarakhand.[34] However, the various Chipko agitations, although the most visible aspect of the movement, represented only so many moments in its history. These discrete episodes should not be considered as representing the totality of the movement as such. While the last Chipko agitation occurred several years ago, the movement's leaders and activists have been busily propagating its message. Within Uttarakhand, foot marchers and environmental camps are organised at regular intervals. There has also been a significant attempt to contribute to the environment debate — both in India and abroad — through lectures, slide shows and articles.

Towards a sociology of Chipko

As an organised social movement, Chipko has marked an important departure from the other movements of social protest that preceded it in Uttarakhand. Not only has Chipko been more enduring but, departing from the localised nature of earlier peasant movements, it has been a significant presence in large areas of Kumaun and Garhwal. The organisational form and greater spread of Chipko has been, in a sense, the logical culmination of a lengthy historical process, a process that has seen the incorporation of a subsistence-oriented peasant society into the orbit of industrial capitalism. The assertion of market forces and the role of the state in directing social and economic change has generated large-scale dislocations in the social fabric of Uttarakhand. During the early phase, protest against these enforced changes — notably, scientific forestry — were loosely organised, but nowadays the growing subordination of Uttarakhand to the wider society has necessitated a more formal and structured response.

The popular conception of Chipko has been of a romantic reunion of humans with nature. The dramatic act — often threatened but rarely brought into play — of hugging the tree to save it from the saw, has been the chief characteristic with which the movement is identified. Once we move away from the public identification of Chipko as an 'environmental' movement to the more private realm of its participants, however, we find a marked *continuity* between Chipko and earlier peasant movements in Uttarakhand. It was the lack of fulfilment of the basic needs of education, health and employment, coupled with the continuing denial of traditional forest rights, that found expression through the medium of Chipko. As one villager, recalling the Badyargarh movement of 1979, succinctly put it: 'Our fields only yield a little grain, and when we could get no wood to cook even what we had, we had to resort to a movement.'[35]

Indeed, Chipko agitations have frequently invoked the spirit and memory of past upsurges against the erosion of customary rights. The key to this continuity lies, as the above quotation suggests, in the failure of the state to guarantee subsistence to the peasantry. In essence Chipko, like other forest-based movements in Uttarakhand, had its genesis in the perceived breach of the informal code between the ruler and the ruled known as the 'moral economy' of the peasant.[36]

Chipko, therefore, can be properly viewed as a constituent element of an overall history of deprivation and protest. In the ecological setting of Uttarakhand, forest management for commerce struck at the very root of traditional social and economic organisation. Moreover, it operated on radically different principles — and for quite different reasons — from the customary use of the forests by surrounding villages. This underlying conflict in its various forms has manifested itself in virtually all the forest movements in Uttarakhand, including Chipko. Through the medium of social protest, peasants have continued to invoke a moral economy of provision in opposition to the political economy of profit that may be said to characterise scientific forestry.

In this connection, a notable feature of the Chipko Movement has been the active participation of all social groups. This has been explained by the obvious fact that all are equally affected by deforestation. During the Badyargarh movement, for example, the Bajgis, a caste of musicians ranked low in the ritual hierarchy, were solicited to mobilise villagers through their *dholaks* (drums). Government servants, such as postal officials and school teachers, and defence personnel also played their part, though by the very nature of their position their support could only be covert. Children, too, joined through the organising of plays and songs while camping in the forest, by going on strike when policemen camped in their school. This created an atmosphere of joyous celebration.

The widespread participation of women in Chipko has been frequently commented upon. Women have always played an important role in local economic life, and their involvement in Chipko has clearly been influenced by the impact of recent economic changes in intensifying their dependence on the natural environment. In Uttarakhand, the participation of women in social movements dates from the anti-alcohol movements in the 1960s. As far as Chipko is concerned, women first came to the fore during the celebrated Reni incident in 1974. In this incident the government was anticipating opposition to forest felling and asked the men of Reni village to assemble in the district town of Gopeshwar in order to collect compensation for land acquired by the state in 1962. When the absence of the men of the village was thus contrived by the local administration, the women unexpectedly came forward to stop loggers from felling the marked trees.[37]

However, despite the important role played by women in Chipko subsequent to the Reni episode, it would be simplistic to characterise Chipko as a 'feminist' movement.[38] In only one instance have women and men come into open conflict: in the village of Dungri-Paintoli in the Pindar valley, conflict occurred when women wished to protect an oak grove which the men, with the help of the Horticulture Department, wished to convert into an apple orchard. In the early mobilisations, however, men played the leading role, while in other instances men, women and children have participated with equal vigour (Joshi 1982).

Chipko's base, then, has not been restricted to any one section of Uttarakhand society. It can be argued, however, as Chandi Prasad Bhatt has,[39] that the women are capable of playing a more dynamic role than the men who, in the face of growing commercialisation, are apt to lose sight of the long-term interests of the village economy. One must nonetheless be cautious in interpreting women's participation in Chipko in terms of a modern conception of feminist self-assertion. As beasts of burden when viewed through the prism of an outside observer, hill women are regarded within their own culture as the repository of local tradition. Indeed, within the orbit of the household, women often make major decisions. Now, more than ever, women are charged with the preservation of family and village culture, for the men have been forced to enter the cash economy in order to provide for the family and are for much of the year physically separated from the village arena. In the act of embracing the trees, therefore, women are acting not in opposition to men (as feminist interpretation would have it), but as the bearers of continuity and tradition in a culture threatened with fragmentation.[40]

Chipko as an environmental movement

Three streams in the Chipko Movement
Chipko's crystallisation as a major social movement has also been reflected in the emergence of several contending wings within it. Constituting, as it were, subcultures of the movement, these groups articulate distinct philosophies of development that also imply alternative styles of environmental activism.

Perhaps the best-known figure in the Chipko Movement is Sunderlal Bahuguna. He views commercial forestry and the close links that exist between contractors and forest officials as solely responsible for the deteriorating Himalayan environment. For Bahuguna, shortsighted forest management is a symptom of a deeper malaise, the anthropocentric view of nature intrinsic to modern industrial civilisation. Thus 'the ecological crisis in Himalaya is not an isolated event. Its roots are in the [modern] materialistic civilisation, which makes man the butcher of Earth' (Bahuguna 1983: 18).

While Bahuguna's group is active in the Bhageerathi valley, the active wing of Chipko in the Alakananda valley is associated with the name of Chandi Prasad Bhatt. Unlike Bahuguna, Bhatt does not deny the villagers' role in deforestation, stressing however that 'this has been a result of separating the local population from the management of the forest wealth'.[41] Further, Bhatt argues that both forest officials and commercial forestry are merely agents of a development process biased in favour of the urban-industrial complex and against local needs. He is also sharply critical of the growing separation between the state and the people, as clearly manifested in the framing of development schemes by urban-centred technocrats. These schemes have little relevance to the realities of rural India (Bhatt 1984).

Interestingly, the two leaders also affirm alternate styles of environmental activism. Bahuguna works in what one might call a *prophetic* mode: attempting to convert the uninitiated with a constant flow of articles, lectures and marches. In an inspired move, he undertook a 4,000 kilometre march across the Himalaya (completed in April 1983), attracting wide coverage on the extent of environmental degradation in hill tracts outside Uttarakhand. Chandi Prasad Bhatt and his group the DGSS, on the other hand, have concentrated more on grassroots reconstruction. Apart from several afforestation camps conducted yearly, they are also working on the installation of bio-gas plants and other low-cost energy saving devices. A remarkable fact about the afforestation camps organised by the DGSS has been the rate of survival of saplings (65 to 80 per cent) — the survival rate achieved in government plantations (around 10 to 15 per cent) seems almost pitiful in comparison.[42]

Interestingly, the rate of survival has shown a rapid rise following the greater involvement of women (Agarwal and Narain 1985).

A third group, the Uttarakhand Sangharsh Vahini (USV), active in Kumaun, adheres to an ideology strongly influenced by Marxism. While respecting Bhatt for pioneering the Chipko technique, the USV is attempting to move away from the public identification of Chipko with the two major leaders. It affirms the view that the human–nature relationship must not be viewed in isolation from existing relationships among humans. For the USV, social and economic redistribution is seen as logically prior to ecological harmony. It follows that the USV refuses to associate itself with state-sponsored development programmes, and in its own work it has occasionally come into sharp confrontation with the administration.[43]

The various streams within Chipko reflect, in a microcosm, different strands in the modern environmental debate. In his rejection of industrial civilisation, Bahuguna comes strikingly close to the American historians Lynn White and Theodor Roszak who stressed the role of religious beliefs in determining human attitudes towards nature. Modern science and technology are largely informed, in this perspective, by Judeo-Christian ideals of human transcendence and rightful mastery over nature. This ethos is contrasted with the value systems of so-called primitive societies which, unlike Western science, view the ecosystem in its totality, thereby ensuring a rational and sustainable use of resources.[44] While accurately pinpointing the inability of Western science to come to grips with the eco-crisis, the alternative proposed by this school implies a return to pre-industrial modes of living — a vision perhaps as elusive as Western science's claim to bring material prosperity for all.

While acknowledging the alienation of modern science from the true needs of the people, Bhatt places a far greater emphasis on alternative technologies which could be more environmentally conscious as well as more socially just. In this respect, his views are similar to the pioneer formulations of the technologist A.K.N. Reddy, who emphasises the role of appropriate technology in an environmentally sound development policy. The criteria of technological choice advocated by Reddy are briefly as follows: technologies that are employment-generating; ecologically sound; that promote self-reliance (both in terms of invoking mass participation and using local resources); that tend to reduce rather than reinforce inequalities; and that build upon, rather than neglect, traditional skills (Reddy 1982). Like Reddy, Bhatt acknowledges the importance of social movements which could bring about a more equitable society — one in which a more ecologically oriented path of development could be adopted.

While the USV does share with the DGSS this vision of an ecologically oriented socialism, the two groups differ in their relative emphasis on political activism. The USV clearly prefers organising social movements that confront the state, to grassroots reconstruction work such as afforestation, arguing that it is the responsibility of the state to reverse the processes of capitalist penetration and environmental degradation. Moreover, it does not share the doctrinal emphasis on non-violence espoused by both Bahuguna and Bhatt.

Widening of Chipko's horizons

With the emergence of three distinct streams, Chipko is at a crucial point in its history. It is imperative that the present atmosphere of mutual suspicion and distrust be replaced by one which would enable a meaningful dialogue between groups committed to different perspectives on the ecology–society nexus. While complete agreement may not be possible, areas of joint action could perhaps be worked out. These could then be integrated with a wider perspective that can view the ecological, social and cultural degradation of hill life in its totality.

Recent developments in Uttarakhand hold out promise for just such a widening of the aims of Chipko. Moving away from the identification in the public arena of the movement as an exclusively 'ecological' one, younger activists (notably in the USV) have begun linking up the forest question with other aspects of social and environmental change. One may also mention in this connection the ongoing movements against the siting of large dams, open cast mining and the illicit liquor trade in Uttarakhand.

Perhaps the most vigorous of these movements has been the opposition to the liquor trade. The widespread consumption of liquor (both licit and illicit) has been linked to a steady erosion of the socio-economic viability of many peasant families. Here, too, the roots can be traced to state-induced commercialisation which has brought in its wake profound dislocation; the liquor contractor (against whom much of the hostility has been directed) has been, like his counterpart in the timber trade, only the most visible symptom. As in the opposition to dam building and mining, activists schooled in the Chipko tradition have played a key role in mobilising support. Liquor, more than forestry, has reflected an incipient conflict between the sexes — in consequence, thousands of village women have demonstrated against the liquor policies of the government (Guha 1985a, chapter 8).

In this manner, the expansion in the scale of commercial penetration and its technological infrastructure — as exemplified by the location of large dams, increased mining and timber operations and the spread of alcohol — in the past decades has been matched almost step-by-step with a sustained opposition in which Chipko has played a major role in catalysing and broadening the horizons of social consciousness. Despite insinuations that Chipko has a localised frame of reference, its aims do not necessarily conflict with the lives of those living in the Indo-Gangetic plain. The bid to rescue hill society from the ravages of capitalist penetration does not call for a narrow regionalism. Since the agriculture of the plains depends heavily on a sustained and assured supply of water from the rivers which originate in the Himalaya, the stabilisation of Uttarakhand ecology and society has far wider implications.

Reds, Greens and Chipko

In this widening of the movement's horizons, changes in forest policy have been conceived as an integral element in the development of an alternative development strategy. In this sense, notwithstanding the differences in style and ideology between its subcultures, one can ascribe a certain unity to Chipko. This unity may be found in the major questions it has raised concerning social change. The existing strategy of state-induced industrialisation, while inherently biased against rural needs, has, as the accumulated evidence clearly indicates, been primarily responsible for the degradation of India's land and water resources.[45] In opposition to this strategy (one prone to view natural resources as inexhaustible), Chipko has implicity been a model of economic organisation that would minimise both social and environmental dislocation. Such an alternative would question not merely the *goals* of the present development policy — rapid industrialisation and urbanisation — but also its *instruments* — namely the reliance on the state and private industry as prime 'agents of change'. What is especially striking about the growth of environmental consciousness in India is the critical role played by movements such as the Chipko Movement.

The movement's two leading spokesmen, Bahuguna and Bhatt, have, albeit in contrasting ways, focused popular attention on one of India's most pressing ecological problems. Interestingly enough, the scientific profession has been largely innocent of ecological concerns. Indeed several scientists have turned their attention to ecologically oriented research as a direct consequence of Chipko. Yet Chipko's significance has hardly been restricted to its catalytic role in making ecology an issue of public debate. As the innovative work carried out by Chandi Prasad Bhatt and the DGSS makes evident, grassroots organisations could also play a leading part in the restoration of ravaged ecosystems.

This decentralisation of political and economic structures advocated by Chipko closely mirrors the Gandhian conception of a 'village-centred economic order' discussed above. As I have shown, nationalist élites in India, by adopting a policy of imitative industrialisation, have chosen to disregard the warnings of Gandhi and his followers. In the decades following Indian independence, there existed a normative consensus amongst intellectuals and political élites on the desirability of rapid industrialisation and technological modernisation. One could argue that this consensus was shared by Marxism which questioned merely the social and political choices made by modernisation theory, and not the model of Western-style industrialisation. In much the same manner as the Greens in West Germany, Chipko has questioned the underlying assumptions of the consensus.[46] What is noteworthy here, as Chipko's affinity with Gandhian perspectives make evident, was the ostensibly 'post-industrial' vision of contemporary environmental movements anticipated in many respects by early critics of modern industrialisation. During the decades leading up to Indian independence the intellectual and political components (of social movements) of the ecological perspectives ran parallel to each other; the fusion of the two in Chipko has lent an added legitimacy and strength.

The potential role of grassroots movements in identifying and addressing environmental degradation raises what is perhaps the most crucial question in the environmental debate: the type of political organisation most appropriate to ecologically sound development. Of central importance here are the different perceptions regarding the role of the state. In one view, the state is seen as a disinterested body which stands above, and indeed mediates, conflicts in civil society. In this view the state represents a higher 'national interest', it is argued, and its intervention in terms of policy prescriptions and programmes is the means by which social conflicts are harmonised and development assured.

Yet the 'national interest', as critics of forest policy in India have trenchantly observed, is usually a thinly veiled guise for the particular interests of the dominant classes in society (Gadgil 1983). In the contrasting, and perhaps more empirically accurate, perspective, the actions of the state are severely constrained by the social structure. As Marx pointed out more than a century ago, the operation of the capitalist state mirrors, to a lesser or greater extent, the conflicts and disproportionalities existing in the wider society (Marx 1975). As such, the ultimate ecological solution must rest on the construction of a more equitable social order.

At this point, Marxist and ecologist (or 'Red' and 'Green') analyses of capitalism take different paths. More accurately, the Marxist critique stops right here, with the belief that the victory of socialism would necessarily put an end to environmental problems.[47] The experiences of the socialist states do not bear out such a sanguine attitude. The half century that has elapsed since the Kumarappas first penned their critique of Soviet Russia strongly reinforces their conclusion that a dogmatic commitment to rapid industrialisation and the fusion of party and state is conducive neither to social justice nor to environmental stability.[48]

Coming to terms with the failure of the communist project, the Greens attempt to do to Marxism what Marx himself did to Hegel: accept what is of continuing relevance in his system of thought while rejecting his false prognosis and many of his key assumptions. Yet it is impossible to conceive of the Green movement in West Germany or Chipko-style environmentalism in India without the historical backdrop of left-wing analysis and political activity against which they have arisen.[49] While accepting the Marxist emphasis on equity and social justice, the Greens take issue with the political and technological solutions offered by state socialism. More innovatively, the 'Greens' argue that environmental degradation also brings in its wake the erosion of distinctive cultural traditions; traditions that are often central to the self-image of a society, its continuity, and the ability to mould its own destiny. In this sense, true 'eco-development' (and the alternate technologies that constitute its core) must build upon the cultural, moral and politico-economic characteristics of individual societies.[50]

The debate between Reds and Greens is as yet in its very early stages. The links between technology and ecology, and politics and culture, will undoubtedly undergo significant changes in the years ahead. In the Indian context, the Chipko Movement and its legacy helped define these issues with a particular clarity and sharpness of focus. It is likely that the continuing evolution of Chipko and its three contending subcultures will help define the outcomes as well.

Notes

The research on which this chapter is based was funded by the Fellowship Programme of the Indian Institute of Management, Calcutta; the writing by the United Nations University/World Institute for Development Economics Research through their project on 'Technology transfer: alternative approaches'. I am grateful to the directors of the UNU/WIDER project, Professors Frédérique and Stephen Marglin, and to Tariq Banuri, Mike Bell, Robert Cassen, Julia Falconer, Sujata Keshavan and Jukka Oksa for their helpful comments on an earlier draft. This chapter is dedicated to Shekhar Pathak, historian, long-time Chipko activist and 'Encyclopaedia of the Himalaya'.

1. The northern hill districts of the Indian state of Uttar Pradesh are known as Uttarakhand. There are eight districts in all. This culturally homogeneous area was divided into two chiefdoms in the medieval period, known as Kumaun and Garhwal.

2. For details see Guha 1985c. The most substantial analysis of *pahari* (hill) society and culture is the ethnographic study by Gerald Berreman (1972).

3. See *British Parliamentary Papers* 1890–92.

4. See *Report of the Task Force for the Study of Eco-development in the Himalayan Region* 1982.

5. *Annual Administrative Report for the Tehri Garhwal state* 1937.

6. For a fuller analysis of 'scientific' forestry see Guha 1985c: 1941–8. These techniques were common to both Kumaun and Tehri Garhwal.

7. *Patti* is an administrative unit comprising a group of villages.

8. See National Archives of India (NAI) 1907.

9. See NAI 1930.

10. See D. No. 10X, dated. 6.2.1917.

11. Among Scott's many stimulating works, see especially his *Weapons of the Weak: Everyday Forms of Peasant Resistance* 1986. I have also found helpful his essay 'Protest and profanation: agrarian revolt and the little tradition' (1977).

12. Differing conceptions of property and use also informed conflicts over forest rights between the peasantry and the aristocracy in medieval Europe. See, for example, Thompson 1975, and Tilly 1986: 15–16.

13. On sacred groves, see Bor 1953: 18; Brandis Working 1987: 12; Edwards 1922: 78–80. On the wide range of traditional conservation mechanisms practised by rural populations in India, see Gadgil 1985b.

14. See, for example, notes by V.A. Stowell, Deputy Commissioner, Garhwal (n.d., probably 1907), Dharmanand Joshi, late Deputy Collector, Garhwal (13.8.1910), and J.K. Pearson (Dec. 1921), all in Forest Department (FD) file 83/1909, Uttar Pradesh state Archives, Lucknow (UPSA); and for fuller citations Guha 1985b: 1940, 1951.

15. For outstanding anthropological studies in the traditional cosmology of forest-dwelling communities in peninsular India, see chapter 3 in this volume; Elwin 1939.

16. In Superintendent, Dehradun, to Commissioner, Meerut Division, No. 340, dated 15.9.1873., in File No. 2, Department I, List 2, Post Mutiny Records, Uttar Pradesh Regional Archives, Dehradun.

17. See Criminal Case 98 of 1915, in Basta (box) for 1928–30 for Chakrata Tehsil, Criminal Record Room, Dehradun Collectorate; Criminal Case No. 7 of 1921, in the court of the District Magistrate, Almora, in Forest Department file 157/1921, UPSA; *Yugvani*, 15.1.1948.

18. For the involvement of soldiers, see FD file 157/1921, UPSA; for headmen see Guha 1985a, chapters 5 and 6.

19. That is government, moneylender and landlord. See Ranajit Guha *Elementary Aspects of Peasant Insurgency in Colonial India*, 1983.

20. For a careful study of the evolution of Gandhi's views, on which the paragraph rests heavily, see Mukerji 1958. I am grateful to Anjan Ghosh for this reference.

21. Bharatan Kumarappa 1965; J.C. Kumarappa 1949. These works have suffered an inexplicable neglect, and present-day Indian environmentalists seem unaware of this anticipation of their concerns.

22. As, indeed, did Marx. See his articles on India in the collection entitled *On Colonialism*, 1976.

23. See Thakurdas et al. 1944. For a fine analysis of the Indian industrialisation debate, see Chattopadhyay 1985.

24. Government of India, Planning Commission 1956: 6. Cf. also Mahalanobis 1963.

25. *National Forest Policy of India* 1952: 2.

26. Uttar Pradesh Forest Department (n.d.).

27. *Uttar Pradesh Forest Statistics, 1978–79*, (n.d.).

28. *Yugvani* issues of 2.4 and 9.7.1967, 14.11 and 21.11.1971, 24.12. and 31.12.1971.

29. G.O. No. V.O.B. 289/XIV–378–56, dt. 23.7.1960.

30. *Report of the Kumaun Forest Fact Finding Committee* 1960.

31. *Yugvani*, issues of 3.4.1960 and 20.11.1966.

32. *Yugvani*, issues of 2.4 and 9.7.1967, 14.11 and 21.11.1971, 24.12. and 31.12.1971.

33. Bhatt 1983: 475.

34. For a description of these different agitations see Mishra and Tripathi 1978; Dogra 1980; Guha 1985a, ch. VII.

35. Interviews in Badyargarh, January 1983.

36. For an elaboration of this theme, see Scott 1976.

37. On the Reni incident, see Das and Negi 1983.

38. See Centre for Science and Environment 1983: 42.

39. Speech at meeting at Bakarkhatia village, Pithoragarh District, October 1983.

40. This is the position (as expressed in personal communications) of two scholars with an unrivalled knowledge of Uttarakhand: Shekhar Pathak and Jean Claude Galey.

41. Bhatt 1983: 477. For an earlier analysis of the divisions within Chipko that in several respects parallels my own, see Berreman 1983.

42. Personal communication to this writer from S.N. Prasad of the Indian Institute of Science, who conducted the study.

43. This paragraph is based on interviews with USV activists in Naini Tal and Pithoragarh, in May and October 1983.

44. Cf. White 1975 and Roszak 1975.

45. For a magisterial survey of environmental degradation in India, see the reports of the Centre of Science and Environment cited earlier.

46. One must, however, distinguish between subsistence-oriented movements such as Chipko and elements in the Western environmental movement concerned more with the protection of habitats for leisure. For some insightful comments on Western and Indian environmental traditions, see Agarwal 1986.

47. For a forceful statement of the classical socialist position, see the writings of Russian social ecologists, for example Laptev 1977. While A.K. Bagchi, in his *The Political Economy of Underdevelopment* (1982), is more cautious, his analysis of environmental problems in the Third World and the celebration of China as an unqualified success are indicative of a belief that centralised planning in a socialist economy would solve such problems.

48. Cf. Bahro 1984. Smil 1984.

49. Let me add that the cultural milieus of the Greens and of Indian environmentalism are quite different. The relationship between socialism and ecology (and its eventual resolution) no doubt significantly differs in the two contexts. In the United States, the radical ecology movement barely addresses the quintessential socialist concerns of equity and social justice, its primary (and sometimes exclusive) concern being the preservation of unspoilt wilderness. See, for example, Devall and Sessions 1985.

Bibliography

Agarwal, Anil (1986), 'Human–nature interactions in a Third World country', Fifth World Conservation ·Lecture, *The Environmentalist*, vol. 6, no. 3.

———— and Sunita Narain (eds) (1985), *India: the state of the Environment, 1984–85: A Citizens Report*, New Delhi, Centre for Science and Environment.

Annual Administrative Report for the Tehri Garhwal state (1937), Tehri.

Bagchi, A.K. (1982), *The Political Economy of Underdevelopment*, Cambridge, Cambridge University Press.

Bahro, Rudolf (1984), *From Red to Green,* London:.

Bahuguna, Sunderlal (1974), *Uttarakhand Mein Ek Sau Bis Din*, in Hindi, Dehradun.

———— (1983), *Walking with the Chipko Message*, Sliyara: 18.

Berreman, Gerald (1972), *Hindus of the Himalayas*, 2nd edn, Berkeley University of California Press.

———— (1983), 'Identity: definition, assertion and politicisation in the Central Himalayas', in Anita Jacobson-Widding (ed.), *Identity: Personal and Socio-cultural*, Uppsala.

Bhatt, Chandi Prasad (1979), *Pratikar ke Ankur*, in Hindi, Gopeshwar.

———— (1980), *Eco-system of Central Himalaya and Chipko Movement*, Gopeshwar: 11–13.

———— (1983), 'Eco-development: people's movement', in T.V. Singh and J. Kaur (eds), *Studies in Eco-development: Himalaya: Mountains and Men*, Lucknow: 475, 477.

———— (1984), 'Himalaya kshetra ka niyojan', in Hindi, Gopeshwar, mimeo.

Bookchin, Murray (1980), *Toward an Ecological Society*, Montreal.

Bor, N.L. (1953), *Manual of Indian Forest Botany*, New Delhi.

Brandis, D. (Working 1987), *Indian Forestry, British Parliamentary Papers* (1890–92), 'Correspondence relating to the scarcity in Kumaun and Garhwal', vol. 59.

Centre for Science and Environment (1983), *India: the State of the Environment 1983: a Citizens' Report*, New Delhi.

Champion, H.G. and F.C. Osmanston (1962), *E.P. Stebbing's Forests of India, vol. IV*, Oxford: chapter IX.

Chatterjee, P. (1984), 'Gandhi and the critique of civil society', in Ranajit Guha (ed.), *Subaltern Studies III*, New Delhi, OUP.

Chattopadhyay, R. (1985), *The Idea of Planning in India 1930–51*, unpublished Ph.D. thesis, Australian National University, Canberra.

D. no. 10X, dated 6.2.1917, from Divisional Forest Officer, North Garhwal, to Conservator of Forest, Kumaun Circle, in General Administration Department, file no. 398/1913, Uttar Pradesh state Archives, Lucknow.

Das, J.C. and R.S. Negi (1983), 'Chipko Movement' in K.S. Singh (ed.), *Tribal Movements in India, Volume II*, New Delhi.

Devall, Bill and George Sessions (1985), *Deep Ecology: Living as if Nature Mattered*, Salt Lake City.

Dogra, B. (1980), *Forests and People*, Rishikesh.

Edwards, S.M. (1922), 'Tree worship in India', *Empire Forestry*, vol. 1.

Elwin, Verrier (1939), *The Baiga*, London.

Forest Department (FD) file 83/1909, Uttar Pradesh state Archives (UPSA), Lucknow.

Forest Department (FD) file 157/1921, UPSA.

G.O. No. V.O.B. 289/XIV–378–56, dated 23.7.1960, from the Assistant Secretary, Government of Uttar Pradesh, in Office of the Conservator of Forests, Tehri Circle, Dehradun.

Gadgil, Madhav (1983), 'Forestry with a social purpose', in Walter Fernandes and Sharad Kulkarni, (eds), *Towards a New Forest Policy*, New Delhi.

—————— (1985a), *Conservation of catchment areas of river valley Projects on the Western Ghats*, Bombay Natural History Society, January: 30–1, mimeo.

—————— (1985b), 'Social restraints on resource utilisation: the Indian experience', in J.A. McNeely and D. Pett (eds), *Culture and Conservation*, Dublin.

—————— S.N. Prasad and R. Ali (1983), 'Forest management and forest policy in India: a critical review', *Social Action*, vol. 33: 127–55.

Gandhi, M. (1908), *Hind Swaraj*, Navajivan Publishing House, Ahmedabad.

Gandhi, M.K. (1966), *Industrialise and Perish*, compiled by R.K. Prabhu, Ahmedabad: 26, 28, 31–2.

Government of India, Planning Commission (1956), *Second Five Year Plan*, New Delhi.

Gross, P.H. (1982), *Birth, Death and Migration in the Himalayas*, New Delhi: 184.

Guha, Ramachandra (1983), 'Forestry in British and post British India: a historical analysis', *Economic and Political Weekly*, 29 October and 5–12 November.

—————— (1985a), Forestry and Social Protest Movements in Uttarakhand, fellowship thesis, Indian Institute of Management: Calcutta.

—————— (1985b), 'Scientific forestry and social change in Uttarakhand', *Economic and Political Weekly*, annual number, Bombay: 1939–40.

—————— (1985c), 'Forestry and social protest in British Kumaun, c. 1893–1921', in Ranajit Guha, (ed.), *Subaltern Studies IV*, New Delhi.

—————— and Madhav Gadgil (n.d), 'Forestry and social conflict in British India: a study in the ecological bases of agrarian protest', unpublished manuscript.

Guha, Ranajit (1983), *Elementary Aspects of Peasant Insurgency in Colonial India*, New Delhi.

Hearle, N. (1888), *Working Plan (WP) for the Tehri Garhwal Leased Forest, Jaunsar Forest Division*, Allahabad: 1, 16.

Joshi, Gopa (1982), 'Men propose women dispose', *Indian Express*, 14 January.

Kumarappa, Bharatan (1965), *Capitalism, Socialism or Villagism?*, Varanasi.

Kumarappa, J.C. (1949), *Why the Village Movement?*, 5th edn, Wardha.

Laptev, I. (1977), *The Planet of Reason*, Moscow.

Mahalanobis, P.C. (1963), *The Approach of Operational Research to Planning*, Calcutta.

Marx, Karl (1975), 'Critique of Hegel's doctrine of the state', in Lucio Colleti, (ed.), *Karl Marx: Early Writings*, Harmondsworth: Penquin Books.

—————— (1976), *On Colonialism*, Moscow.

Mishra, A. and S. Tripathi (1978), *Chipko Movement*, New Delhi.

Mukerji, D.P. (1958), 'Mahatma Gandhi's views on machinery and technology', in his *Diversities*, Bombay.

National Archives of India (NAI) (1907), Foreign Department, nos. 37–9, Internal-B, Progs, October.

National Archives of India (NAI) (1930), file no. 458-p/1930, acc. no. 22 (on microfilm), Crown Representative Records.

National Council of Applied Economic Research, *Growth Centres and their Industrial Potential: Chamoli*, New Delhi.

National Forest Policy of India (1952), New Delhi: 2.

Nehru, Jawaharlal (1946), *The Discovery of India*, London: 346–8.

Pathak, C.S. (1980), *Uttarakhand Mein Coolie Begar Pratha, 1815–1849*, unpublished Ph.D. thesis, Department of History, Kumaun University: 461–2.

Pearson, Dr F. (1866), 'Report on mhamuree and smallpox in Garhwal', in *Selection from the Records of the Government of the Northwest Provinces*, vol. II, Allahabad: 300.

——— (1869), 'Forests in the Bhageerathi Valley', in *Selections from the Records of Northwestern Provinces*, 2nd series, vol. II, Allahabad: 121.

Reddy, A.K.N. (1982), 'An alternative pattern of Indian industrialisation', in A.K. Bagchee and N. Bannerjee (eds), *Change and Choice in Indian Industry*, Calcutta.

Report of the Kumaun Forest Fact Finding Committee, The, (1960) Lucknow: 26f.

Report of the Task Force for the Study of Eco-development in the Himalayan Region (1982), Planning Commission, New Delhi, mimeo.

Roszak, Theodor (1975), 'The sacramental vision of nature', in Robin Clarke (ed.), *Notes for the Future*, London:.

Sarkar, S (1983), *Modern India, 1885–1947*, New Delhi.

Scott, J.C. (1976), *The Moral Economy of the Peasant*, New Haven Yale University Press.

——— (1977), 'Protest and profanation: Agrarian revolt and the little tradition', *Theory and Society*, vol. 1: 1–38, 211–46.

——— (1986), *Weapons of the Weak: Everyday Forms of Peasant Resistance*, New Haven Yale University Press.

Singh, V.P. (1967), *WP for the West Almora Forest Division, Kumaun Circle, 1966–67 to 1975–76*, Nainie Tal; Agrawala, N.K.

——— (1973), *WP for the Kedarnath Forest Division, Garhwal Circle, 1972–73 to 1981–82*, Naini Tal.

Smil, Vaclav (1984), *The Bad Earth: Environmental Degradation in China*, White Plains, NY.

Stebbing, E.P. (1922–27), *The forest of India* (3 Vols.) London.

Smythies, E.A. (1914), 'The resin industry in Kumaun', *Forest Bulletin No. 26*, Calcutta.

——— (1925), *India's Forest Wealth*, London.

Thakurdas, P. et al. (1944), *Memorandum Outlining a Plan of Economic Development for India*, 2 vols, Bombay.

Thompson, E.P. (1975), *Whigs and Hunters*, Harmondsworth: Penguin Books.

Tilly, Charles (1986), *The Contentious French*, Cambridge, MA.

Uttar Pradesh Forest Department (n.d., prob. 1971), *Forest Development Project, Uttar Pradesh, India*, Lucknow: 117–21, mimeo.

Uttar Pradesh Forest Statistics, 1978–79, (n.d.) Lucknow.

Verma, V.P.S. (1973), *WP for the Tehri Forest Division, Garhwal Circle*, Naini Tal.

—— (1981), *WP for the Tehri Forest Division, Garhwal Circle, 1973–74 to 1982–83*.

Visvesvaraya, M. (1920), *Reconstructing India*, London: 273–4.

Voelcker, J.A. (1897), *Report on Indian Agriculture*, 2nd edn, Calcutta: 135–6.

Von Monroy, J.A. (1960), *Report to the Government of India on Integration of Forests and Forest Industries*, Food and Agricultural Organisation, Rome: 8.

White, Lynn (1975), 'The historical roots of our ecological crisis', in Robin Clarke (ed.), *Notes for the Future*, London.

Yugvani, Hindi weekly from Dehradun, issues of 15.1.1948, 3.4.1960 and 20.11.1966, 2.4 and 9.7.1967, 31.10.1970, 14.11 and 21.11.1971, 24.12. and 31.12.1971.

5. The benign encounter: the Great Move and the role of the state in Finnish forests

Jukka Oksa

Introduction

Finland, the most northern country examined in this study, has a widely spread rural population which practises both agriculture and forestry. The rapid structural change of the economy and society during the past ten years has led to a heated debate between the forest industry and the rural population. This debate, over what some have called the 'green gold' of Finland, centres within the contrasting views of the forest held by the forest industry, on one hand, and the rural population, on the other. The forest industry views the forest strictly as a source of raw material. This view contrasts with other views of the forest by the rural population, such as the forest as a base for local communities, as a landscape to be used for recreation and pleasure, or as an archetype (mother nature) to be respected.

This chapter discusses the changes which have taken place in the Finnish countryside and the nationwide debate regarding the breakdown of the two rural forms of economy. Based upon observations conducted by a village research group from the Karelian Institute of Joensuu University, the experiences of North Karelia highlight these national discussions. As one of the most underdeveloped provinces in the country, North Karelia has been characterised as a 'forest periphery'. This characterisation is justified, I believe, because its major social and economic problems are connected with the extraction of roundwood and the future of the labour force. The rural population in North Karelia has reacted to the upheavals of the economy and society, and therefore in their daily lives, by both political protests and by looking for new forms of social action.

The chapter expands these national discussions to an international level and must therefore consider particular national characteristics. The first of these is the strong impact of the state on rural development, an impact which cannot be ignored. Rooted in the formation of independent Finland, state legislation ended the concentration of private forest lands in the hands of forest companies. Although the farmers' land ownership currently remains protected by legislation, in the past the state gave land to crofters and rural workers in order to reconcile deep class conflicts. These conflicts eventually led to a civil war in 1918, but it was not until after World War Two that the last (re)settlement programmes for evacuees and men returning from the war were discontinued.

During the period after the war, new estates were founded, and the population in many periphery villages increased until the end of the 1950s. These landowners, who had been resettled, were considered the last significant generation to have cleared land for farming (within a European framework). During the 1960s when it seemed as if the state had forsaken them, this rural population channelled their protest through the Finnish political democracy in order to react as citizens and not as outcasts. Other forms of protest were viewed as less desirable because of the Finns' deep trust in the state and their strong commitment to citizenship (although political officials are deeply mistrusted).

Another specific consideration deals with the Finnish forest industry. This industry has been export-oriented from its creation. Corporate strategies instigated at the global level have begun to loosen what have traditionally been tight connections within, and to, local rural communities. There is a growing concern among many prominent officials that as a result, corporations will also begin to loosen ties to national responsibilities. This could increase the tensions already apparent in rural communities.

Discussion about the Finnish forests cannot take place without considering the large regional variation in forest ownership. Currently about two-thirds of Finnish forest land is owned by private smallholders — an exceptional fact when compared with other important forest production countries. This private ownership has become threatened in the last twenty years with the transfer of land to non-agricultural owners. Inheritance has resulted in the loss of over half of all private forest lands. This rapidly changing ownership pattern must remain under close scrutiny in any discussion.

Finland has been characterised as a 'forest sector society' (Koskinen 1985). The two wings of the forest sector, the private forest owners and the forest industry, have not only played a central role in defining the interests of the Finnish nation, but have also become the basis of the political system as well. These conflicting sectors, and their political connections, have been viewed in Finnish class analyses as contributing to the profound conflicts in this country and must remain an important part of studies of the 'green gold' of Finland.

The formation of the two forms of rural economy
In order to understand the functioning and consequences of the decay of the two forms of the rural economy, a brief historical perspective is necessary. The formation of the rural economy, and concentration of forest lands and forest industries begun in the last century cannot be separated. Early forms of the rural economy included fur and animal

hunting, fishing and slash-and-burn cultivation. Forests were the source of many necessities in the family economy including firewood and building materials. This led to disputes in the long-time frontier territory of Karelia. Set between the Swedish and Russian empires, Karelia had been depopulated and resettled several times. As the number of farms increased, disputes arose over the rights to continue slash-and-burn cultivation. Later the slash-and-burn disputes were continued by the owners of sawmills.

The structure of land ownership

The Swedish Crown began the division of public lands, including forest lands, into private peasant farms in the late 1700s. By the early nineteenth century this process had begun in Karelia. However, large areas of frontier land were not divided and given to farmers, but were left to the Crown. These large state forest lands are a unique feature of northern and eastern Finland, and its significance for the regions' development must be emphasised even today.

Karelia remained in a state of isolation until Finland was annexed to Russia as an autonomous Grand Duchy in a 1809 treaty. It opened the border to the south and east. In North Karelia, ironworks processing lake ore, and sawmills exporting timber, began to develop rapidly, especially in the latter half of the 1800s after the liberalisation of the economy. The latter brought about new uses for forests. Ironworks, especially favoured by the Crown, needed charcoal for refining the lake ore, and sawmills demanded lumber. At first industry was not established by local entrepreneurs, but was built by the office holders of the Crown, and investments were strictly regulated by mercantilistic state policies. The Crown granted concessions and sometimes supported new ventures with loans.

The division of land turned forest lands into private property which could be bought and sold. The industries operating in the area started securing their raw materials by buying forests. Often peasants, who did not understand the future value of their lands, sold their lands for what seemed to them a fortune, but was unfortunately a smaller compensation than they had realised.

The concentration of merchant and industrial capital in North Karelia started relatively early in the Finnish context. So even before the liberalisation of the economy, which took place after the middle of the 1800s, a single industrial owner became almost the only large-scale industrialist and forest owner in the county. He owned the largest ironworks and sawmills, built two separate export routes of his own, and even paid wages with his own paper money before the Bank of Finland started printing Finnish Marks.

Table 5.1 Forestry land ownership (%) in Finland, southern
Finland and North Karelia

	Private	Companies	State	Others	Total
Southern Finland	77.7	10.4	7.4	4.5	100.0
North Karelia	56.6	21.4	18.4	3.6	100.0
Forest Karelia	36.8	25.9	34.4	3.0	100.1
Finland	56.8	6.9	32.3	4.0	100.0

Sources: Official Statistics of Finland XVII A:15, National Forest Inventory
1971–1976 Land Ownership Statistics, Farm Register and Forest Estate
Register.

Note: 'Forest Karelia' here includes the municipalities of Lieksa and Ilomantsi.

After the liberation of the economy, there were three decades of prosperity
for the merchant houses of the newly founded (1848) town of Joensuu.
By the end of the century a small group of merchant families owned the
sawmills, ironworks, sailing ships and steamers. They benefited from
Karelia's proximity to Petrograd, because export of iron and timber
brought profits and wealth. These merchant houses kept on buying large
forest lands from the farmers, often making the earlier
peasant-landowners their workers and tenants. The number of landless
workers, mobile and looking for work, grew.

The period of prosperity for the Joensuu trading families came to an
end at the turn of the century. The forest industries became concentrated
on the national level. The rocky ore displaced the lake bed ore and the
large ironworks of Karelia had to be closed down. One sawmill after
another, each with its vast forest reserves, was sold to the large companies
of southern Finland. These companies built their big plants at the southern
ends of the best floating routes; the Gutzeit company was first to introduce
the new technique of bundle floating, lowering the cost of long-distance
roundwood transportation. Of the numerous sawmills of Joensuu, only
the largest remained operative under new ownership.

At the beginning of this century, all the extensive forest properties
(about 400,000 hectares owned by the Joensuu merchants) were bought
mainly by two large national companies, Gutzeit and Kaukas. In some
eastern communes of North Karelia the companies owned, and still own,
almost 30 per cent of the area. On the basis of this large-scale ownership
of land, to which must be added the vast state-owned forests, the eastern
and northern parts of North Karelia differentiated into a special region
sometimes called 'Forest Karelia' (as opposed to 'Agricultural Karelia'
in the south and the west). There developed in Forest Karelia a particular
occupational structure and type of farming.

Regional division of labour: formation of forest periphery

The role of North Karelia in the regional division of labour was determined both by the new role of Finland in the international division of labour and by the position of North Karelia in the Finnish national economy.

After the October Revolution in Russia and the granting of independence to Finland, Finnish industry turned its trade towards the Western market. The earlier extensive trade of paper and foodstuffs to Russia dropped to practically nothing.

In the next decade the position of Finland in the international economy was crystallised through the export of raw wood and half-finished products. North Karelia became the backward country of the big wood processing and exporting companies. The companies that now owned the North Karelian plants and large forests located new and modern plants near the export harbours on the south coasts. Kaukas Ltd gradually stopped all processing of wood in North Karelia. Also Gutzeit located its main plants in southern Finland but kept some medium-sized plants around the waterway of Lake Pielinen in North Karelia. Around the 1930s North Karelia's proportion of the total value of Finnish forest production was over 8 per cent, and its proportion of floated timber was as high as 15 per cent, but its share of forest manufacturing was only around 2 per cent.

Between the two world wars, the economy of Finland was very diversified, its labour force doubled and many consumer industries grew rapidly. This growth led, however, to an accelerated regional concentration of industry in the centres of southern Finland. In the 1950s, when economists were rejoicing at the thought of Finland having grown up into 'a real industrialised country', North Karelia was a region characterised by underproduction in almost every category of manufactured consumer goods.

The peripheral position of North Karelia in the regional division of labour was reflected in the occupational structure of the population. The proportion of industrial occupations remained low and limited mostly to wood industries and mining. In contrast, the proportion of agricultural occupations remained high. State settlement policies continued to populate Finland's remote rural areas until the 1950s.

How to use the periphery's forests and labour: two forms of local economy

The structure of Finnish agriculture has adjusted to take care of the tasks of forest work and timber transportation. In Forest Karelia, where wage labour was necessary in the state and company forests, the average area under cultivation per farm became, and remained, consistently lower than in Agricultural Karelia. However, it was the task of the whole region to provide raw timber for southern companies. The majority of the farms in Agricultural Karelia were also small in size and depended on extra income from forests. Their relation to a wood-buying company was that of a small proprietor to a big buyer.

Figure 5.1   The position of the two rural forms of economy in relation to the central economic structures

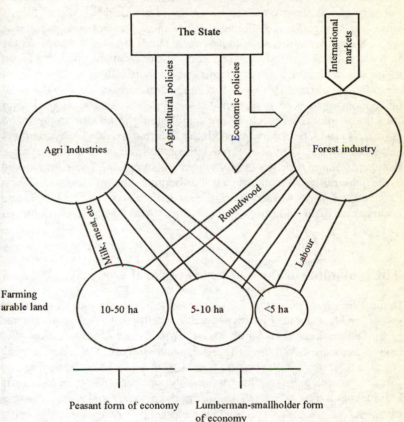

Before the 1960s the Finnish rural population was tied to the villages mainly through two different forms of economy: (1) the peasant form of economy, and (2) the lumberman-smallholder form of economy (see figure 5.1). They represent two different ways of combining agriculture and forestry — it is worth emphasising that both these forms are combinations of agriculture and forestry. Their difference arises from the different local land ownership structures.

In those regions where private peasant land ownership prevails (especially southern and central Finland), forestry is a natural part of farming. The peasant family derives its basic income from cattle and farming. The forest has been a guarantor of peasant independence, helping to finance farming investments: mechanisation and purchase of additional land. It also pays for the education of the children to enter new professions. Forestry also offered possibilities for more efficient use of the farm's work force, horses and machinery. When there was not enough farming work, the farmers, their sons and the farm hands could do forestry work. In those parts of Finland (east and north) where state or company forest ownership is strong, small farming is subordinated to the role of reproduction of forestry's work force. The lumberman-smallholder form of economy has been typical in these regions. The sociological term 'functional' describes precisely the smallholding in relation to the forest industry's production of roundwood. Small farms provided forest workers and work horses. The wives carried on small-scale farming (cattle, pigs, hens, etc.) mainly for the family's own consumption. The men worked in the fields during the summer. The lumberman-smallholder combination survived as long as forestry work demanded a lot of seasonal labour and horses, and other industries did not draw away the peripheral labour force.

The crumbling of the two forms of rural economy

In the 1960s state policies were reoriented to serve the aims of industrial growth and to adapt the Finnish national economy to the new requirements of the international division of labour, first in EFTA co-operation, and later in agreement with the EEC. At the same time profound centralising changes took place in the organisational framework of both farming and forestry. On the one hand, the farmers, the agribusinesses, the foodstuffs industry and the state agencies formed an integrated agro-industrial complex. In agricultural policies there was a move away from subsidising small farms and a move towards structural policies — emphasising productivity, specialisation and mechanisation.

On the other hand, the forest industries, forestry organisations and state forest agencies campaigned for intensive forest production, providing more raw material for board, pulp and paper exporters. Also the forest sector was emerging as an integrated system, with complicated internal relationships (both conflicts and common interests). There were new pressures to reorganise forestry production and to cut down the cost of roundwood, not only in company- and state-owned forests, where wage labour was used, but also in the private forests of the farmers.

In the 1960s both rural forms of economy in the forest periphery began to disintegrate, but according to different timetables, and with different social consequences. The obvious causes of the disintegration are the technological changes in agriculture and forestry. In my opinion, however, we have to focus on agents of action (organisations, institutions) adapting and introducing these technologies, using some of the technological possibilities and disregarding others. In our case of forest periphery the important institutions taking advantage of the mechanisation were: (1) the state forestry organisation, (2) the forest industries, and (3) peasant farms. The forest industries have been most keenly interested in cutting down the costs of cutting and transportation of roundwood. (The state forestry organisation has this same goal, but it also has to take into consideration other pressures. Its representatives emphasise their commitment to sustained yield forestry planning and also their sensitivity to the local needs of employment and multiple forest use.) The peasant farm uses the forest as one part of the farm economy, either as a source of personal income or for financing the development of agricultural mechanisation. Because of these differences of interest, the special technology for peasant-scale forestry has not been developed.

During the 1970s, modern large-scale forestry used forms of planning and work organisation which discouraged farmers from cutting and transporting timber in their private forests. The companies wanted to guarantee an effective and intensive use of their own cutting and transport organisations. In the 1980s, as the result of a lively public debate, some emphasis and attention were given to smaller-scale forestry. Cheaper tractors and other machinery were developed ('soft technology' is the slogan for marketing forestry tractors) and price agreements and taxation were altered to favour the farmer's own work in his forest.

In the 1950s, at the same time as smallholdings were still being founded in eastern and northern Finland, the mechanisation of agriculture was already gathering momentum. The mechanisation of farms began on large and medium-sized farms and reduced the need for farm workers and family members in order to produce crops. In the 1950s a noticeable part of the labour force released through agricultural mechanisation was able to find other local work; at that time many roads and several hydroelectric plants were being built in the forest periphery. In the next decade the state started promoting the mobility of labour and the restructuring of family agriculture. The peasant form of economy was beginning its thorough transformation. Many smaller farmers could not make ends meet from their farm income; on the farms classified as profitable, to which was directed the support of state agricultural policy, families needed fewer children to work on, and carry on, their farms. The peasants in a higher income bracket were able to help their children to move away by educating them for new occupations, often for white-collar employment. On the other hand, the children from small farms were often in the same position as the forest workers' children: they had to look for work without occupational training.

The mechanisation of forestry began in North Karelia about ten years after that of agriculture. The chainsaw replaced the handsaw. This did bring some new strata of skilled machinists to forest workers' camps, but it did not yet drastically reduce the number of workers. Besides, the first power saws were heavy and clumsy. A more important change was the replacement of the horse by the tractor. This change was important, because the horse was a link between farming and forestry. Horses were raised on farms, whilst tractors were made in factories and consumed gasoline. Although, at first, farming tractors were also used in forestry, new specialised tractors for forestry were soon developed.

The most important factor about the introduction of forest tractors was the new organisation of work. State and forest companies began organising lumbering and transporting on a year-round basis. The number of temporary and seasonal jobs decreased rapidly.

Figure 5.2   The monthly variation in the number of forestry and floating workers in the years 1958 and 1981 ('000 workers)

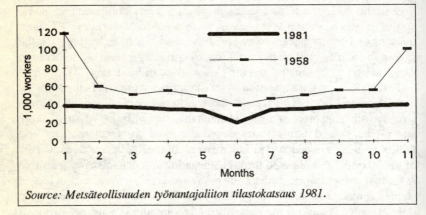

Source: Metsäteollisuuden työnantajaliiton tilastokatsaus 1981.

The seasonal lumberjack was replaced by the professional, full-time forestry worker. The lumberman-smallholder form of economy was phased out over roughly ten years, and with dramatic social consequences.

The smallholders, and especially their children, were forced to find new occupations in southern Finland or Sweden. Earlier, the state had organised jobs for the unemployed in the remote areas, but now its labour market policies helped transfer the labour force to southern Finland. There was a labour drain straight from the forest periphery to the factories and construction sites in industrial Finland (see figure 5.2).

So a major part of the younger generation in the forest periphery participated in the Great Move of the period 1960–75, as a result of which urban, industrial Finland was created. The size of North Karelian age cohorts under 15 years in 1950 (born in 1936–50) shrank to only 39 per cent in 1975.

The lumber-smallholding was crushed in a little over ten years, transforming forest work into a new, specialised and mechanised profession, without any economic ties to farming. The modern forestry worker may have social and emotional ties with the villages, but these ties do not differ much from those of first-generation town-dwellers.

Figure 5.3 The crumbling of the two forms of rural economy and its consequences in the social structure of the villages.

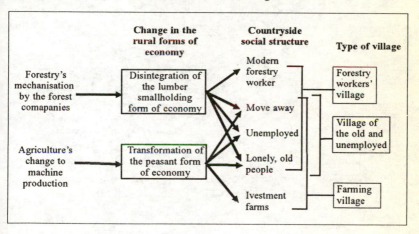

Also first-generation workers living in the provincial towns have maintained many rural features in their way of life, like countryside leisure activities (fishing, hunting, gathering berries and mushrooms, boating, etc.) and have not integrated in the cultural or consumer institutions of town life (see Ahponen and Järvelä 1985).

Figure 5.4 The location of the case villages.

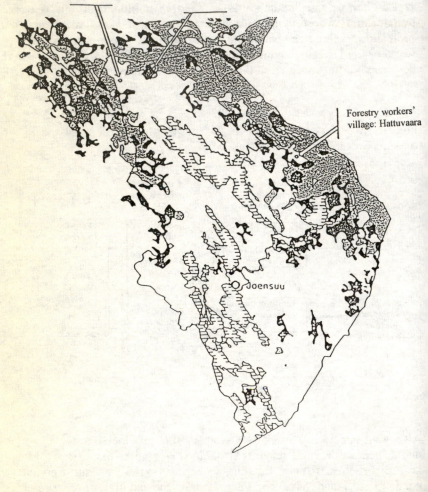

State-owned forest land

Company-owned forest land

Farming village: Rasimaki

Village of the old
and unemployed: Sivakkavaara

Forestry workers'
village: Hattuvaara

Joensuu

Villages with different local socioeconomic structures have gone through these general changes in different ways. If we leave out the villages where daily commuting to service or industrial centres is a common practice, we can easily distinguish three basic types of forestry periphery village. I shall clarify each type with a case description.

Case studies: three villages in the forest periphery

Our research group in the Karelian Institute of Joensuu University has made case studies of different types of villages. They are all located in North Karelia, representing different paths of development in the forest periphery. The first village, Rasimäki, is inhabited by the most typical Finnish family farms of milk producers. The second village, Sivakkavaara (Sivakka), is a remote traditional village of lumberman-smallholders without modern forestry workers. The third village, Hattuvaara (Hattu), is a village of modern forestry workers. (See figure 5.4.)

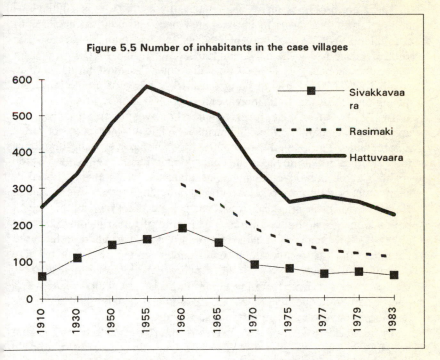

Figure 5.5 Number of inhabitants in the case villages

As figure 5.5 indicates, all three villages have gone through a drastic loss of population since the 1950s. But because of their different local structures and different links to the Finish society and economy, they went through the time of the Great Move in different ways. They also participated in the common reactions of the countryside to these changes, the political protest and new forms of local action, but also these processes were moulded into different forms in each village.

The dairy farmers' village

Our first case study village represents the most typical agricultural production of eastern and northern Finland — dairy farming. Rasimäki was a farming village of approximately 140 inhabitants in 1983. Its lands were cleared mainly after World War Two and evacuees were settled there by the government. The land contained naturally beneficial conditions for cattle farming. The farms in our research area are part of a united field area of about 600 hectares. It is too remote for even small-scale industry. Probably for the same reason, specialisation in fresh produce for townspeople (greenhouse produce, berries, etc.) has not developed there. The village has persisted as a producer of milk and meat, the raw materials for the dairy and the slaughterhouse.

There are no big farms in the village of Rasimäki. It is a village of family farms. No farms in the research area had over 20 hectares of arable land in 1970, and only two farms had less than 5 hectares. The bulk of farms had 7–15 hectares. Earlier, up to the 1960s, on a farm where the economy was based on dairy cows, as most farms were in North Karelia, there had to be at least 10 hectares of arable land, but during the 1970s this limit increased to 15–20 hectares.

In 1970, Rasimäki's forest ownership was distributed roughly according to land ownership. The farms each had 40–60 hectares of forest apiece, but the primary form of forest ownership was quite unique: a forest common was founded in connection with the settlement which covered about 2,200 hectares. It was managed by an elected board of share owners. This meant that the running of village forests was separated from individual farming decisions. For private share owners this meant both advantages and discomforts. The timing of forest income does not always follow the needs of active farmers, who would often prefer more income at the time of investment requirements on the farm. For inactive elderly farmers who used their farm primarily as a place of residence, the continuous income from the common forest was welcome. It was a good addition to their pension, provided social benefits and made the pensioners' lives more comfortable and secure.

In Rasimäki we can see two waves of internal polarisation. The first began in the late 1960s. Some of the farms, mostly because of small field acreage, dropped out of production with the help of the state programme of 'field packaging'. In the mid-1970s came the second wave of polarisation, the change to a new type of 'industrial' farming. There is a new division between those who have gone through this change, and those who have kept the former way of farming. (See Table 5.2.)

Table 5.2 The number of farms in Rasimäki according to economic activity, 1970 and 1981

	1970	1981
Modern investing farms	–	8
Farms of the 1960s	32	8
Low production farms	1	2
No production but land in ownership	5	13
No production, and land sold away	1	8
Total number:	39	39
– milk production	33	12
– other specialised production	–	6

In the village a new division of field acreage is also taking place. The number of large farms has increased, that of smallholdings has decreased, and the total number of active farms has decreased from 33 to 18 (see Rannikko and Oksa, p. 26). Agriculture thus secures a better income, but for fewer families than before. On the darker side, some farms have completely ceased production. Some families sold their lands but kept the farmhouse as a residence or for holiday use. Most people on these farms are retired or unemployed.

As the traditional family farm changed to 'industrial' agriculture, it underwent several changes. The farm had to be formed into a specialised and sufficiently large production unit. For Rasimäki cattle raisers this has meant almost doubling their field acreage. Specialisation has often meant investment in the agricultural part of the farm and de-emphasising the forestry part. Forestry development has been left to other organisations. However, investment in agriculture calls for extra income (from forestry); so the needs of the farmer in relation to his own forest are contradictory.

The farm has to be provided with enough modern buildings, machinery and equipment, and also pedigree livestock. On the Rasimäki investment farms this meant a rapid move into debt. On eight investment farms the average amount of debt rose twentyfold in ten years. An older farmer, unsure of his future capacity for work, cannot undertake such long-term commitments.

The farm has to form a labour unit of the right size and quality for this new mechanised farming. Agricultural policies tend to develop one-family farms, which are based on the nuclear family's two-adult work input. Family forms other than the nuclear family seem unsuccessful in developing production. For example, bachelor farmers often continue the traditional method of farming, without making modernising investments.

The future for Rasimäki depends on the future of agriculture. About one-fourth of the farms have made investments in specialised production. They have farming families of good working age. However, this stratum of farms is not enough to support permanent basic services in the village. The village school is under threat of closure because of the small number of children. The number of this type of farm is not likely to increase. In the village there are good fields and also farms willing to invest, but the state policy of milk production quotas make it very difficult, almost impossible, for new farms to join the group of efficient producers.

The traditional lumberman-smallholders' village

Our traditional forestry workers' village, Sivakka, is among Valtimo's oldest settlements, the area having been settled since the 1600s. The fields are small, stony, scattered and rather unproductive. The population has lived mainly from forest work and to a smaller extent from farming.

The increase in the demand for timber abroad, and the forest purchases by timber companies at the turn of the century, put an end to the peace and quiet of the earlier close-to-nature culture of Sivakka. Development in the area began to be linked to the money and market economy. The timber companies' and the state's vast lumber sites brought to Sivakka's environment lumbermen mainly from east Finland. There were enough large forest work sites for several decades.

To Sivakka, forest work was of particular significance and to most Sivakka families forest work was the main source of livelihood. The greater number of forest workers — or rather their wives — farmed and kept cattle on a modest level (one or two cows), mostly for the family's own consumption. For them it was impossible to live off farming alone, since the holdings usually had only 1–2 hectares of arable land.

The population of Sivakka reached a peak at the end of the 1950s. Many forest workers who had come to the lumber sites stayed and started families with young Sivakka women. For the periods of 1950–54 and 1955–59 the birth boom in Sivakka was noticeably larger than in the years 1945–49, which was the typical birth boom period in Finland as a whole. Of the present dwellings more than half were built in the 1950s.

Due to these new residents there was a loosening of the firm kinship network which had become intertwined round several families of long standing in the village. The outside world introduced new lifestyles and attitudes to the traditional village populace.

Nowadays, Sivakka has become a dwelling place of the old and unemployed. The consequences of the change in forest work are very evident in Sivakka. The final collapse came in the early 1970s, and thereafter only three to five persons had any noticeable income from forest work, whereas the corresponding figure for 1970 was about 20.

In addition to the change in forestry work, the depopulation of Sivakka's type of village has been hastened by public housing policies. In the early 1970s, the community built the first public rental housing in the centre of Valtimo. Sivakka's large families, which had lived in small, shabby cottages, were given these new apartments. The first community-built rented housing became known as the 'new Sivakka'.

The new professional forest workers have become independent of farming and tend to live in population centres. One-third of those employed in Valtimo community's forestry were living in the community centre in 1980.

Although the drain of population has slowed down in recent years, the losses of earlier years have had the effect of 'ageing' the village until it approached a final collapse. In 1982 Sivakka's school was closed as the number of pupils dropped to six (from over seventy in the early 1960s). At present the majority of inhabitants are pensioners or are unemployed. Only a quarter of Sivakka people belong to families whose income is not dependent mainly on social income transfers of society. Thirty per cent of Sivakka's population are already over fifty-five years old. A typical inhabitant is a grandmother living alone in her cottage, while her children are scattered around the country (see Rannikko and Oksa 1985: 29).

Table 5.3 Sivakka's population structure, 1983

Under school age	7
School age or students	12
Pensioners	21
Employed	9
Unemployed	16
Housewives, or otherwise at home	8
Total inhabitants	73

It is difficult to conjure up a future for Sivakka's type of remote village, where the core of operating farms is missing. A central problem in the near future will be caring for those elderly people who live alone. There is a danger that many of these former forestry villages may become wildernesses, where here and there some of those who have turned their back on the system live apart from the 'achieving' society.

The modern forestry workers' village

After studying these two villages our research group gathered data on a modern forestry workers' village, Hattuvaara, a settlement of about 240 inhabitants (1984) on the outskirts of the forest industry town of Lieksa. In these parts of the periphery, the network of administrative community centres does not sufficiently cover the forest lands. In the vast tracts of land near the eastern border, where the state is the largest landowner, a few of the old lumber-smallholding villages have taken a part in housing the new forest workers. Here the state Forestry Board has built ten apartments for the forestry workers to rent. The village is used as a centre for organising cutting and transport in the area around the village, about 40–50 kilometres in every direction. Collective transportation to the felling sites is organised by the employer.

The core of forestry workers has been adequate for the maintenance of the basic public services (school, post office, meeting hall, shops) and even some new ones (pub, bank, taxi drivers). The service centre of the area has been able to increase its population. The commune has built eight apartments for pensioners and young families with children. Also the small farmers in the village have made some extra income from forestry and were therefore able to survive, while in other areas small farms may have been almost totally closed down.

Table 5.4 The socioeconomic position of the heads of households in the service centre of Hattuvaara in 1984

Forestry workers of state Forestry Board	15
Other forestry workers	3
Forestry tractor contractor	1
Farmers (in the service centre only)	3
Working in the services in Hattuvaara	6
Working in the town centre (40 km away)	2
Pensioners (mostly from forestry)	13
Unemployed (long term)	2
Other	1
Total number of households	46

Source: Data collected and analysed by my colleague Pertti Rannikko.

A summer school of the Nordic Planning Institute (Nordplan) made a short visit to the village of Hattuvaara to conduct fieldwork in 1980. Nordplan recognised that the size of farms was small, and that mechanised forestry could be combined with farming. They concluded that this village has no future and that it will lose its population during the coming years.

We have criticised that conclusion as being too narrowly tied to the idea of small farming as the foundation of the village. The study did not recognise that the core of this village is modern forestry and that its workers are employed in the state forests.

The future of this village type is, however, threatened by plans to introduce the new generation of technology in forestry. New forest harvesters and combines would further reduce the need for forestry workers. These machines are already in use in some companies' forests, and plans have been made to introduce them into state forests. There is strong opposition to them inside the state Forestry Board organisation, among the local and district officials, and of course among the village inhabitants.

The search for new economic layers

In today's situation the future of villages in the forest periphery is uncertain. Because of production surpluses, agriculture faces production quotas. Industry's job growth has slowed down, Finnish enterprises are turning their investments towards international operations, and the pace of technological change is speeding up. This threatens both the traditional and the new manufacturing industries in developing regions. Political pressures to restrict public spending on welfare programmes and to streamline regional policies have increased. These factors have revived the threat of centralisation.

Solutions are being looked for in local projects. The state is pushing programmes of self-employment, creating small enterprises in rural areas, and encouraging adaptation to the use of new technology. These projects have created new hopes and expectations, but their effects have so far remained modest in proportion to the problems.

Forms of reaction and action

The reactions of the inhabitants can be divided into two periods. During the Great Move there was nationwide political protest, bringing into the limelight the Finnish Rural Party, SMP, which declared itself the party of the 'forsaken masses'. The second period started in the latter half of the 1970s, when rural migration became stable for almost a decade. Then the idea of village committees started spreading. During this process over 2,000 village committees were organised in the Finnish countryside, changing the rural atmosphere from anxiety to hopefulness.

Political protest through the SMP

In each of our three village cases, the SMP became the channel of political protest. The ideological profile of the SMP can be characterised as populist. It is located in the political centre and was started as a small-farmer oriented splinter of the Agrarian Party (now the Centre Party). It emphasises the good old values of petty producers, is strongly anti-socialist, anti-corruption, and very Finnish-nationalistic. It is strongly identified with the character of its leading figure, the founder of the party, Veikko Vennamo, whose son is continuing as the chairman of the party. The colourful style of the leading personalities is skilfully publicised through the media.

Although during the 1980s the SMP, like other parties, has emphasised some of the 'Green' issues (like opposition to nuclear power) and has recruited some local activists on environmental issues, the SMP is much too anti-intellectual and too rural to be considered Green. The Greens of Finland, as elsewhere, are a loose grouping of educated, modern and young people, who are looking for an alternative way of life and world-view (some of them seeking solutions from the rural past of their society). The SMP is the reaction of those who live in real rural poverty today but are not able to dream of a better life in the cities.

Figure 5.6 contains results of the parliamentary elections, in so far as they can be counted, on the district voting level (comparable to villages). A small minority of votes go to individual candidates and so cannot be attributed to political parties, which explains why the numbers do not always add up to 100 per cent. In the 1960s, 70 per cent of the population in the farmers' village, Rasimäki, voted for the Agrarian Party (today the Centre Party), but in 1972, when one-third of the village acreage was going out of cultivation under the state field package programme, 50 per cent of the votes went to the SMP. Later, when the new investment farms had again stimulated village agricultural production, the Centre (former Agrarian) Party was able to win back the largest proportion of votes in the village. Some activists from the earlier protest movement have themselves modernised their farming and returned to the Centre Party.

The traditional forestry workers' village, now a village of the old and unemployed, was politically to the left in the 1960s. It could be called a stronghold of backwoods communism, with 45 per cent of votes going to the People's Democratic League (which includes Finland's Communist Party) and 36 per cent to the Social Democratic Party in the 1966 Parliamentary election. The SMP, which received only 30 per cent support in the early 1970s, increased it to 46 per cent at the expense of left-wing parties in the 1983 election, when the economically active population had almost vanished.

In the modern forestry workers' village, the SMP protest was quite strong in 1972 (40 per cent of the vote), but with the revival of the village the votes have returned to the Centre Party, to the Social Democrats and partly to the People's Democratic League. Inside the left, however, the modern forestry workers have given their votes more and more to the

Figure 5.6 Distribution of votes in parliament elections in the three case villages.

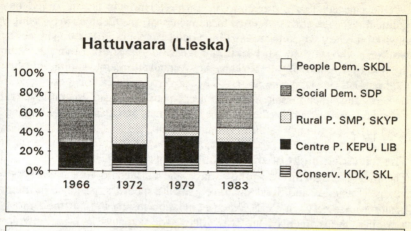

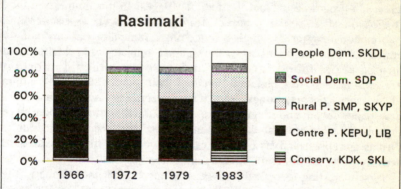

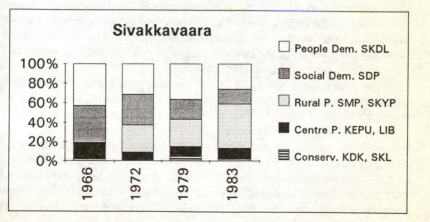

Social Democratic Party, which has grown to be equal in power with the Centre Party.

One can say that socioeconomic differentiation is accompanied by political differentiation. Modern farmers support the Centre Party, while modern forestry workers support the Social Democratic Party. The poor workers, who worked hard and only received meagre incomes, as was the lot of traditional lumberjacks and small farmers, supported the Communists in large numbers. The poverty-stricken or poor small owners, and other forsaken groups (poor pensioners and unemployed), are prone to vote SMP. When facing new threats and crises, the villagers seem prepared to change their voting patterns.

The television night of the small farmers' wives

The inhabitants of the farming village and of the old forest workers' village (Rasimäki and Sivakka) have gained a special experience of their position in society. In 1975, when population losses were at their most alarming, the women of the two villages participated in a nationwide television programme about the fate of villages. In this connection they studied our first research report from 1973 as well as background information on agrarian policies. In the programme they put surprisingly critical questions to members of the Cabinet (minister of agriculture and minister of social affairs) and also to other important decision-makers. They had also prepared their own cultural programme of sketches, poems, songs, etc. The programme initiated a heated newspaper debate about agricultural policy and the role of cooperative organisations. It brought the women of these two villages into public forums as representatives of rural people. Later this strategy was used actively in local politics in village committees.

It is interesting to note the division of labour that took place in the television show. The women of the protesting farming village Rasimäki were active in formulating sharp and sometimes angry questions about agricultural and social policies. They formulated their position in terms of politics. The women of the traditional forestry workers' village, Sivakka, were active in the cultural part of the show, reading poems of their own, singing, acting in sketches, etc.

Seppo Knuuttila, a folklorist in our research group, has analysed the significance of this television programme for the traditional forest workers' village, Sivakka. The villagers felt that the show was a rare possibility to express their hopes and demands for a better life to a nationwide audience. In this situation the villagers' strategy turned out to be representative of 'poverty culture'. The strongest common element in the poems and manuscripts written for the programme was the endless toiling of the farmer's wife, and the life-long succession of hard working days, from early morning till late at night. 'Sometimes I feel so empty, because this work does not seem to amount to anything at all. Always you have to work, and it never ends.' A small piece of hard dark bread in a child's hand is a common symbolic element. Other repeated themes were: the burden of taxes, difficulties in paying debts, youth moving away from the village, disappointment in the upper class and decision-makers who think only of the interests of their own and other rich people. Those belong to the 'evil world' outside the village (Knuuttila 1984: 151).

One feature of the 'poverty culture' is the absence of planning in life. One has to admit, from a practical point of view, that a village like Sivakka has no means of producing a development plan of its own. The development of the village has been 'planned' elsewhere, and one television show or even village committee action cannot change those plans from being realised, writes Knuuttila (1984; 151).

The village committees

Since the mid-1970s about 2,000 so-called village committees have sprung up in the Finnish countryside, in almost every settlement of at least 200 inhabitants (see Rouhinen 1981 and 1983). The committees have tried to enliven the social and cultural life in rural areas. So far, their achievements have raised morale more than improved the economic premisses for rural development, but the committees have received widely favourable publicity.

As social phenomena, village committees are a mixture of two contradictory tendencies, neither one of which should be forgotten. Village committees were founded through a nationwide campaign by a central organisation of rural communities, university research groups, adult education networks and local planning bodies (and often local banks). It was a well-run programme of action research. Its leader, Professor Lauri Hautamäki, declared: 'The purpose of village studies is to help the rural inhabitants to improve their living conditions. The purpose is to create action, not papers ...' (*Kylät ja...* 1980: 42). The idea was to create new regional planning on a village level. The significance of this new planning level was expressed in a contradictory manner. On the one hand, there were speeches about making the village into an autonomous subject — a planner of its own development. On the other hand, the aim was to integrate the village level into a modern system of planning, with communal planning specialists instructing the villagers in what the village committee action actually means.

Another equally important side of the matter is that the villages were ready to accept the village committee campaign. After the years of political protest, villagers were divided and disappointed in political leaders outside the village. There was a need even in small things for a new community and for co-operation; and in fact there were, at least in the beginning, many things left undone, that could be done with the united effort of the local inhabitants.

In all of our three case studies there are village committees. They differ, however, in their role and also in their style of activity. In the farming village, the village committee consists of active women, either wives of investment farmers or widows with large amounts of leisure time. The men of the investment farms tend to carry on their social activities outside the village, as is the case with the young people, too. The role of the women taking care of the household has widened to the village level and a small group of women is involved in organising festivities, skiing contests for children, theatre excursions, training courses in gardening, etc. The unemployed feel, and are seen by the activists, to be outcasts in relation to the village committee.

The old forestry workers' village also organised a village committee, although later than the others. It has been hard to find a chairperson. Often an unemployed person is elected as chairman when he has a lot of time and energy for many activities. The old pensioners have time, but not always the strength and health. So the group of activists is necessarily small, although no group in the village is excluded. 'We are all poor and almost all relatives.' This village also organises fishing contests, meetings and demands to the community to save the bus service or to get a taxi-driving licence for the village shopkeeper.

The modern forestry workers' village has a large active population consisting of several organised groups. The village committee has a coordinating role in the village. It coordinates all the organisations, the Foresters' Union, the Agricultural Producers' Association, the local shopkeepers, the bank branch office, the Hunting Association, etc. Its action is typical of village-level activities: clearing the sports ground and cleaning the village beach, organising the beach festival, preparing initiatives for the community to get electric lights for a village skiing and jogging track. This committee's working style is said to be very male, as is its composition, men representing the different interest groups of the village.

These examples describe the nature of village activities. Many of the successes that created the bases for rural optimism were indeed small improvements in the environment, or just the organising of local social life such as festivals (midsummer night, mother's day, harvest), fishing and skiing events, etc. Much more complicated is the question of making demands to local officials. Here the ties to the local political power groups tend to set the tone of these demands.

After five years of activities many people have become disillusioned. Over the years, the village committees and especially their leaders have become institutions of optimistic village spirit. Now the easy things have been done, and the difficult things are still too difficult. The institutionalised village optimism is not able to analyse the possibilities and demands of the new situation.

The village committees, although they cover the whole Finnish countryside, have not gathered their forces into a nationwide social movement, that would promote a rural policy of its own. Cooperation of village committees at a national level is coordinated by leaders of central interest groups and 'friends of the countryside' in Helsinki. The village networks looks more like a centrally organised publicity campaign than a social movement. A social movement would have plenty to do: state policies towards rural areas consist of unpredictable and inconsistent elements. Many development and employment programmes simply do not reach peripheral villages. The various policies (on agriculture, the labour market, housing, etc.) have been conflicting, even contradictory, in their effects.

The struggle over the Forest Karelia project

In 1985 the village committees of the state forest district participated in common action and public debate about the so-called Forest Karelia project. The background to the situation is that the one and only cellulose plant in North Karelia at Uimaharju was becoming obsolete. The province's politicians were trying to ensure investments to renew and develop the plant. As an answer to the province's demand, the owner of the plant, Enso Gutzeit, a state-majority stock company, one of the largest forest industry companies in Finland, published its own plan, the Forest Karelia project. In this plan the company proposed a fusion of all the major sawmills to a new cellulose corporation. This would help to rationalise the local sawmills and, what is more important, it would put the corporation into an almost monopolistic position among the local buyers of roundwood. In addition, the company also proposed that the state should support the project by giving 100,000 hectares of state forestry lands to the company.

This project was strongly opposed by a local social movement. The local inhabitants felt that the company would set limits to everyone's rights to use forest areas for recreation, fishing and hunting, picking berries and mushrooms, etc. The village committee of Hattuvaara participated in this campaign and the village forestry workers took part in a demonstration rally. Approximately 1,000 people rallied against the plan. The clear messages of the demonstration were: 'The company harvester eats trees and jobs', 'Don't close the forest roads!'

The social basis of the movement was wide: unions of forestry workers and sawmill workers, village committees, district officials of the National Board of Forestry, leaders of the two municipalities involved, and some figures from the local professions (doctors, local journalists, university professors).

On the day of the demonstration the organising group made new plans for continuing the struggle on a nationwide level. They planned how to increase pressures on ministries and also how to influence the members of parliament. About one week later, however, the organising group decided to stop functioning. This voluntary dissolution was a surprise (a disappointment to some and good news to others). After that, different groups in the movement continued with their own limited mini-debates in the local press.

What went wrong? The goals of the movement were getting increasing support, as was revealed later in a county-wide survey by one newspaper. A vast majority of the rural population shared the goal of 'keeping the public forests public'. My explanation is that the leadership of the movement did not know how to cope with politics. Certainly the issue of state forest ownership was a political one but the leaders of the movement could not define a common relationship to political parties. All the district political organisations were lobbying for further investments in the Uimaharju plant and the issue of giving state forests to the company divided the memberships of all the major parties. Different political groups in the movement could be kept together only so long as the movement could be defined as a local phenomenon. When it spilled beyond the local frame, the political issues intensified and contradictory loyalties destroyed local cohesion. The only agreement that could be reached was to dissolve the movement's organising centre.

However, the work of the movement was not in vain. By mobilising public opinion it did help to kill the idea of giving state forests to industry. The planning of the Uimaharju plant had to be conducted from a different starting point, based on regional policy.

Discussing the Finnish experience

I think that lessons can be learned from the Finnish experience, and I agree with David Vail (chapter 6) that these are connected with the triangle of state, forest industry and family farming.

The structure of land ownership is the historical foundation of the power institutions of society. Those institutions are the ones that create the strategies for technology transfer. The distribution of power between them (their more or less contradictory interests) establishes the framework within which the possible alternative technological strategies are to be defined.

For about half a century both the exporting forest industry and the forest-owning peasantry of Finland have identified their interests with 'sustained yield' forestry securing long-term production of roundwood. So it was easy for the state to accept this as the official forest policy of the country and easy to believe that rural settlement programmes, which provided land for farmers and labour for forestry, were all the rural policy that was needed.

The significance for Finland's history of combining forestry with agriculture (both in the form of private forests and in the form of the lumberman-smallholder) can hardly be overemphasised. The private forest properties lengthened the life of family farming in Finland. These private properties were a base for small enterprise forestry and later challenged the industry's way of organising forest work and developing technology. In some issues of silviculture the private properties have been an ally to the urban environmental activists in opposing the representatives of forest industry. Family farming has been the foundation for a strong Agrarian Party with power within the Finnish state. The lumberman-smallholder was a blend of forestry labourer and petty property owner. For a long time this group constituted an important part of the working class, but which supported peasant politics.

The contradictory relationship of the power institutions in Finland came to light when they started introducing new technologies, each according to their own interests: forest industries to increase the material output and to lower its cost; peasants to strengthen the important second cornerstone of rural life, the economy; forestry workers (coming from the small farms) to improve their earnings and working conditions; and the state to integrate these elements into the economic growth policy of the nation.

The state of Finland is currently able to make use of a quite complicated collection of measures within the welfare state, which I think will be very important in future years. Two examples will suffice. When the farmers thought that too much of their own forests were cut by company forestry workers, the state allowed a tax-free quota of roundwood to farmers cutting and transporting wood from their own forests. Now the forestry workers are accusing farmers of taking away their jobs. Another example is the threat of the real job-eaters, the new combines and harvesters, which are intended to bring a new period of productivity to forestry. They are usually owned by private small contractors, who finance them by loans, and run them with the risk and self-exploitation typical to small entrepreneurs. This means that they do well only when a full year of operation can be guaranteed. In this case the process of introducing forest harvesters and combines could be, to some degree, influenced by the terms of loans and taxation. On the other hand, the burden of forestry job losses could also be lightened by lowering the retirement age of forestry workers (their union has proposed fifty-five years).

Of course, whether the state will decide on such measures or others will be determined through social and political struggles. What I want to emphasise is that the welfare state creates a certain field of possibilities to integrate some social policy strategies with the process of technological transfer, and also with other processes of restructuring the economy. Of course, a sensitive system of representation of various social interests is needed. Some scholars emphasise the importance of local and traditional communities in realising such social policy strategies. In Finland, as in other Nordic countries, local communities and kinship networks have been severely damaged in the process of rapid increase in social and geographic mobility and in the privatisation of life. Because there is no possibility of return to the former communities, the functions of the local municipalities have expanded. The municipality has also gained importance in the field of economic policies: employment programmes, industrial development and the restructuring of agriculture have become arenas for social struggles about alternative methods.

As sources of alternative modes of technology transfer, we must consider those social institutions able to use or at least challenge those with power over the restructuring of the economy. The capability and the will of these institutions are shaped by social forces, e.g. active groups, communities and classes striving to make their goals and values into realities while creating and defending their own cultures.

Bibliography

Ahponen, Pirkkoliisa and Marja Järvelä (1985), 'From country to town and from small farm to factory: study on changes in the way of life of factory workers', in J. Oksa (ed.), *Papers on Social Change in North Karelia*, Joensuu: University of Joensuu, Karelia Institute, Working Papers 12/1985: 59–73.

Kiiskinen, Auvo (1961), 'Regional economic growth in Finland 1880–1952', *Scandinavian Economic History Review*, vol. IX, no. 1: 83–104.

Knuuttila, Seppo (1984), 'Mitä sivakkalaiset kertovat itsestään: kansanomaisen historian tutkimuskoe' (What Sivakka people tell about themselves: an experiment in oral history), in *Yhteiskunta kylässä: Tutkimuksia Sivakasta ja Rasimäestä*, Joensuu: University of Joensuu, Publications of Karelian Institute 61: 131–175.

Koskinen, Tarmo (1985), 'Finland: a forest sector society? Sociological approaches, conclusions and challenges', in Kari Lilja, Keijo Räsänen, and Risto Tainio (eds), *Problems in the Redescription of Business Enterprises*, Helsinki: Helsinki School of Economics, Studies B-73: 45–52.

Kunnas, Heikki J. (1973), 'Metsätaloustuotanto Suomessa 1860–1965' (The production of forestry in Finland 1860–1965), *Suomen Pankin julkaisuja* (Publications of the Bank of Finland), Helsinki.

Könönen, T.A. (1971), *Penttilän saha 1871–1971 100 vuotta* (The Penttilä sawmill: 100 years), Joensuu: Pohjois-Karjalan Kirjapaino Oy.

Kylät ja kaupunginosat yhteiskunnan alueellisina perusyksikköinä (Villages and Town Communities as Territorial Elements of Society), (1980), University of Tampere, Aluetiede, tutkimuksia, Sarja A 2. Tampere: Finpublishers.

Metsäteollisuuden työnantajaliiton tilastokatsaus (Statistical Review of the Association of Forest Industry Employers) (1981), Helsinki.

Official Statistics of Finland, Population Census 1959, 1960, 1970.

Official Statistics of Finland, Population and Housing Census 1975.

Oksa, Jukka (1986), 'Social change in Finnish forest periphery communities: cases from eastern Finland', paper presented to the 13th European Congress for Rural Sociology, Braga, Portugal, April.

———— (ed.) (1985), *Papers on Social Change in North Karelia*, working papers 12/1985, Joensuu: Karelian Institute

———— Heikki Eskelinen and Pertti Rannikko (1985), 'Structural change in the Finnish forest periphery and its effects on young people', paper prepared for European Expert Meeting on Young People in Remote Rural Areas, Luz Saing Sauveur, France, in J. Oksa, (ed.), *Papers on Social Change in North Karelia*: 5–14.

Pohjois-Karjalan uittoyhdistyksen uittotilasto (The floating statistics of North Karelian Association).

Rannikko, Pertti and Jukka Oksa (1985), 'The social consequences of the differentiation of agriculture and forestry: a case study of two villages in Finnish forest periphery', in J. Oksa (ed.), *Papers on Social Change in North Karelia*: 15–32. Also published in *Acta Sociologica*, vol. 31 (1988), no. 3: 217–29.

Rouhinen, Sauli (1981), 'A new movement in search of new foundation for the development of the countryside: the Finnish action-oriented village study and 1,300 village committees', *Acta Sociologica*, vol. 24, no. 4: 265–78.

———— (1983), *Village Action and New Forms of Local and Regional Policies*, XII European Congress for Rural Sociology, Budapest.

Yhteiskunta kylässä: Tutkimuksia Sivakasta ja Rasimäestä (Society in the village: studies of Sivakka and Rasimäki villages) (1984), University of Joensuu, Joensuu: Publications of Karelian Institute 61.

6. The internal conflict: contract logging, chainsaws and clear-cuts in Maine forestry

David Vail

Maine's 'paper plantation': a corporate capitalist forest system

Forest industries in the northeastern United States exemplify the uneven development of knowledge in capitalism, a process driven in this case by the corporate objective of extracting raw materials at the lowest short-run financial cost. As an example of industrial resource extraction, this case illustrates the logic and the cumulative impact of capital's dominance over nature and over workers — in the presence of capital mobility and global competition and in the absence of a strong countervailing labour movement or a resource conservation ethic.

New England is one of America's most urban and industrial regions, but inland from the Atlantic seaboard lies a vast, sparsely populated forest hinterland. The state of Maine, at the region's northeastern extremity, is almost 90 per cent wooded. Its 7 million hectares of forests have been thought of and treated as a virtually limitless, commercially valuable resource since the seventeenth century, when the colonial state began the expropriation of native forest-dwellers, and 'the king's broad arrow' marked tall pines reserved for ship masts of the Royal Navy. Three centuries later, ownership of half the state's land area by seven industrial forest owners has led Maine to be described as a 'paper plantation'. The state's heavy economic dependence on $3.5 billion annual sales of forest products by multinational corporations has prompted the label 'chilly banana republic' (Osborn 1974, Lack 1986).

Since the pre-industrial era, primary products from Maine's farming, fishing and forestry have supplied both the urban northeast and export markets. However, the predominance of forestry should be underlined. As early as the American Revolution, 'the effort to get trees to market was the central industry in Maine. Nearly every family in the state received economic benefit from the woods. Those who were not participating directly helped supply those who were' (David C. Smith 1985: 3). Until early in this century lumber was the major export commodity. Then, deteriorating competitiveness of northeastern lumber combined with technological innovation in wood pulping and paper making to launch a new epoch of rural industrialisation. Paper corporations bought out the land holdings of the 'lumber barons' and erected giant pulp mills on Maine's rivers. The vast 'unorganised territories' of northern Maine, site of the 'limitless' spruce fir stands, had no local government apart from the corporate owners. By 1914, vertically and horizontally integrated paper/lumber corporations were the state's largest employers and a dozen paper mill communities were classic examples of the 'company town'.[1] The 'paper plantation' was, in sum, a rural manifestation of the USA's transition from competitive to monopoly capitalism. A paradox which this chapter attempts to explain is that technology and the labour process in timber extraction long resisted the logic of large-scale industrialism.

In more recent times, the economy of forest regions has evolved in two new directions. First, affluent urban dwellers with abundant leisure time increasingly look to the mountains, lakes and streams of northern Maine for recreation. Second, rising energy costs and growing disillusionment with nuclear power have revived the age-old use of wood for fuel, but now to generate electricity on an industrial scale. At the present juncture — a time of capital accumulation crisis in the paper and lumber industries — these new demands on forest resources have unclear economic, ecological and cultural implications.

This chapter in the political economy of knowledge seeks to explain the uneven development and application of knowledge in forestry. At a general level, it addresses the broad range of forestry practices which constitute a management system. Central tasks are to explain the qualitative degradation of timber resources through three centuries of 'mining and neglect', to probe the meaning of the euphemism 'scientific forestry' as applied to corporate land holdings, and to grasp the ecological implications of recent innovations described by their advocates as 'intensive management'. More concretely, the task is to understand the delayed development and only partial diffusion of mechanised harvesting technology. Here three interconnected phenomena require explanation: incomplete 'industrialisation' of the labour process, reflected in the persistence of motor–manual tree felling carried out by small, semi-proletarian logging crews; the coexistence of several technologies and distinct production relations; and 'human obsolescence', manifested in poverty earnings, high injury rates, middle-age 'burn-out' and rising unemployment. An observation that is not intuitive and merits explanation is why the early phase of mechanisation coincided with a regression from capitalist to pre-capitalist production relations.

Where economic growth degrades resources and makes workers and traditional cultures obsolete, one might expect the rise of Green or Red movements to challenge the power of industrial landowners and corporate employers. A basic historical fact, however, is the weakness of ecological consciousness (greenness) and class-based organisations (redness) in the Maine woods. This has profoundly affected the corporations' capacity to dominate the state, as well as the forests. Several deep-seated values seem to underlie the paucity of Greens and Reds. First, the forests are private property and the trees are commodities.[2] The ideology of private property rights pervades Maine's history and is reflected in state and local land use statutes as well as past governments' vigorous efforts to sell or give away huge public lots. The sanctity of private property is cemented by the petty-landowning status of most Maine households (the majority own their house lots today; one-fourth own small woodlots as well) (Howlett: 81). In America's commercial culture, an instrumental view of nature has always held sway. Forest land is valued largely, if not exclusively, for the stream of raw materials it generates and for anticipated capital gains when it is sold. De Tocqueville's wry observation, during his visit to the United States 150 years ago, was close to the mark: Americans may be farmers, merchants and mechanics, but they are all land speculators at heart. In such an ideological environment, it has been difficult for the notion of common property rights and the ethic of land stewardship to maintain a degree of countervailing influence in political discourse.

A second profoundly influential value is economic progress, measured principally by growth in material production. A corollary of this materialist teleology is the belief that capitalist 'free enterprise' — grounded in private property, competition and self-interest — is the most efficacious means of promoting progress. Progress is fostered by a pragmatic, problem-solving orientation towards nature. Perfecting the means of controlling nature, in order to increase the flow of 'outputs', is a wholly appropriate expression of human reason. New conceptual systems for manipulating nature, like 'scientific forestry', and new tools, like motorised chainsaws, are examples of reason harnessed to self-interest, in order to bring about progress. It is believed that most problems or constraints that arise in the course of economic progress have technological solutions. The prevalence of such unproblematic notions of material progress and technological advance, and the little-questioned instrumental value of capitalist relationships have also narrowed the scope of discourse about forest management and the role of the state.

A third cultural value, the 'American dream' of self-employment, has influenced relationships between corporations and forest workers, and thereby the trajectory of technological development and forest management practice. Loggers' strong attachment to the fictions of independence has also adversely affected their material conditions. Despite a radical change in the American social formation since Thomas Jefferson's day, his pre-industrial vision of self-reliant, property-owning rural citizens still animates many people. In particular, a species of frontier individualism, manifested in the desire for (nominal) self-employment, appears to characterise many loggers. It helps explain their class 'unconsciousness', generally ineffective political and economic organisations and limited geographic and occupational mobility. As we shall see, rather than resist this ethos, the paper corporations have taken advantage of the disposition to self-employment. Both the workers' contradictory consciousness and the actual production relations in Maine forestry are analogous to tenant farming in some Third World settings. There, too, the subordination of tenants stems in part from uneven distribution of land and finance capital, but also from the peasants' resistance to proletarianisation and their strong ties to place.[3]

Finally, state intervention has deeply influenced the development of forest knowledge systems and the diffusion of forest management practices. The state is, of course, neither an 'exogenous' nor a monolithic force: its role is complex, contradictory and changing through time. Simple conceptions of the state, whether as the 'executive of the bourgeoisie' or as the rational executor of 'the public interest' are misleading. Thus, over the past thirty years the US Federal Government on forest labour regulations has evolved from being essentially a captive of corporate/landowner interests into a pluralistic terrain, contested by workers, environmentalists and recreation industries. Though promotion of capitalist economic growth remains the state's central function, interest-group contention, along with signs of cumulative forest degradation, have shifted the balance from unbridled promotion towards regulation.

A detailed comparison between Maine's paper plantation and the Indian and Finnish cases described by the other authors in this volume is reserved for a concluding section. However, a preliminary observation about technology transfer is in order. A basic, though often only implicit, premiss of most discussions regarding technology transfer from industrial economies to the Third World is that the technologies are beneficial and sustainable on their 'home turf '. The forest management systems and timber harvesting technologies used in Maine have indeed produced tangible 'outputs', like jobs, tax revenues and profits, along with glossy magazine paper and cheap toilet tissue. But there is compelling evidence to support the conclusion that the system has also entailed exploitation of loggers, degradation of forest ecosystems and erosion of traditional rural ways of life. If this knowledge system has had such problematic consequences at home, one must seriously doubt its capacity to improve material well-being and be compatible with ecological sustainability and cultural integrity in a pre-industrial setting. The rapid decimation of natural and cultural ecology in the Amazonian rainforest stands as a stark reminder of the awful destructive power of chainsaws, skidders and bulldozers when they are harnessed to the profit-making schemes of multinational corporations and their allies in parasitic 'host nation' governments.

The ambiguous entailments of particular technologies are suggested by evidence from Scandinavia. In Sweden, for instance, several of the same forest management practices and machines employed in Maine, like chainsaw and clear-cutting (harvesting that removes at least 70 per cent of timber from a stand), are embedded in and mediated by an institutional environment which encourages their positive contributions without most of their negative entailments (Andersson 1984; Hermelin 1981; Swedish Institute 1984, 1985). Nonetheless, it is unclear whether fragments of an industrial knowledge system can be decoupled from their parent social formations and reassembled as an 'appropriate technology' in the Third World. I return to this dilemma at the chapter's conclusion.

Forest management, technology and the logic of capital accumulation: 1900–1970

In the 1890s, when Maine's paper corporations built the first great pulp mills and assembled holdings of hundreds of thousands of hectares in the unorganised territories, forestry remained a pre-industrial craft. The paper industry inherited a lumbering tradition in which the northern spruce fir forest was treated like a limitless, self-regenerating wild land, rather than as a scarce domesticated resource. This was reflected in the practice of highgrading: 'cutting the best, and leaving the rest' (the poor-quality trees and less desirable species) to become the foundation for the future forest. For seventy or more years between harvests, most lots were simply left to nature. Getting the logs 'from stump to mill', not harvesting them, was the central constraint in forest management and the focus of technological innovation prior to World War Two. In 1900, most logs were floated to mills on the spring floods of Maine's many rivers. This dependence on natural forces restricted harvesting far from rivers or mills; thus parts of the forest remained unexploited while others were already being depleted of high-quality timber (Parenteau 1986: 21; David C. Smith 1972: 334).

The prevalent pattern of 'mining and neglect' stood in sharp contrast to principles of 'scientific forestry' and 'sustained yield management', which were being developed and advocated by the first cohorts of professional foresters. At the turn of the century they were prominent in a national conservation movement and well represented in Maine's academic and political life. But they were never able to exert much influence on private land use practices. Echoing the appeal of national leaders like Gifford Pinchot, Maine's conservation-minded foresters espoused long-term planning and the application of new biological discoveries to commercial forestry. The prime objective of scientific management was to increase and sustain timber yields, in order to raise the rental incomes of progressive landowners and the supply of low-cost raw materials to growing industries. The logical implication of so-called scientific methods was a domesticated forest environment: a plantation. In sum, the conservation ethic was future-oriented, anthropocentric and utilitarian. Its partisans had little respect for 'unscientific' traditions from the past and there was little altruism in their conception of resource stewardship. 'Sustained yield forestry' was the catchphrase for a reductionist conception of nature (Hays 1959: chapter 3; David C. Smith chapter 13).[4]

In Maine's 'paper plantation', the conservation ethic was honoured more in rhetoric than in practice. The combination of unchecked property rights, 'economic exigencies' and heavy discounting of distant future profits effectively discouraged sustained yield management (Cox 1981). A basic fact, then as now, was that a transition to sustained yield entails higher costs and lower yields in the short run, in return for uncertain long-run returns. Two conditions made Maine a particularly unattractive setting for such an approach. First, industrial woodlot managers 'insisted that the supply was inexhaustible' and that high-value spruce stands would regenerate adequately without human assistance (David C. Smith 1972: 337). Second, beginning early in this century, growing competition from Canadian newsprint producers and low-grade paper mills in the southeast United States was the 'economic exigency' forcing mills to concentrate on minimising their immediate raw material cost, rather than maximising long-run timber yields (Irland 1984). In sum, corporate managers recognised neither the need for nor the feasibility of intensive management. The most important legacy of the early conservation movement was the state's expanded role as promoter of industrial forest development. At both the federal and state levels, debates raged between the conservationists who advocated a regulatory role for the state and those who advocated a more supportive role. In Maine, corporate lobbying ensured that the latter approach would prevail. The fledgling Forest Service became the extension agent, providing technical assistance to large landowners; the legislature funded a School of Forestry to do scientific research and train foresters (Irland 1982: chapter 11).

In this epoch, timber harvesting was centred in company-owned logging camps. The typical three-man crew was composed of 'farm boys', who came from both sides of the US–Canadian border. During the winter months they lived in remote camps, following a rugged, masculine frontier life romanticised in the 'Paul Bunyan' stories and other regional folklore. The concentration of harvesting in winter stemmed from the seasonal availability of labour and horse teams from the farms, and the ease of 'skidding' logs from the stump to river landings along frozen trails. Although crews were employed by the companies and typically were paid a monthly wage, they had a high degree of functional autonomy.[5] A crew planned its own cutting 'chance', set its division of labour and controlled its work pace. Lumberjacks frequently owned their hand tools and horse teams. Harvesting, loading and skidding logs relied on simple tools (the axe, crosscut saw and peavey), horse power and sheer physical effort. Men worked from dawn to dusk in rain, sleet or snow, and hard manual labour in hazardous conditions took a heavy toll of life and limb. As long as safety records have been kept, logging has had the highest injury rate among Maine occupations. At the point of peak timber demand in 1910, nearly 30,000 semi-subsistence farm men were thus employed. For young farmers on the northeast frontier, a few winters of logging were part of a traditional rhythm of the seasons and the family life cycle. Loggers were quite unreceptive to organising efforts by labour unions. This helps explain why the industrial landowners were not inclined to move towards direct control over the details of harvesting. With only minor changes, these patterns held until the early 1950s (Ives 1985: 5–6; Parenteau 1986: chapter 2).

1900–40: from boom to Depression

Table 6.1 indicates broad trends in the two principal forest industries, lumber and paper. After 1910, Maine's sawmills rapidly lost competitiveness to cheap lumber from federal lands in the Northwest.[6] Timber consumption by paper mills surpassed that of sawmills during World War One, but was insufficient to sustain total demand for timber. The Great Depression sharply reduced demand for both products, and even on the eve of World War Two, timber consumption had barely recovered to the level of 1900.

Table 6.1   Volume of timber harvested in Maine, 1900–1940 (million rough cords) [a]

	1900	1910	1920	1930	1940
Pulpwood (paper)	0.4	0.9	1.4	0.9	1.4
Saw timber	1.9	2.7	1.2	0.5	1.0
Total commercial harvest	2.3	3.6	2.6	1.4	2.4

[a] One cord equals 3.53 cubic metres (Irland 1981: 50).

Highgrading spruce and natural regeneration remained the common practices in conditions of depressed demand and low profitability. The *laissez-faire* state did nothing to offset this pattern either by enforcing or by subsidising long-term resource conservation.[7] Nonetheless, a forest inventory, following a heavy spruce budworm attack between 1910 and 1920, did raise the spectre of long-run spruce depletion. Perceptive foresters were beginning to recognise that repeated highgrading undermines forest quality. Later when systematic inventory methods were developed, it became clearer that the average tree diameter was declining and the species mix was shifting towards unmarketable hardwoods and budworm-susceptible fir (Lansky 1986).

Confronted by erratic demand and declining profit in newsprint and other low-grade paper products, a principle goal in this period was to minimise raw material cost. The principal tactic was to transform the system of transport from stump to mill. To open up high-quality spruce forests farther from rivers and mills, the paper companies invested in a mix of spur railroads and haul roads. They began to use trucks for long-distance hauling and promoted university and private sector experiments with prototype equipment for yarding logs. By 1940, one-third of pulpwood reached the mills over land (Irland 1981: 40; David C. Smith 1985: 4).

For the most part, organisation and technology remained unchanged in logging. With more or less unrestricted access to French Canadian workers, the logging camp operators could usually find adequate labour. They coped with any large increase in timber demand by recruiting transient workers in northeastern cities. As a cost-cutting tactic, the paper companies gradually shifted from a fixed rate to piece-rate pay in the late 1920s and 1930s. This change, which has had profound long-term consequences, was evidently not resisted by the core workforce of 10,000 experienced Maine and Quebec loggers. The camp operators apparently took advantage of their patronage role, assigning the best cutting 'chances' to their most skilled and reliable loggers. As a result, their pay initially increased with the shift to piece rates. Later, during the Great Depression, the loggers' desperation for work led them to accept reductions in the piece rate. This dispersed and seasonal labour force showed few signs of militancy (Falk 1977: 19–22; Parenteau 1986: 142).

In response to the abundance of labour in the 1930s paper companies experimented further with the organisation of timber procurement. First, Great Northern Paper took advantage of farmers' dire economic straights by offering to buy 'cash wood' from their small woodlots at low prices. This inchoate shift towards older, self-employed loggers presaged much greater organisational shifts in pulp procurement to come. Second, when federal New Deal labour laws of the latter 1930s threatened to increase labour costs on company crews, a few paper companies began to write contracts with independent crews to harvest the industrial forest. Using nominally self-employed contractors allowed the companies to circumvent laws regarding child labour, accident insurance and overtime pay (Parenteau 1986: 100). These incipient changes in labour relations can be interpreted as alternatives to new technology, as means of cutting raw material costs and keeping paper mills solvent in a depression. (Parenthetically, contract logging and cash wood procurement *were* critically dependent on a new consumer technology: the automobile.)

Selective mechanisation: 1940–70

With the war, labour abundance quickly turned to shortage, as young men left for the military and high-paying manufacturing jobs. At the war's end, few returned to the woods. The forest labour shortage was reflected in a doubling of pulpwood prices (the piece rate) between 1940 and 1945, followed by a further 28 per cent increase by 1950. Over the ensuing two decades, the exodus from Maine's farms perpetuated a 'seller's market' in logging. Labour costs were further increased by enforcement of the New Deal labour laws and by new restrictions on recruitment of Canadian loggers. These actions reflected the influence of organised labour in national, but not state, politics. With a veritable boom in the paper industry and a gradual recovery in lumber (see Table 6.2), rising labour costs threatened profits.

Table 6.2 Volume of timber harvested in Maine, 1940–70 (million rough cords[a])

	1940	1950	1960	1970
Saw timber	1.0	1.2	1.3	1.6
Pulpwood	1.4	1.5	2.4	3.2
Total harvest	2.4	2.7	3.7	4.8

[a] One cord equals 3.53 cubic metres (Irland 1981: 50).

This nexus induced a wave of labour-saving technological innovations which eliminated three-fourths of the labour time per cord of wood in less than twenty years.[8] Between 1955 and 1970, a three-component technology became predominant throughout New England and eastern Canada. Motor–manual chainsaws replaced axes and hand saws for felling, limbing and bucking trees. Diesel-powered skidders replaced horses for yarding logs and truck-mounted hydraulic loaders replaced manual labour in handling logs.[9] Together they represented a quantum leap in the power and speed (as well as the noise and violence) of logging. For loggers, they appeared to promise liberation from low income, physical exhaustion and devastating injuries.

Chainsaws came first. Costly and cumbersome prototypes were used experimentally in Maine by the 1920s, but it took rising labour costs and war-related technological breakthroughs to stimulate a burst of innovations in the light engines industry.[10] Between 1945 and 1950, chainsaw weight was reduced 50 per cent to less than 15 kilograms and price was cut 60 per cent to less than $250. Within five years, chainsaws had wholly replaced hand saws for felling industrial timber (Parenteau 1986: 86–8) Loggers adopted the new method with alacrity. Like their pragmatic and mechanically minded forebears, they were not inhibited by subjective attachments to traditional techniques. Chainsaws meant progress: less arduous work, fewer accidents and higher earnings. Chainsaws doubled productivity in felling and limbing. Combined with a stable piece rate in the 1950s, they led to nearly a doubling of loggers' median earnings in a ten-year span. Moreover, chainsaw work did not de-skill cutters or impinge on their control of their immediate working conditions: efficient felling and equipment maintenance challenged loggers' dexterity and mechanical know-how; and the autonomous three-man crew remained intact (Falk 1977: 9; Parenteau 1986: 86, 92–3; Swift 1983: 130).

The negative aspects of chainsaw cutting — noise levels that stifled communication and damaged hearing, accidents resulting in severe cuts, and vibrations causing 'white finger disease' (a chronic nervous system disorder) — did not seriously concern most loggers until some years later.

By the latter 1950s, heavy equipment producers were developing fully mechanised harvesters for North American forests. Design engineers predicted that these 'monsters of the forest' would rapidly usher in assembly line extraction (Parenteau 1986: 90). In fact, mechanised harvesting spread only slowly and in a limited range of conditions The reason lies in the simultaneous spread of contract logging with diffusion of high-productivity chainsaw cutting. This procurement system was initially imposed by paper companies primarily to avoid the compliance costs of federal regulations, but it proved to have several additional advantages for the corporations. Their position as monopolistic landowners and monopolistic timber buyers in much of Maine gave them considerable leverage over the two critical aspects of pulpwood contracts: the stumpage fee (rent) contractors paid to cut on company land and the price of timber delivered to the mill (contemporary forest economics texts expressed the suspicions that companies also colluded to depress wood prices). Furthermore, the courts' interpretation of federal anti-trust laws was that contractors, as independent businesses, could not bargain collectively with the corporation.

There seem to be several objective and subjective reasons why loggers readily accepted 'de-proletarianisation' under such circumstances:

- Company crews were laid off, logging camps were shut down, and north-woods loggers who wanted to keep their jobs had to purchase equipment and accept contracts.
- Contractors who resisted company-imposed terms were threatened with importation of Canadian labour or found their contract unilaterally cancelled.
- Mill managers often cemented their relationship with favoured contractors through patronage: loans for equipment, allocation of the best cutting chances, advance payments against future deliveries.
- The new technology 'package' had no significant scale economies to disrupt the traditional three-man crew.
- Thousands of loggers appear to have been happy to exchange the life of wage earners in isolated logging camps for that of self-employed commuters.
- Last, but not least, contracting was introduced in a period of rapidly increasing earnings for loggers (Falk 1977, Irland 1981, Parenteau 1986, Swift 1983).

At the war's end, company crews harvested over 70 per cent of pulpwood. In 1956, the proportion was less than 50 per cent and by 1968, less than 20 per cent. In the latter year, small contractors (with a single truck and skidder and a maximum production of 3,000 cords per year) accounted for 90 per cent of contracted pulpwood (Falk 1977: 3, 14–29; Parenteau 1986: 100–1)

Once chainsaws were in common use, horse skidding and hand loading of trucks could no longer keep pace with the increased volume of felled logs. The dependence of horse skidding on frozen ground also impeded the incipient shift to year-round logging. As of the late 1950s, crews filled the gap with farm tractors and a motley array of other vehicles, but these were also too slow or ineffective on rough terrain. The need for a specialised skidder was widely discussed at forestry conferences and in trade journals. Such was competition in the heavy equipment industry that by 1956 twelve firms were test-marketing prototypes. The design that ultimately prevailed in Maine was diesel-powered, had four-wheel drive and wide tyres for all-terrain traction; it had an articulated frame for manoeuvrability in tight spaces, and a cable winch for handling logs. Despite a price of $60,000 (in 1986 dollars) contractors invested heavily in the new tool in the 1960s, tapping their profits and finding rural banks ready to lend for logging equipment. By 1970 nearly all commercial timber was yarded by skidders. Loggers took readily to mechanised skidding. Like horse teamsters before them, skidder operators were highly skilled, though seldom formally trained. It was a challenge to harness so much power to the tasks of laying out efficient haul routes and manoeuvring loads without destroying residual trees. Keeping a complex machine running called for considerable mechanical ability (Falk 1977: 42–57; Parenteau 1986: 88–90).

The skidder-chainsaw combination tripled a crew's productivity, which created a bottleneck at landings where logs were loaded onto trucks. This was quickly remedied by attaching hydraulic loaders to the trucks. Mechanical handling greatly reduced physical effort and saved labour time by permitting the shipment of tree-length logs, instead of four-foot lengths suitable for manhandling.

The combination of new technology and contract procurement entailed several major changes, including the creation of a petty capitalist stratum in the forest workforce, a tremendous increase in the volume of wood extracted by a crew, and the possibility of year-round logging.[11] Indeed, the high fixed cost of skidders and trucks made full-time logging a necessity. Wholly apart from the fact that paper corporations gave them no choice in the matter, thousands of men were attracted to full-time forest work by the rapid increase in their earnings. To be sure, logging was badly paid compared to unionised paper mill jobs. Loggers' relative earnings improved steadily from the war's end until the 1970s, rising from 62 per cent to 76 per cent of the average for manufacturing workers (Falk 1977: 8–9, 43–4).

There is little doubt that new technology and new production relations also contributed to the corporate objective of minimum raw material cost in a period of labour shortage and rising timber demand. Despite a 25 per cent decline in the forest workforce between 1950 and 1970, timber procurement doubled. Pulpwood prices, after rising sharply from 1940 to 1950, thereafter held roughly constant in real terms. Pulp procurement cost as a fraction of overall paper industry costs fell from 31 per cent in 1956 to 25 per cent in 1964. In this period of renewed competition between mills producing low-grade paper products in different US regions, cost containment prolonged the profitable operation of older mills and generated surplus to underwrite massive investment in high-grade paper capacity in the 1970s (Parenteau 1986: 117). The effectiveness of this industry-wide cost containment strategy largely explains why paper companies were not attracted to fully mechanised harvesting. The chainsaw–skidder method demonstrated its versatility and high productivity in diverse logging situations, whereas the early mechanised harvesters were suited only to clear-cutting on fairly even terrain.[12] These half-million dollar 'monsters of the forest' were also prone to costly breakdowns, in a situation where high overhead costs necessitated continuous operation. Small contractors, in contrast, could be subordinated to the corporations' market power; they accepted the 'invisible foreman' of piece-rate pay; they were exempt from costly labour regulations that applied to mechanised company crews; and they were willing to absorb the risks associated with breakdowns, poor weather and slack demand. In sum, small contractors delivered pulpwood more cheaply and accounted for 95 per cent of timber supply in 1970. Mechanisation, though still largely experimental, served as a warning to contractors: if they resisted company terms they could be mechanised out of existence (Hoffman, Irland and Magnusen interviews).

Forest management knowledge and practice

Forestry research in Maine has been conducted in both the private and public sectors. In practice they are closely linked, since the University of Maine Forestry School's Cooperative Forestry Unit (CFU) is jointly financed by the state and industry. In consequence, its agenda has been heavily weighted towards applied research on immediate or anticipated problems facing industrial landowners and the timber products industries (Hoffman, Seymour and Soule interviews). During the period in question, for example, considerable resources were allocated to inventorying the spruce fir resource, testing pesticides for control of spruce budworm, skidder engineering, efficient design of haul road networks, and research on optimum tree spacing in plantations, and methods of pulping hardwoods. However, the School of Forestry was not simply a handmaiden to industry. Since the 1940s, there have been university scientists who doubted the long-term sustainability of highgrading and natural regeneration on a very long rotational cycle, arguing instead for managed regeneration and light 'selection' harvesting at short intervals. CFU's minimal budget for studies of forest ecosystem dynamics made any definitive resolution of this controversy impossible. This effectively prevented a rigorous scientific challenge to 'mining and neglect' (Lansky 1986). The focus of CFU's very limited ecosystem research was sustainable commercial timber yields, and few scientific man-years were allocated to topics like the impact of alternative management systems on wildlife habitat, soil erosion and siltation of streams (there was even less research into the wages and working conditions of loggers).

Material conditions and meanings: the lives of Maine loggers circa 1970

The paucity of scholarly descriptions and analysis of the work life, family life and community life of forest workers is a striking example of the uneven development of knowledge about the forests. Entire university departments and government agencies analyse timber resources, yet almost no one in either setting studies the people whose livelihoods depend on timber. This reflects the priorities of a state that is foremost a promoter of capitalist economic growth. The existing studies of loggers' conditions take two main forms: empirical studies needed to enforce labour regulations (Public Affairs Research Center 1968, Maine Bureau of Employment Security) and historical studies, many of which rather uncritically reconstruct work life in 'the good old days' (Sheldon David C. Smith 1972). Few historical and social science studies are grounded in a critical perspective (Falk 1977, Irland 1975, Parenteau 1986). Logging represents a particularly puzzling gap in the work of rural sociologists, the academic bearers of America's populist ideological tradition. They have not subjected logging to anything like the scrutiny applied to farming (Goldschmidt 1978, Summers 1983). Much of what is known about loggers has been assembled from fragmentary statistical evidence and a wealth of anecdotes. Because of these limitations, one can only speculate about the answers to many questions about loggers: who chose to work in the woods? what were loggers' social and economic relationships with each other and with other members of their communities? what were their material living standards? what values and beliefs gave meaning to their lives? and why did they fail to act collectively, like members of an industrial working class? In attempting to answer these questions, we look first at the better-documented aspects of logging.

The size and character of the forest workforce changed fundamentally between 1900 and 1970. In the former year, most of the 20,000–30,000 loggers were 'farm boys' doing seasonal work for fixed wages. Their horse teams and tools were adapted to both farming and logging (depending upon whose data one accepts). They were considerably older and two-thirds were full-time workers earning piece-rate pay; 1,500 were self-employed contractors who owned highly specialised machinery. Loggers' median schooling was 9.0 years (compared with 12.3 years for the entire adult labour force), which indicates that many of them dropped out of high school to work in the woods. The forest was still a 'man's world'; indeed, as paper companies shut down their logging camps, the proportion of women in forest occupations shrank from 10 to 3 per cent (Benson 1985: table 5; Falk 1977: 5–9; Irland 1975: 204–6).[13] These generalisations mask the diversity of the workforce. It contained both a core minority who were permanently attached to logging and a majority who shifted between logging and other jobs several times in a working life. It ranged from healthy high school dropouts, looking to save some money before moving on, to burnt-out middle-aged illiterates, with declining earnings but no alternative job prospects. Skilled, hard-working — and lucky — loggers earned more than the paper mill 'labour aristocracy', yet many others scraped by with poverty earnings. Some cutters were content to hire out on a crew, but many an aspiring entrepreneur pursued the 'American dream' of riches as a self-employed contractor. A few contractors rose from the ranks to manage several crews and own fleets of trucks, while numerous others could not make their skidder payments and fell back into the ranks of cutters. Potato farmers who cut spruce in winter on their own 100-hectare lots coexisted with professionals who cut 300 days a year on Great Northern's million hectares (Cottell 1975: 63–5; Public Affairs Research Center 1968; Young and Newton 1980: 204–6).

In sum, loggers at one extreme were upwardly mobile petty capitalists, and at the opposite extreme were rural sub-proletarians, academic failures and social misfits. Yet there was typically no sharp class distinction between contractor and crew member. They dressed, talked and drank alike; lived in the same neighborhoods at a roughly comparable living standard; switched status with some frequency; were not set apart by a mental vs. manual division of labour. Indeed, contractors had a reputation for putting in the longest hours, working nights and weekends to keep their machinery running (Butler, Chase, Falk and Irland interviews). Nonetheless, the economic relationship between contractor and crew was inherently contradictory in the piece-rate procurement system. Everyone's earnings depended on the whole crew's productivity, but since contractors bore the overhead costs, their net income was especially sensitive to crews' efforts. Thus, though class distinctions were blurred, contractors became *de facto* agents of corporate exploitation — and piece-rate pay was indeed an 'invisible foreman': 'It is a vicious circle. The paper company pushes the contractor and the contractor drives his crew. The end result is many strained backs and a high number of injuries' (Hardison 1984: 9).

Prosperity or poverty?

Median earnings of full-time loggers more than doubled between 1950 and 1970 and, as we have seen, incomes also rose substantially relative to other manufacturing jobs. On average, full-time loggers earned about $5,400 in 1970 ($14,000 in 1986). However, the earnings distribution was extremely variable, depending on the number of days a crew worked and on its average productivity. Days worked fluctuated with weather conditions, machinery failures, injuries and demand for timber. Productivity varied with the crew's skill, effort, physical fitness and the quality of 'stumpage' (timber stands) secured by the contractor. Industry sources insisted that skilled, hard-working crews 'made good money', but to do so year-in and year-out required luck to stay healthy and 'connections' to get consistently good cutting (Falk 1977: 51). Inefficient, unlucky and 'unconnected' crews made poverty incomes, as indicated by 1970 census data: nationally, the households of 25.1 per cent of full-time loggers fell below the official poverty line, compared to 5.1 per cent for all full-time male workers (Irland 1975: 205).

There are few data on contractors' profits. Up to 1965, soaring productivity and a steady or rising price of timber made contracting modestly profitable for the typical contractor. Some time after 1965, contract logging appears to have become subject to over-entry, which drove down profits by depressing timber prices and generating unutilised capacity. Simultaneously, the 'Vietnam inflation' pushed up operating costs and after the adoption of skidder technology the pace of productivity growth slowed. Parenteau estimates that contractors' average profit decline was $1.00 per cord in 1961 but only $0.62 in 1971 (Parenteau 1986: 120).[14] In the latter year, profits of a contractor delivering 3,000 cords a year might thus have been $1,800 on a $50,000 investment (i.e. 3.6 per cent) — less than the interest paid on a riskless bank account. 'Unlucky' contractors must have had negative returns on their investment, though they might continue to survive as petty capitalists through 'self-exploiting' eighty-hour working weeks.

Sick and tired

Logging has always been among the most hazardous industrial occupations. Felling, limbing and manhandling trees, especially in poor weather and rough terrain, are inherently risky. Neoclassical economists deduce that, other things being equal, hazardous jobs must pay more to attract workers. Higher labour costs, in turn, give employers an incentive to make work safer. The case of contract logging suggests flaws in this logic. It is true that chainsaw modifications, mechanised timber handling and new safety gear did reduce accident rates after 1958. Yet in 1970, the frequency of accidents in Maine remained 37 per cent above the national rate for logging, and nearly three times the rate for all manufacturing. One worker in eight suffered a disabling injury each year, losing on average a half-year of work. At least twenty loggers were killed yearly by falling trees, chainsaw kickbacks and other hazards. Not reported in the injury data were low-grade chronic ailments — impaired hearing, lower back pain, arthritis, and 'white finger disease' from prolonged use of chainsaws (Falk 1977: 9–11, 18; Irland 1975: 201).

Until the passage of Occupational Health and Safety legislation in the late 1960s, the principal political reaction to dangerous work was not to mandate safe conditions, but to require employers to carry workers' compensation insurance. High accident rates meant high insurance premiums — insurance costs reached 20 per cent of payroll for company logging crews in the 1970s — so there should have been a strong incentive to improve safety. But injury rates have not fallen sharply and the reasons have been a subject of much dispute. Blame has been laid on excessively high compensation payments (thought to induce injured workers to stay off the job), inadequate safety training and 'moral hazard' (carelessness prompted by the existence of insurance). However, nearly everyone, including insurance companies, agrees that piece-rate pay is a major culprit. It pressures loggers to speed the pace of work, to cut when they are fatigued, to work in treacherous conditions and to neglect cumbersome safety apparel (Hardison 1984; Irland interview). Evidence supports this argument, since paper company crews, using the same technology as contract crews, but paid an hourly wage instead of a piece rate, had less than half as many accidents per man-year of work (Falk 1977: 18; Parenteau 1986: 124). High accident rates were certainly not inherent in chainsaw cutting: in Sweden, where an hourly wage was paid and the state enforced strict safety codes, loggers were injured no more frequently than factory workers. Indeed, the high priority given to workplace safety in Sweden brought about developments in safety apparel and safer harvesting equipment (Anderson 1981). Cheap toilet paper and corporate profits did not require a high toll of death, injury and chronic disability in the forest.

The question arises: who ultimately bore the costs of accidents? Since, under prevailing law, small contractors were allowed to carry little or no accident insurance, several thousand loggers had only minimal coverage. These loggers thus 'internalised' the 'external diseconomies' of injuries, bearing both the economic risk and the physical agony of crushed legs and gashed heads. A documentary film, *Cut and Run*, depicts how the logger's risk and anxiety were shared by other family members. A middle-aged logger's wife expresses her constant fear that one day he will be brought home on a stretcher: 'When you gonna leave the woods? His reply, "Nothin' else for me to do."'

Fatigue, along with risk, was logging workers' constant companion. Indeed, many accidents occurred at the end of the day, when bone-weary loggers pushed themselves to cut one more cord before total darkness set in. Career loggers scoff at the notion of a forty-hour working week. Sometimes there was no work at all, as in the spring 'mud season' and periods of slack demand, but when there was cutting it was dawn to dusk. Adding time for commuting and equipment repairs, a ten-hour day and fifty-hour week were the minimum. As noted, contractors routinely worked sixty to eighty hours a week. A hint of what the intense pace and long hours of work meant for leisure activity and social life is given by a logger's self-description: 'I'm just a machine. I sleep, eat and work ... I'm about the dullest guy my wife's ever met' (*Cut and Run*).

The French Canadian underclass

For half a century, French Canadian loggers, 'a distinct ethnic group, set off by language and custom', have been a convenient scapegoat for the genuine problems of Maine timber workers (Parenteau 1986: 121). Between 1956 and 1970, the state certified 1,500 to 5,000 'bonded' Canadians each year to cut in situations where (the industrial landowners claimed) Americans were not willing to work. Though firm data are non-existent, it appears that 'bonds' cut 20 per cent to 40 per cent of Maine timber. They came primarily from depressed Quebec farming parishes just across the border from northern Maine. Like alien migrant workers in other parts of the world, they were indentured and permitted to work only for the employer who posted their bond. Operating from the old logging camps, they typically harvested five days a week and commuted home at weekends (Falk 1977: 39).

After 1945, the wages and work conditions of alien workers were regulated, ostensibly to prevent their employment from undermining the position of *American* crews. In practice, regulatory enforcement was lax in the remote northern camps. Court testimony shows bonds to have been largely ignorant of their rights. Desperate for work, they tolerated practices which exploited them and, indirectly, Maine loggers. They worked fifty- to sixty- hour weeks while accepting pay for forty hours. They neglected to file insurance claims for many injuries and accepted the corporations' demands that they supply their own saws and skidders. They also tolerated crowded and unhealthy camp conditions.[15] To justify requests for bonded workers, crew operators reputedly discouraged Maine contractors from applying for jobs by giving them the worst cutting chances. Instead of consolidating worker solidarity against the paper companies, this 'divide and rule' tactic only intensified ethnic hostility between Yankees and Quebecois (Butler interview; Falk 1977: 34–9; Irland 1984: 23; Parenteau 1986: 121–2). In sum, the evidence supports Parenteau's conclusion about this 'reserve army' of impoverished and underemployed Quebec farmers: 'While Canadian bonded workers played a major role in the degradation of native woodsmen, they were victims rather than perpetrators of the system' (Parenteau 1986: 122).

Why work in the woods? 'Little universes of meaning'[16]

Why did thousands of rural Mainers choose an occupation likely to leave them burnt out or disabled — if not dead — by the age of fifty? Why head for the woods before dawn each day — in rain, sleet or snow — when the pay was lower and the hazards far greater than at the nearby paper mill or in many urban service jobs? Why stake the family home as collateral to purchase logging equipment when the risks were high and the probable returns low? Few studies have addressed these motivational questions, but it is possible to make plausible conjectures by combining fragmentary Maine evidence with insights from the broader literature on work in America.

Expected material rewards were certainly relevant to occupational choices in the 1950s and 1960s. Real earnings were increasing rapidly and there was widespread local knowledge about contractors who 'made good money'. One can grasp why healthy rural youths, bored with school, might drop out, invest in a chainsaw and take work on a contract crew.

Within a few years, they would find themselves either moving up to contractor status or locked into logging by their lack of formal credentials for other jobs. The farmer's rationale for seasonal logging on his woodlot is also clear. Indeed, for a wide range of rural men, part-time logging fitted into a long tradition of diversified livelihood. It was still common in 1970 for rural families to combine subsistence activities (hunting, growing food, cutting firewood, building homes, repairing vehicles) with cash-earning activities (logging, construction work, truck driving, clam digging). The choice of a diversified, resource-based livelihood can be interpreted several ways. It may be a low-risk subsistence strategy for rural people who have not been seduced by mass consumption culture. It may be an affirmation of traditional frontier values like self-reliance, integration of mental and manual labour, closeness to nature, and ties to place. Certainly working in the woods coloured many aspects of loggers' existence. Their dooryards were filled with equipment parts; weekend 'leisure' was catching up on sleep and repairing equipment; relaxation meant hunting, snowmobile rides in the woods or a few beers with the boys at a local bar. In Sahlins' words, 'the pragmatic logic of work forms a grid of material constraint to which all relations and conceptions are functionally submitted' (Sahlins 1973: 40).[17]

On the other hand, a 1968 survey of cutters in the far north supports a less affirmative view of logging work. The majority of respondents claimed to be loggers only for lack of better options. By and large, they did not consider logging to be either a rewarding or a respected job; and they tended to blame themselves for their limited career choices, stressing poor education and geographical immobility as constraints to finding better jobs. Table 6.3 indicates the range of reasons for being a logger.

Table 6.3 Loggers' principal response to the question: 'Why did you take this job?'

Insufficient education to get a better job	31%
Could not find any other job (nearby)	21%
Like the work	20%
Best-paying job available	15%
Have always done this work	12%

Source: Public Affairs Research Center PARC 1968.

Loggers and their neighbours alike held forest work in low esteem. However, the loggers' perception of the stigma generally attached to their work may have biased them towards self-deprecating comments. Sennett and Cobb's study of urban workers reveals just such a contradictory self-image:

> Rissarro believes people of a higher class have a power to judge him because they seem internally more developed human beings; and he is afraid, because they are better armed, that they will not respect him.... [But] when he thinks just of himself, and is not comparing himself to his image of people in a higher class ... all of this is set against ... a feeling that manual labour has more dignity. (Sennett and Cobb 1973: 25)

'Manual labour has more dignity.' Young and Newton characterise lumberjacks in the Pacific Northwest as men who 'strive for a mode of production that is based on craft work, autonomous from the boss, and [allowing] self-control of production knowledge' (Young and Newton 1980: 9). This stress on craft and self-reliance also seems applicable to Maine. Asked to describe the best features of their work, 63 per cent in the PARC survey stressed 'occupational freedom'. The second most common response was 'the outdoor nature of the work' (only 9 per cent had nothing positive to say). To an observer familiar with the workings of the contract system, this self-reliance appears largely illusory: the terms of employment were largely dictated by giant corporations: high fixed costs and piece-rate pay — the 'invisible foreman' — severely constrained loggers' freedom of action.

The perennial willingness to go into contracting, despite its high risks and low returns, warrants special consideration. It is perhaps best understood as the result of two powerful American traditions: the frontiersman's gambling instinct and the yeoman's drive for self-employment. Popular history is replete with tales of the 'American Dream', ranging from the California gold rush to Maine's own potato farming boom. There remain several million petty commodity producers in industrial America — working hard and risking all for 'the main chance'. Even though the life expectancy of small businesses is only a few years, logging contractors — like fast food franchisers and contract poultry farmers — continue to invest. What these petty business operators have in common is that they perform the least profitable tasks in a division of labour determined by vertically integrated corporations. Social critics may apply terms like self-exploitation, semi-proletarian exploitation, indirect subordination to capital or false consciousness to this condition. In any case, it is as American as apple pie.

Why no 'reds'?
Periodically, Maine loggers have shown a capacity for militant action against the paper corporations. This has taken three typical forms:

vigilantism against logging camps employing French Canadians, political organising around specific issues like workers' compensation, and unsuccessful attempts to unionise company crews. These scattered episodes do not suggest a strong trade union consciousness, much less a broader working-class consciousness. Objective and subjective factors combined to inhibit the development of such consciousness. Objectively, forest workers occupied multiple positions in a complex network of production and exchange relations which ran from the chainsaw cutter to the millyard manager. There were Yankees and Quebecois, company and contract crews, small and large contractors, small woodlot owners, truckers and wood dealers. They coexisted in a web of partially common and partially conflicting economic interest. Solidarity was further impeded by a high rate of labour force turnover and the two-way status mobility between contractors and crew members. As always in petty capitalist competition, there were economic winners and losers, and thus some who had a stake in the status quo and others with an interest in changing the procurement system. The historical record is not clear to what extent these were deliberately created by the paper corporations.

At base, solidarity among loggers was also obstructed by their nearly universal acceptance of the fundamental ideological tenets of liberal capitalism: private property, individualism and competition (US workers' captivation by these values has impeded the effectiveness of the labour movement in general). On Maine's forest frontier, a mystified espousal of capitalist values was compounded by a residue of archaic notions of classlessness, self-reliance and masculinity. The self-defeating implications of such an ethos are captured by James O'Connor:

The discrepancy between the economic reality and the consciousness of that reality by the victimised workers and small producers is especially poignant in 'frontier' economies where ideologies of hard work, individual initiative, self-help and the like have been hegemonic from the beginning. Nativism and frontier extremism are seen as defenses against rural proletarianisation, defined as being displaced and feeling unneeded. The false beliefs that working people adopt, which derive from idealised visions of the past, are in fact necessary for their own emotional survival and well-being. The range of deceptions and self-deceptions runs from a strong sense of self-hood and faith in the efficacy of hard work to rather grotesque images of 'supercowboy' and 'superlogger', which function to conceal the powerlessness of ordinary people without a sense of collective solidarity and power. Although permitting workers and small producers to retain some shred of dignity, these beliefs and the almost angry persistence with which they are held totally obscure the real causes of economic and social misfortune. This is especially true of the various 'blame the victim' ideologies which operate with particular viciousness in the cases of [extraction industries]. (Young and Newton 1980: x)

The forest as a contested terrain

For a century, the economic and political hegemony of Maine's industrial landowners went largely unchallenged. In the vast unorganised territories, local government was synonymous with the landowner. In state government the legislative and executive branches were dominated by the pro-business Republican Party. Beginning in the 1930s, new interventions to protect the forest workers' interests stemmed largely from the federal level, where organised labour was influential in the Democratic Party's majority coalition. Until the latter 1960s, intervention to protect forest ecology and promote use-values other than timber was essentially non-existent. Then, from quite distinct angles, corporate dominance came under increasing attack by loggers and the nascent environmental protection movement. This section first traces the rise and fall of large-scale labour militancy. It then interprets the growth of environmental activism in forestry. It will be seen that these challenges have been confined within quite narrow limits. Nonetheless, the state's growing regulatory role in the 1970s is a gauge of their success and an indicator of the state's transition from a captive of corporate interest to a terrain contested by competing interests. In the 1980s, the state executive has evolved further to become a 'pro-choice' planner for 'sustainable multiple-use forestry'.

Militancy, mechanisation and clear-cutting

Cohesive and sustainable state-wide organisation has always eluded Maine loggers. Successive episodes of militancy foundered on a combination of concerted corporate opposition and the loggers' geographical dispersion, their ethnic antagonisms, individualism and contradictory class relations. Thus, from 1904 onward, attempts to unionise logging crews were stymied by Canadian–American hostilities, farmer-loggers' petty bourgeois consciousness, the isolation of crews, and the companies' vicious union-busting tactics (Parenteau 1986: 95). It is especially noteworthy that there was no significant worker resistance to new technology or piece-rate contract logging in the period after World War Two. Until the 1970s, elimination of Canadian bonded labour was the single political issue around which Maine loggers could be mobilised. Their highly publicised mass rallies and vigilante actions against camps employing bonds became catalysts for a gradual tightening of immigration restrictions after the mid-1940s.

In the early 1970s two distinct struggles took shape. Union organising reappeared in northern logging camps along the Allagash River, and a group of contractors tried to form a collective bargaining unit, the Maine Pulpwood Producers Association. In 1975, several accumulated grievances brought these proletarian and semi-proletarian loggers together to form the Maine Woodsman's Association (MWA). As so often before, opposition to Canadian labour was a rallying point. Loggers also protested that the paper mills rigged scaling (measurements) of pulpwood deliveries. The industrial landowners were accused of charging exorbitant stumpage fees (rents) to harvest their land, and mills were accused of colluding to depress timber prices at a time when contractors' operating costs were undergoing rapid inflation. The underlying fact was that men who had committed their lives to logging and had experienced thirty years of rising earnings now found their economic condition deteriorating. The last straw was the paper companies' practice of unilaterally cancelling contracts and laying off crews when the demand for paper fell in the 1974–75 economic recession. Hundreds of contractors, already suffering a 'cost–price squeeze' and beset by skidder payments, faced a survival crisis.

The MWA's tactics met with considerable success so long as grievances could be politicised. Supported by Democratic Party politicians and given sympathetic coverage in some news media, loggers overcame heavily financed corporate lobbying to win a uniform scaling law, more extensive workers' compensation coverage and virtual elimination of bonded Canadian labour. State government was evolving into a mediator of class conflict. Capitalising on their political success and the loggers' economic crisis, MWA leaders mobilised several thousand members — probably half of Maine's loggers — in a matter of weeks during the summer of 1975. Their decisive test came in the autumn of 1975, with a decision to challenge the paper companies' monopoly over contract terms. The concrete issues were high stumpage fees, depressed timber prices, arbitrary allocation of bonuses for fulfilled contracts, and unilateral termination of contracts. Piece-rate payment *per se* was not questioned. The MWA's tactic was to embargo timber deliveries to the mills, a resolution backed by mass picketing at the mill gates. The strike (as they called the embargo) lasted three weeks and was a failure. The paper companies made no concessions on the central issues. MWA's strident rhetoric and violence against recalcitrant loggers eroded public sympathy. The members became divided and demoralised, and MWA soon disappeared as a major force in politics and the woods. According to Parenteau, MWA was 'a union brought together by the force of expediency, rather than a unified, well planned, coherent entity. [It] proved to be no match for the powerful paper industry' (Parenteau 1986: 136, 144). The story is in fact more complex. For example, the strike's outcome was largely determined by immediate economic conditions and subtleties of American labour law. The 1975 recession was not an opportune time to strike. Even though MWA picketing reduced the flow of timber to a trickle, the paper mills had large inventories and faced slack demand for paper. They were therefore not vulnerable to a raw material shortage. In contrast, the contractors, with no strike fund, few personal assets to live on and inexorable monthly equipment payments, could not survive a long work stoppage. The question of who could hold out longer became moot when the Maine Superior Court banned picketing at the mill gates. This robbed the MWA of its most powerful tool for preventing 'scab' contractors from supplying the mills. The court ruled that MWA members could not picket or bargain collectively because they were not employees of the paper companies (legally many MWA members were employed by other members). It was precisely the complexity of relationships in the timber procurement network that prohibited the MWA from acting as the agent for wood workers as a whole. According to Parenteau, the paper corporations had promoted this complexity with the knowledge that such legal obstacles would ultimately prevent loggers from mounting an effective challenge to their power (Parenteau 1986: 146–7).

Legal proceedings revealed the state's internal contradictions: loggers were counselled by a federal legal aid agency while the paper companies were supported by Maine's anti-labour governor and attorney general. The MWA, for its part, remained substantially isolated from potential political allies. It was not strongly backed by national labour unions. In fact, during the strike two unions moved opportunistically to compete with the MWA for the allegiance of company logging crews. The MWA was also unsuccessful in forging permanent ties with progressive political organisations; and except for one minor episode, loggers did not join forces with environmentalists, who were contesting paper company power at the same time.[18]

Most important, MWA's internal solidarity began to erode even before the end of the strike, as objective and ideological cleavages between the more and less proletarian loggers became apparent. The former group, concentrated in the far north, included a shrinking group of wage earners on company crews and a growing number of men forced to purchase skidders and sign contracts simply to get work. They tended to view large contractors and wood dealers in their part of the state — many of whom belonged to the MWA — as paper company 'puppets [for whom] it has always been much easier to take from their workers ... than to get more money per cord from the companies' (Hardison 1984: 13). Tactically, they were not adverse to using intimidation and violence to protest against exploitative employment conditions. Having shed any illusions of independence, they developed a trade union consciousness. In fact, some leaders of their MWA faction took union organising jobs while the 1975 strike was still in progress. For them, the strike's defeat was the beginning of a successful unionisation drive. (By late 1975, some of the paper companies saw the virtue of stable labour relations and encouraged the conservative United Paperworkers' International Union to form bargaining units.) By 1980, 40 per cent of loggers on large crews were unionised; today the figure is 100 per cent. The notion that loggers achieved their economic objectives through unionisation is problematic, however, since the corporations eliminated most company crews and mechanised the rest to 'squeeze out labour'. Today only 5 per cent of loggers are corporate employees (Magnusen interview).

Petty capitalist contractors, who made up the bulk of MWA membership, had what might be termed a 'producer cooperative mentality'. They resisted the idea of becoming hired employees in order to improve their material conditions. Their goal was countervailing power through collective bargaining. The defeat of the 1975 strike effectively broke their organisation: at present they still remain divided.[19]

A central thesis of this chapter is that changing production relations influenced the diffusion of technology. Paradoxically, the results of the MWA strike both stimulated and inhibited mechanised harvesting. As company crews became unionised, the piece rate was replaced by a negotiated hourly workers' compensation rate induced by mechanisation. (Experts estimate that roughly one-fourth of timber is now harvested by machines, compared with perhaps 5 per cent at the time of the strike.) Feller-forwarders and other types of harvesting and handling equipment cost $250,000 to $500,000, or several times as much as a chainsaw and skidder. But in ideal clear-cutting conditions, they fell and bunch 100 trees per hour, ten times as much as a chainsaw cutter. Investment in such capital-intensive methods stimulated yet more changes in timber extraction, including computer-planned logging, larger-capacity haul roads and labour-saving equipment for yarding and processing logs. In large-scale clear-cuts, mechanised extraction has indeed come to resemble the factory assembly line, as predicted by equipment designers in the 1950s (Corcoran, Magnusen interviews).

Machine harvesting had several advantages for loggers on company crews. Jobs were secure and relatively well-paid. Operating heavy equipment was a skilled and challenging task, and harvesting trees from a heated cab, with the stereo playing, was far safer and more comfortable than chainsaw cutting in hip-deep snow. On the other hand, mechanisation rendered hundreds of older and less-skilled loggers redundant (Kurelek 1984: 94; Irland interview)

In the small-contractor sector, which still accounted for about 80 per cent of pulpwood harvesting in the early 1980s, piece-rate pay and the chainsaw–skidder technology prevailed. In general small contractors were discouraged from investing in mechanised harvesters by their initial cost, stagnant timber prices and unreliable demand.

With hindsight, a few hundred forest workers appear to have gained economically from the struggles of the 1970s. But in the absence of complete statistical data, it is difficult to assess earnings precisely. A paper industry spokesperson, citing government figures, is thus able to assert that skilled, industrious loggers earn upwards of $25,000 a year (and that lower-paid loggers have themselves to blame). The same data have led a state labour specialist to conclude that only a small fraction of loggers, primarily those on mechanised crews, achieve such high earnings with any regularity. Injuries, bad weather, rising input costs and declining timber quality mean lower earnings for the great majority. Survey data from large operations suggest that, on average, loggers' real wages have declined since 1975. Finally, Irland calculates that a 'cost–price squeeze' has further depressed contractors' already low returns since the mid-1970s (Falk 1977: 9; Irland 1984: table 3; Maine Bureau of Employment Security 1981; Butler, Hagan, Irland and Magnusen interviews).

Production relations influence the relationship between 'man' and nature as well as between man and man. Evolving procurement relations, along with their impact on harvest mechanisation, contributed to a shift towards large-scale clear-cutting which occurred after 1970. (A clear-cut is a harvest which removes at least 70 per cent of timber from a stand.) By the late 1970s, mechanised crews were making true 'silvicultural clear-cuts', mowing down 100 per cent of the trees on stands covering thousands of hectares and leaving behind what one observer described as 'pockmarked moonscapes'. Clear-cutting now amounts to nearly 50,000 hectares annually and generates over half of pulpwood volume. Its consequences for timber stand quality in the short run and forest ecology in the long run are controversial. Certain types of clear-cut, like the 'patch', 'strip' and 'seed trees' methods used widely in mature Scandinavian softwood forests, appear to enhance long-run yield. Clear-cuts of dead and diseased trees and low-value species, when followed by managed regeneration of high-value species, have been shown to increase the long-run commercial value of stands dramatically. Indeed, much of Maine's large-scale clear-cutting has been dictated by just such labour-saving mechanisation. In recent years most of these operations have involved salvage of fir and spruce damaged by a recent spruce budworm epidemic and clearing of overstocked spruce fir stands that grew back after an earlier epidemic around 1910. (Selection harvesting in these tightly spaced stands is often impossible. Even if techniques existed for extracting selected trees without damaging the rest, the residual stand would not be 'wind-firm'.) It should of course be understood that the devastated forest conditions which dictate clear-cutting are results of past 'mining and neglect'.

The shift to clear-cutting is not limited to mechanised operations. Contract loggers, cutting for piece-rate pay and threatened by a cost–price squeeze, contribute equally:

> When you're after that spruce or fir in a thicket, then nine times out of ten a dozen trees bite the dust to get out one or two. A good selective cut area where a man should reach in with the skidder and pull out one tree at a time ends up being flattened. Why? Because in order to make any kind of a day's pay you must get out and limb 100+ trees a day. Every day. That cannot be done when you have to slow down or do a good careful job. The forest would benefit and so would the health of the workers, but that's not the way we cut wood today. (Hardison 1984: 10)

Only in the past few years has scientific research begun to verify what many practitioners had been arguing for years: that large-scale clear-cuts without carefully managed regeneration may seriously deplete the commercially valuable spruce resource. Until then, critics were greeted by a litany of assertions from corporate apologists, including numerous Forestry School faculty, that clear-cutting would not deplete soil nutrients and that Maine's cool, damp conditions were ideal for natural spruce fir regeneration following clear-cuts. It has now been demonstrated that heavy harvesting machines crush most of the young spruce undergrowth on which regeneration depends, while the vast open spaces left by clear-cuts promote restocking with sun-loving broadleaf 'weed' species rather than shade-loving conifers. At a minimum, such clear-cutting sets back regeneration, and therefore the next harvest, by ten to twenty years. At worst, stands will not grow back to high-value spruce. As a result of all these past practices, Maine faces an imminent spruce shortfall, despite the fact that the potentially sustainable yield is twice the present harvest (Bley 1986; Chaisson 1985; Lansky 1984; Seymour 1984; 1985; D.M. Smith 1981).

The ascendency of clear-cutting in the past decade has revealed the ethics of professional foresters in the corporate forest. Paper company foresters have not been able to convince their employers to invest in managed regeneration on a scale that would prevent spruce depletion; nevertheless they have been conspicuously unwilling to condemn large-scale clear-cutting. In the words of an eminent Yale University forestry professor, 'There are so many foresters accustomed to taking orders from on high that they don't question. They just go on drawing their pay and saying it's not their fault' (Austin 1986). Almost all large landowners have engaged in some 'intensive management', but the following estimates reveal its negligible extent. For the most part, management simply means spraying herbicides to kill the weed species that are favoured by clear-cutting. According to one estimate, herbicide use has increased to nearly 20,000 hectares in 1986, about half the clear-cut acreage (Austin 1986). The only management practice *ever* used on a large proportion of the forest was aerial insecticide spraying against spruce budworm. It reached a level of one million hectares per year in the late 1970s.

Great Northern Paper's president rationalises: 'There are more important problems than resources ... the company has to think of surviving in the short-term' (Bailey et al. 1986). Within the logic of short-run profit maximisation, clear-cutting and neglect make good sense. Selection harvesting, especially in poor-quality stands, reduces productivity and managed regeneration costs several hundred dollars per hectare. It has no payoff for thirty years and most of the return does not come until regrowth matures after fifty or more years: such a long-run pay-off is discounted to insignificance by corporate accountants. In the event, the mix of contract logging, new technology and clear-cutting has cut raw material costs dramatically. Real timber prices have declined since 1975 and pulpwood costs as a fraction of paper mill sales have fallen dramatically, from 25 per cent in 1964 to 6 per cent today.[20] What ethic guides these corporate practices? International Paper's forest manager put it thus: 'There isn't anything unethical about a company limiting forest improvement efforts. That's just business' (Austin 1986).

Table 6.4 Managed regeneration of clear-cut stands (1982).

Clear-cut acreage	47,000 ha
Seedbed preparation	1,000 ha
Fertilisation	–
Seedling plantings	3,370 ha
Manual thinning/pruning	3,140 ha
Herbicide spraying	9,600 ha

Sources: Natural Resources Council of Maine 1985: Table 1; Lansky 1984: 27.

Bourgeois environmentalists demand a 'multiple-use forest'

The lure of the forest wilderness as a hunting, fishing and camping retreat for a few hardy urbanites was evident by the 1850s, when H.D. Thoreau popularised his experiences in *The Maine Woods*. Early in the present century, rail and road access enabled thousands of the urban middle class to vacation at forest camps and head north for the autumn hunting ritual. Since most of the north woods were owned by absentee landlords, much of this activity took place on their property, with access via logging roads. As a goodwill gesture, paper companies were typically liberal in allowing recreational use of their lands.

Both nationally and locally, the 1960s were a watershed in the development of recreational forest uses and in the emergence of the environmental protection movement as a political force. This revival of conservationism combined a 'wilderness ethic' with alarm at the mounting evidence of environmental degradation. Most of this new generation of conservationists viewed the wilderness as 'an aesthetic heritage that must be cherished *and experienced*' — rather than as a pristine ecosystem into which humans should not intrude (Burch 1986: 36). The central practical issue was how commercial forestry could best coexist with the leisure activities of an affluent population. In Burch's interpretation, forests came to be conceived as 'stage settings for enacting certain fantasies and having certain family diversions'. From that conception, it is but a short step to a domesticated 'wilderness', commodified as corporate ski resorts and white-water rafting outfitters. Parenthetically, Burch notes that 'It took the debates of the 1960s to impress on [the forestry profession] that trees had values other than as timber' (Burch 1986: 36, 38).

Maine environmentalists attributed both metaphysical and instrumental meanings to the forest and combined altruistic and self-interested motives for resource conservation. They had a problematic relationship with rural residents who customarily used the forests for hunting, fishing and snowmobiling; and with loggers, who increasingly depended upon unaesthetic clear-cutting for their livelihoods. Environmentalists were generally rather oblivious to the view and the economic plight of these indigenous rural people, and, until quite recently, they had little awareness of the timber resource degradation caused by past 'mining and neglect'.

Since 95 per cent of Maine's forests are private, environmental causes inevitably clashed with the paper companies' property rights. This was dramatised by two early cases, whose resolution indicated the main policy options available to the pluralist state. The cases involved river log drives and unique wilderness lands in the Allagash region. For a century, log drives had blocked many rivers to other users for several months each year. Accumulations of chemical residue and sludge from floating logs had also undermined the aquatic food chain, destroying sport and commercial fishing on many streams. In a ground-breaking 1971 victory over the paper companies, the conservation lobby won state legislation to enforce the Federal Clean Rivers Act by banning log drives as from 1976. (By 1971, paper mills had already largely converted to truck transport; the new law merely completed the process.) Public awareness and sentiment raised by the rivers issue created the political climate for further regulation, and a Land Use Regulation Commission (LURC) was created in 1971. LURC's citizen members were charged to represent the public interest in the corporate-owned unorganised territories. In practice, LURC has little authority over forest management and logging operations and few resources to enforce its limited mandate. It must depend largely on voluntary compliance by logging crews and landowners. Its central achievements have been in preserving forested buffer zones along ponds and streams and in regulating the layout of haul roads and skidder trails to limit soil erosion and siltation of water bodies.

In the Allagash River valley, long a symbol of unspoiled wilderness, the state employed a different approach to conservation, by purchasing land and conservation easements in a narrow strip along the river. Recreational users were thereby reassured that they would not be subjected to unsightly logging operations and polluted waters while canoeing, camping and fishing. Instead, they are subjected to each other. Today the Allagash Wilderness Waterway has become easily accessible by logging road. Its thousands of annual visitors create canoe traffic jams and campsite congestion, belying its wilderness designation. In the meantime, the Bureau of Public Lands has acquired several more pieces of unique or scenic forest wilderness, through purchases and 'swaps' with industrial landowners. Roughly 5 per cent of the forest is now owned by the state and private conservation groups.

Despite occasional opposition to corporate interests and espousal of wilderness values, the environmental movement basically accepts corporate ownership and commercial timber extraction. Since the mid-1970s, it has been riven by controversy over the appropriate response to new forms of industrial disruption of the forest ecology. These became evident in the mid-1970s when the largest environmental groups initially supported a state subsidy for aerial insecticide spraying against a spruce budworm infestation of the corporate forest. Government and industry representatives had portrayed the epidemic as a life-or-death situation for wildlife as well as industry. At the time, knowledge of practical alternatives to insecticides, like biological pest controls — or inaction — was minimal. Scientific evidence about the effect of blanketing the forest with poison was virtually nil. Only after several years of taxpayer-supported spraying did the Natural Resources Council (NRC) accumulate sufficient evidence of its own to reverse its stand and join a few environmental fringe groups in opposition to large-scale chemical spraying. This experience alerted NRC to the pro-industry bias of government-financed research and the necessity of conducting its own studies on critical issues. Maine's largest conservation organisation, the Audubon Society, never opposed spraying (Butler, Irland and Lansky interviews).

One measure of the environmental movement's success in legitimating the public interest in private forests is the movement of numerous environmental activists into the state's executive branch and regulatory boards. One might infer that the conservation ethic has been securely established as a core value in public life. However, the capacity of conservationists, as state employees, to take principled stands on behalf of the public interest and ecological principles is compromised in several ways. Most importantly, they accept the premiss that a central function of the state is to promote economic growth. (Those who dispute this imperative do not attain responsible positions in government.) In practice, all competing values become relative and subject to compromise: preservation of a threatened wildlife species has no prior claim over the pleasures of downhill skiing; resolution of conflicts between private and collective goods and between present and future use-values is not subject to any clear formula; and the legal–ethical boundary between private and collective property rights is opaque. These ambiguities, combined with corporate political 'clout', reduce environmental politics to an arena of only incremental change.

Perhaps with some reservations, the most influential conservationists accept basic capitalist premisses: land is a commodity, profit is a valid human motivation, and market competition is a useful mechanism governing social relations and relations between humans and nature. This ideology is consistent with the bourgeois class interests of most active conservationists. The Maine Audubon Society, in particular, has been compromised by the presence of paper company executives and scions of landowning families in its leadership and by its reliance on corporate financial contributions. This is reflected in Audubon's indecisiveness about budworm spraying, large-scale clear-cutting, herbicide use, and most recently biomass harvesting (on which more below) (Hewett 1985, Lautenschlager 1986). In contrast to Europe's Green movements, with their comprehensive social, economic and environmental agendas, Maine's environmental organisations have paid little heed to the material concerns of working people and have been limited to a typical American single-issue politics.

The corporate response: resistance and 'good citizenship'
At each turn, the paper companies have resisted regulatory encroachment upon their prerogatives. Public statements stress the necessity of a compromise between conservation goals and profitable forestry, conveying a thinly veiled threat: if government interference drives pulpwood costs too high, the corporations will consider abandoning their Maine operations (Yacavone 1983). The present illiquidity of forest land assets and the corporations' multi-billion dollar investment in paper mill modernisation since 1970 cast doubt on corporate blackmail efforts. Nonetheless, politicians and industrial workers do not treat these as idle threats. Paper and lumber industries worldwide are going through a shake-out and several Maine mills are losing money. Their parent firms

could shift to alternative timber supplies and paper mills elsewhere. Moreover, the large number of recent plant closures in traditional rural industries such as shoes and textiles has reinforced workers' fears and inclined rural legislators to make concessions. This has been vividly demonstrated in recent years as working people and politicians in northern Maine strongly backed Great Northern's application to build a hydroelectric dam on the Penobscot River. The justification for damming a unique stretch of 'wild' river was the need for cheaper electricity to save 1,500 threatened paper mill jobs. A coalition of southern Maine conservationists and wilderness recreation businesses defeated the dam proposal when expert testimony revealed most of Great Northern's claims to be spurious. But their evident disregard for the livelihoods of northern Mainers aroused bitter regional hostility which has already jeopardised future conservation efforts.

A very different industry tactic is promoting goodwill by portraying itself as the patron of sportsmen and naturalists. Low-cost actions, like swapping recreationally valuable lands for state forests, protecting deer lots and nesting trees visible from hiking trails, and replanting a few thousand hectares of clear-cuts each year have been heavily publicised. Waterfront building lots are leased inexpensively to fishing and hunting enthusiasts, and the paper companies' 20,000 kilometres of haul roads have become veritable highways into the wilderness for 100,000 visitors each year. However, in the past few years, low profits and the rising cost of complying with LURC regulation have led most industrial landowners to restrict free access and to consider commercial recreation developments. They have also launched a political offensive, arguing that citizens who demand wildlife protection and recreational access to paper company lands should be prepared to defray the cost through tax relief or public subsidy. This will undoubtedly be on the political agenda of the recently elected Republican administration in Augusta (Bartlett 1984).

A rational state in a plural society?
The technical experts and bureaucrats who currently staff the state's exclusive agencies perceive themselves as playing dual roles as mediators among contending interests and as promoters of multiple-use forest management (in 1986, yet another quasi-public body, the Citizens Forestry Advisory Council, was created to hammer out compromises between industry and environmentalists). As mentioned, a growing number of influential policy makers have backgrounds in the environmental movement. Like conservation-minded foresters at the beginning of this century, they are imbued with a commitment to 'progress' through judicious application of scientific principles to resource management. This conviction is expressed by the present Conservation Commissioner:

I see the adversary relationship between large landowners and environmental groups, which has existed over the last fifteen or twenty years, gradually changing to a more cooperative spirit. Large landowners and mill operators have solved a lot of problems in the past fifteen years. I think that's a positive accomplishment we can all look back on. We sometimes complain about the bureaucracy, complain about the legislative process and about regulations. But if we all stop and look at what has happened in the last fifteen years, we would all agree that there must have been a lot of things that were done right. (Anderson 1981: 120)

A more critical interpretation of recent events suggests that the rational state is an illusion. Pluralistic contestation, compromise and non-deterministic outcomes on specific issues all tend to mystify the state's structural role: promoting capitalist economic growth. This prevents any fundamental challenge to the handful of corporations that own nearly half of the state's land and direct the $3 billion forest products industry. This interpretation is aptly summarised by George Scialabba:

This is not a conspiracy theory. Business leaders do not meet in secret to decide how best to delude the public mind and thwart the public will. In a capitalist democracy, business control over the state is assured structurally. Most people are economically vulnerable — they depend on employment ... to survive — so the best predicter of their voting behaviour is likely to be the state of the economy at election time. Overall, the state of the economy is determined by the level of investment. Since investment decisions in a capitalist economy are made privately, governments must nurture that most delicate of blossoms, 'investor confidence'. (Scialabba 1986: 19)

It needs only to be added that 'business leaders' in the paper industry do meet behind closed doors to map out their political tactics. In the 1980s, their leverage over the state derived largely from the widespread fear that they would 'cut and run' — to Alabama or Brazil.

The future of industrial forestry: a 'technological fix'?

Maine's forest industries are in a period of economic crisis and appear to be on the verge of an ecological crisis. The symptoms abound: paper mills have laid off 2,000 of their 18,000 workers since 1984, dozens of small sawmills and wood products factories have closed their doors, employment in logging has shrunk 25 per cent since 1979, numerous past clear-cuts are regenerating to weeds and 'junk' wood, and a spruce fir shortfall before the end of the century appears inevitable (Bailey et al. 1986; Seymour 1985). Consistent with the analysis developed in this chapter, the causes of crisis are complex. However, past and present capital accumulation strategies of multinational paper corporations are decisive in any explanation of the present conjuncture. Likewise, the state's contradictory roles as promoter and regulator of economic growth loom large in future predictions.

Accumulation crisis in forest industries

The corporations that dominate Maine's lumber and paper industries compete in 'mature' (slow-growing and intensely competitive) international markets. In recent years several factors have reduced the competitiveness of older mills. Macroeconomic policies raise the value of the US dollar, pricing marginal mills out of some markets. Aggressive export promotion by Canadian and Scandinavian paper companies cut into Maine's market share in high-grade papers that have been its comparative advantage. Low costs in Third World countries have also cut into Maine's markets for lumber, veneer and low-grade paper. Low Third World costs stem from a potent mix of state-created and natural conditions: low wage labour, lax workplace safety standards, state-subsidised stumpage (low land rent), tax holidays, minimal environmental safeguards, short tropical forest rotations, and a temporary abundance of fibre from virgin forests. In this competitive environment two forces, the state and the multinational corporation, are especially important. While this chapter has stressed the Maine government's structural role as a growth promoter, it is nonetheless clear that the state in industrial nations imposes far more stringent regulations and tax burdens on forest industries than are common in the Third World. In much of the Third World, the aggressive agents of forest 'development' are the very same corporations that have mined Maine's forests and resisted workers' demands — International Paper, Champion International Georgia Pacific, and so on (Business Week 1986; Irland 1986).

Maine's mills are now merely branch operations of multi-plant paper companies. These in turn are subsidiaries of conglomerate corporations. The lawyers and accountants who run the parent corporations from distant offices have reacted in varying ways to changing competitive conditions and ominous timber supply forecasts. One might expect them to take a long-run view, considering that collectively they carry roughly $1 billion in illiquid forest land assets on their books and have invested several billion dollars in paper mill modernisation and new haul roads since 1979.[21] Indeed, a few corporations have indicated their commitment to stay by increasing investments in forest regeneration, mill modernisation and development of new end products from low-quality wood fibre.

However, the stock market's and corporate leaders' notorious preoccupation with short-run profit has prompted 'cut and run' behaviour by other companies. A classic case is International Paper's denuding of 50,000 hectares which were then sold for their 'salvage value'. Great Northern Nekoosa, after publicising its dedication to protecting jobs and forest for many years, has announced plans to eliminate one-third of its jobs (1,400 of 4,000) and terminate replanting and timber stands improvement programmes. Given such behaviour, the best hope for averting a spruce fir shortfall may, ironically, be a depression in the lumber and paper industries (Austin 1986).

Forest system dynamics: 'TSI' or further degradation?

University of Maine research professor Robert Seymour points out that 'Most of the events that will determine the forest's fate [in the coming thirty years] have already occurred.' As most Maine forests enter their fourth rotation of commercial cutting, that fate looks ominous. In northern Maine, much of the commercially valuable spruce fir forest has either been clear-cut in the past twenty years or is heavily stocked with mature, dead or dying trees. That means a glut of softwoods now and an inevitable decline in mature stands for many years beginning in the 1990s. This condition derives largely from industrial landowners' responses to cycles of spruce budworm predation. Today's overstocked, mature, even-age stands stem from unmanaged regeneration after a major epidemic in 1910–19. The enormous volume of dead and dying softwoods, about 20 million cords or the equivalent of five years of harvesting, results from a recent epidemic that is just now abating. Some analysts believe far-sighted actions could still avert a sharp decline in harvestable spruce. But this would mean foregoing clear-cuts wherever selection harvesting is feasible, an action that would significantly increase short-run raw material costs. Sustaining yields could also require a major investment in herbicidal weeding and pre-commercial thinning of the 'new forest' that is growing up in the wake of past clear-cuts. The calculus of short-run cost versus long-run return leaves no one optimistic that timber stand improvement (TSI) will occur on such a scale (Lansky 1986; Seymour 1984; 1985).

Outside the northern spruce fir region, Maine's mixed hardwood and coniferous stands are generally 'an unmanaged mess'. (Irland 1981) The lack of profitability in hardwoods and the absence of either a private ethic or a public mandate supporting resource stewardship have resulted in enormous inventories of poor-quality trees and low-value species.[22] Note that this preview of the future forest does not take account of possible changes in forest ecology caused by unchecked regional and global industrial growth. Acid rain, ozone poisoning and the 'greenhouse effect' of carbon dioxide accumulation could profoundly change forest conditions in a matter of decades.

Because there are major gaps in knowledge about forest ecology, scientists and foresters disagree about the long-term implications of past and present management practices. Nonetheless, experimental findings in Maine, and nearly a century of experience in Scandinavia, support a consensus that timber yields could be sustained well above the current level. Although the Acadian forest has been degraded, in David Smith's words, it is 'forgiving' (Bailey et al. 1986). However, there is no sign that Maine's industrial landowners will adopt the practices that have raised yields in Scandinavia — intensively managed regeneration following clear-cuts and TSI in established stands — unless there is a dramatic shift in the profit–loss calculus (Yacavone 1983, Seymour et al. 1985). Scandinavian forest policy, combining rigorous land use regulations with carefully targeted subsidies, appears to be politically unfeasible here.

The state promotes a 'technological fix'

An investigative journalist has pointed out that, in the past, 'new technology' has bailed out bad forest practices' (Austin 1986). Thus chainsaw harvesting overcame the threat of falling labour productivity when highgrading began to deplete large-diameter trees; and machine harvesting coped effectively with overstocked and budworm-damaged stands after 1970. Today policy makers and many professional foresters are again counting on technology to bail out the industry and even contribute to the elusive goal of a high and sustainable yield forest. According to its advocates, a new three-component technology 'package' may save the paper companies from their own rapaciousness and myopia. Small, highly mobile feller-bunchers shear up to 100 trees per hour and lay them in neat bunches for skidding. Compared to chainsaw felling, fellers reduce labour time and workers' compensation costs by about 80 per cent. Compared to earlier 'monster' harvesters, their small size and versatility permit selection harvesting, instead of 'flattening everything in sight'. Second, mechanical chippers at forest landing reduce whole trees to small chips which are blown into trailer trucks at a rate of 10 tons per hour. Third, on the user end, industrial biomass boilers burn millions of tons of chips from otherwise unmarketable hardwoods, thinnings, 'junk' trees and slash to produce electricity. Maine's Conservation Commissioner and the state Forest Service see the combination as a panacea:

- A huge stock of heretofore unmarketable timber can finally be harvested profitably. Culling low-value trees improves both the species mix and the growth rate in residual stands.

- The feller's high productivity and the chipper's ability to process whole trees finally permits cost-effective thinning of young stands. This releases high-quality trees from competition and accelerates their growth. Thinning is viewed as one key to minimising the spruce fir shortfall early in the twenty-first century.
- Whole-tree chipping cuts waste of previously unused slash (tree limbs and tops). This constitutes up to 30 per cent of total biomass from harvested trees.
- Whole-tree culling and thinning improve the aesthetic appeal of stands and the habitat for some wildlife species.
- Biomass harvesting creates jobs in economically depressed regions. As noted, mechanised crews tend to have safe, secure and relatively high-wage jobs. Building biomass boilers will generate temporary construction work for thousands of people and hundreds of permanent jobs to revitalise northwoods communities.
- Electricity from biomass reduces dependence on imported oil. (Anderson interview; Allen 1985; Maine Forest Service 1985)

Whole-tree harvesting for biomass is not a pipe dream. In recent years, it has grown from negligible volume to nearly one-third of the total harvest. At least fifty crews — roughly 500 workers or 13 per cent of the full-time forest workforce — are equipped with fellers and chippers; and at least ten biomass boilers, including five electrical generating plants, have come on line. This represents an investment exceeding $0.5 billion (Anderson interview; Allen 1985). As in the past, the state has had a pivotal role in this technology diffusion. In particular, investment in biomass boilers, which creates the demand necessary for profitable whole-tree chipping, has been driven by state capital subsidies, federal investment tax credits and guaranteed electricity prices.[23]

There is a growing conviction that 'high tech' forest management is the key to economic survival. This is a latterday version of the nineteenth century's 'scientific forestry' creed. A host of new technologies is under development, running the gamut from integrated past management and genetically engineered tree seedlings to infrared satellite photography and computer models of haul road layout. New end-uses for wood fibre are also being developed in corporate and university laboratories. They include hardwood pulp, silvichemicals, and construction materials reconstituted from low-grade wood chips (Knight and Schottafer 1984; Young 1984). Of all these innovations, mechanised whole-tree harvesting is the best example of a technological 'fix' for the economic and ecological contradictions inherent in past practices. Even a severe critic of past industrial forest management accepts that 'whole-tree harvesting is the most powerful silvicultural tool available for managing Maine's forests' (Hewett 1985: 38).

However, there is mounting evidence that *in practice* whole-tree harvesting is often used in clear-cutting operations rather than for timber stand improvement. This means the removal of virtually 100 per cent of forest biomass and gives new, more literal meaning to the notion of mining the forest. As was true of the earlier version of clear-cutting in the 1970s, a profound change in forest management appears to be taking place without prior research to determine its long-term consequences for the regeneration of various species, nutrient depletion, soil erosion and wildlife habitat. Yet some whole-tree clear-cut sites have completely failed to regenerate softwoods. These lots are likely to be quickly overstocked with low-value hardwoods which are suitable only for short rotations of mechanised 'mowing' and burning (burning is the lowest-value use of wood fibre). If this practice were to become widespread, the logging profession, recreational use of forests and wildlife habitat would all be jeopardised (Allen 1985; Cooperative Forestry Unit; Hewett 1985; Hoffman and Seymour interviews). The critical issue is thus not whether whole-tree harvesting and chipping for biomass have desirable effects under optimum conditions, but rather their probable effects when adapted to the existing mode of production.

The state does not regulate whole-tree harvest, relying instead on 'market signals' and the profit motive (abetted by heavy public subsidy of biomass energy generation). These, of course, are the forces which brought the forest to its present state. Such is the faith in technology and the fear of economic depression in rural Maine that political leaders have accepted the logic — and the ethic — of a paper industry scientist who concludes: 'Since we don't know [the long-run effects] we should proceed ... this is too good an opportunity at this point to stop this kind of harvesting' (Saviello, quoted in Allen 1985).

The future of work in the woods

The crisis in Maine's forests and forest products industries has prompted a seemingly endless flow of conferences, scholarly papers and journalistic feature stories. The plight of loggers, in contrast, is seldom given more than a passing nod except when workers present a 'problem' — like high workers' compensation costs. Yet their future too hinges on the competitiveness of the lumber and paper industries, on the severity of the spruce fir shortfall, on the spread of whole-tree chipping, and on the growth of biomass demand. The basic facts about the loggers' current condition (as best it can be gleaned from shaky data) are that the number of full-time jobs fell from 5,300 to 4,000 between 1979 and 1985; that real earnings have been falling for the past ten years; and that 20 per cent of loggers' households continued to live in poverty in 1980, compared to 13 per cent of Maine and 11 per cent of all US households (Bailey et al. 1986; Benson 1985; Maine Bureau of Employment Security 1981).

Since the forest workers' future is clouded by so many uncertainties, eight experts were asked to sort out the factors shaping employment and work conditions up to the end of the century. Their opinions fall into two broad categories which can be labelled the 'optimistic' and 'majority' opinions. As logging moves towards total mechanisation and professionals such as foresters and engineers become more numerous in the age of 'intensive management', the two optimists expect to see far fewer but substantially better jobs. Further mechanisation will result from several forces: a shrinking pool of rural school dropouts who opt for logging, prohibitive accident insurance costs, the ascendency of large contractors in spruce fir regions; economic superiority of mobile felling machines over chainsaws in the many poor-quality stands, and the related growth of biomass harvesting (labour militancy is not expected to play a role in choice of technology). The number of logging jobs will probably be cut in half, largely through attrition of retiring middle-aged loggers ('retirement' is a euphemism, since there are no pension funds for contract loggers).

The majority of respondents expect employment to decline too, but less sharply and influenced more by the spruce fir shortfall than by mechanisation. Chainsaws will still be used for at least half of the harvest because there will still be plenty of small contractors willing to supply timber under the piece-rate contract system. These observers tend to be sceptical about future growth of biomass demand; it was noted that several contractors who invested in feller-bunchers and chippers appear to be losing money. Neither the state, through tougher labour regulations, nor loggers, through collective bargaining, are expected to influence technology or production relations significantly.

At base, the predictions of both groups imply a rather grim future for some thousands of loggers. Either many will lose their jobs, without obvious alternative employment in their depressed communities, or they will continue to suffer low pay, many injuries and middle-age burnout.

Vision versus praxis

Twenty people with expertise in forestry or forest policy were asked whether a transition to high, sustainable yield forestry is possible; whether current levels of timber extraction are compatible with demands for recreation, aesthetic amenities, wildlife habitat and ecological stability; whether new technologies such as whole-tree chipping could be employed without adverse environmental consequences; and whether the level of forest employment could be maintained, but with less poverty, injury and burnout. In the abstract, most responded affirmatively. They tend to believe that existing scientific and technological knowledge is adequate to make substantial progress on these challenges. However, few respondents had much confidence that there are politically and economically feasible means to these ends. It appears that most foresters, political leaders, industry representatives and loggers are limited to a discourse of incremental reform, even as they begin to sense the necessity of fundamental change to bring about equitable, sustainable, multiple-use forestry.

The few who articulate a more radical vision are not yet take seriously (Lack 1986; Lansky 1984). However, crisis in the forest and the paper mills is beginning to liberate more actors from the 'free enterprise' mystique. In interviews, this was reflected in repeated references to Scandinavia as an example of vigorous state intervention making capitalist forestry conform to the public interest;[24] a few suggested that increased public landownership may be a precondition of sane forest management. And a few hinted that worker and community shares in paper mill ownership may be necessary to deter corporate 'cut and run' tactics. These notions, subversive of the prevailing economic order, may presage an emerging Green and Red consciousness as the crisis deepens.

Maine's forestry and technology transfer

The dominant system of knowledge in Maine forestry — symbolised by chainsaw–skidder harvesting, large-scale clear-cutting and unmanaged regeneration — stands as a warning rather than a model to Third World nations. Even if forests were considered solely as sources of raw material, it is evident that successive technologies and management systems have exploited and degraded the resource, to the point where the sustainability of forest industries is imminently threatened. Even if loggers were considered only as economic agents, it is evident that they too have been exploited, both physically and financially. When forests and loggers are considered in broader ecological and cultural terms, the failure of Maine forestry — and the absurdity of extending its methods to the Third World — is all the more clear.

In considering the implications of Maine's experience for technology transfer, it must be borne in mind that its technology, production relations and forest management methods evolved interdependently and in a unique social formation. Maine contrasts so greatly with the north Indian situations discussed by Guha and Savyasaachi that there are few obvious bases for comparison. The chapters on the Hill Maria and the Chipko Movement describe indigenous peoples' resistance to external aggression. Colonial Maine passed through that stage more than 200 years ago, when forcible expropriation of indigenous peoples (ironically, called 'Indians' by the colonisers) created the precondition for commercial forestry. Prior to that infamous episode, native tribes followed a holistic way of life in the forest quite analogous to the Hill Maria. Forests were the basis of their material existence; their pattern of hunting, gathering and shifting cultivation was ecologically stable. Yet the forest had more than instrumental value; cultural ecology was much more than sustainable resource cycling. In the native American cosmology, nature was suffused with transcendent spiritual meaning. Every practical use of the forest had a ritual dimension, and useful knowledge was bound to symbolic meanings in a tightly woven web.

The alliance between the British state and resource-exploiting colonisers, which expropriated Maine's tribes, bears a strong analogy to capitalist penetration of Uttarakhand Himalaya in the nineteenth century, as described by Guha. The Indian state's aggressive promotion of industrial development since independence, predicated on the instrumental conception of forests as sources of raw material, is also similar. The obvious difference between the two situations is the Chipko Movement tenacious struggle to preserve traditional forest livelihoods and environmental stability. In contrast, Maine's 'red men' were relatively easily dispersed, annihilated, or resettled by 'white men' armed with British property law, modern weapons and an ideological shield of racism. Loggers and conservationists — protagonists in my interpretation of Maine forestry — certainly do not possess Chipko's holistic conception of forest-based livelihood and ecological balance. Indeed, after reflecting on this aspect of the Chipko Movement it is easier to understand the incapacity of Maine loggers' militancy and environmentalists' single-issue politics to confront or overcome the fundamental contradictions of industrial forestry in corporate capitalism.

Comparison between Maine and Finland are more germane and probably more instructive. The two areas share quite similar geoclimatic conditions. Forest industries have historically dominated both economies. Paper and lumber corporations are part of the same international competitive nexus. By and large, the same system of silvicultural knowledge and equipment technology is available to both. As Oksa ably demonstrates, Finnish forestry is beset by its own characteristic contradictions and faces critical problems for the future. Still, there are striking differences, notably Finland's long-standing national commitment to sustained yield forestry, in contrast to Maine's unregulated 'mining and neglect'. Finland's relatively secure, safe and well-paid forest occupations also contrast with Maine's exploitative contract logging. To my mind, the most obvious divergence is in the role of the state, specifically Finland's seventy-year tradition of pervasive intervention to shape forest management practices. Indeed, there is probably no other nation where professional foresters and forest issues have been so prominent in political life. As Oksa stresses, this is not simply a quantitative matter of more regulation, more research and more public subsidy, but the embodiment of a national ethos. The folk tradition summarised in the phrase 'Forest Finland' centres on a land ethic incorporating non-production values, a shared sense of responsibility to past and future generations, and a commitment to equity for farmers, loggers and other rural dwellers in a rapidly urbanising society.

Oksa has vividly portrayed the historical underpinnings of the 'Forest Finland' ideology and traced its implications. Here, I would simply point out Finland's obvious and critical contrasts with Maine in land ownership, class-based mobilisation, and the historic moment of national independence. Thus, for example, legal restrictions on corporate penetration have kept most Finnish forest land in the hands of resident smallholders. By custom, property rights are shared between the title holder and the community. In Maine, native tribes were expropriated and the state sold or granted much of the forest land to the bourgeoisie, establishing the dominance of large absentee landowners long before the industrial era. In the unorganised territories, private property rights were, until very recently, unimpeded by common property notions. Finnish peasant forest owners were the backbone of an agrarian party and loggers were supported by a trade union federation and leftist parties. Therefore the values and material interests of people whose livelihoods depended upon the forest were well represented in parliamentary politics. In the USA, forest interest groups — other than capital — have tended to be poorly organised and only weakly linked to national farmers' and workers' movements. Finnish independence occurred at a pivotal time in the development of industrial forestry, when restricting the domain of foreign corporations was a major nationalist commitment. Maine has never experienced a similar effort to contain the power of external capital.

These contrasts suggest a provocative conclusion about technology transfer. Finland may not be a paragon of humane and ecologically sound forestry. Yet, compared to Maine, its system of forestry knowledge appears to have served social and environmental ends rather effectively. Since the knowledge system and the natural environment are much the same in the two places, this seems to imply that particular aspects of a given knowledge system can, in principle, be decoupled from one social formation and appropriated by another without serious negative entailments. After all, Finnish loggers use chainsaws with low accident rates; clear-cutting is part of Finland's sustainable yield forestry; Finnish whole-tree chipping for biomass does not appear to cause regeneration failures; and industrial timber extraction has been compatible with 'everyone's right' to use the forest for subsistence and recreational activities.

Notes

1. A horizontally integrated firm has several production units producing the same commodity, e.g. several paper mills in different locations. A vertically integrated firm carries out distinct stages in a multi-stage production process, such as forest management, timber harvesting, pulp making and paper manufacture.

2. Roughly 3 per cent of Maine's forest land is publicly owned; 2 per cent is held in trust by conservation groups. The privately owned 95 per cent is divided in roughly equal fractions between large industrial owners and smallholders. The spruce fir forest of northern Maine, prime source of industrial raw material, is nearly all large private lots.

3. Indirect subordination of self-employed workers by corporations is more common in the United States than is often realised. For example, several million workers are employed in contract farming, home knitting and retail franchises. James O'Connor and J.K. Galbraith argue that corporations find it functional to 'spin off' high-risk, seasonal or labour-intensive tasks to 'self-employed' workers and petty capitalists. Market power, exercised through the terms of contract, reinforces the superior profitability of contracting-out.

4. Conservationists were not exclusively concerned with optimal resource exploitation. Most also expressed concern about preservation of wildlife habitat and enhancement of recreational amenities. This anticipated the concept of 'multiple use forestry' championed by environmentalists today.

5. In addition to cash income, turn-of-the-century loggers received room (crude, unsanitary log huts) and board, and enormous volumes of starchy, sweet and fatty foods.

6. The flood of low-cost Pacific Northwest lumber into East Coast markets early in this century underscores the decisive role of the state in the forest industries. Low stumpage fees (rents) on federal forest lands and completion of the government-financed Panama Canal were decisive in undermining Maine's comparative advantage in lumber.

7. Under the US constitution, land use is governed largely by the states. Maine's governors and legislators, bankrolled and heavily lobbied by the paper industry, granted industrial landowners virtually total freedom to use their land in the unorganised townships as they saw fit.

8. The demand for labour-saving logging machinery was universal in the paper-producing nations, as they all experienced labour shortages after the war. Governments, forest industries, universities and capital goods producers throughout northern Europe and North America were involved in advocating or developing the technologies described here.

9. The continued diffusion of truck transport was another aspect of this innovation process. On the eve of World War Two, two-thirds of pulpwood was still moved to the mills by river. Ten years later, two-thirds was being trucked. In the mid-1970s, Maine enforcement of federal water quality standards eliminated river drives altogether (Falk 1977).

10. Wartime innovations instrumental in the development of the chainsaw included the lightweight gasoline engine, the diaphragm carburettor and new metal alloys for chainsaw bars (Parenteau 1986: 86–8; Swift 1983: ch. 5)

11. Even with skidders, the spring 'mud season' continues to be a slack period in the woods.

12. A 50-ton Koehring harvester was poorly suited to selection harvesting because it tended to destroy residual trees.

13. In 1900 women did much of the domestic work and book-keeping in logging camps. By 1970, most of this labour had been shifted to individual loggers' households, so that the women's contribution was no longer reported as logging employment.

14. Reported profits overstate the true return on investment because they include the implicit return to contractors' labour.

15. Under Labour Department provisions, employers were required to pay bonded workers a fixed basic wage, which varied by task. The easily exploited position of this 'reserve army' stemmed from internally contradictory Canadian government policies. On the one hand, economic policy failed to create wage employment for poor farmers in rural Quebec, leading them to look across the border for work. On the other hand, socialised medicine and subsidised credit for logging equipment made it possible for Quebec loggers to accept safety hazards and low-productivity cutting chances that were not acceptable to local workers. By exporting its unemployment problem, the Quebec government in effect hurt US loggers and subsidised the paper companies. But, at base, it was US immigration laws and Maine's lax enforcement of them that permitted this dual labour market to exist (Butler interview; Falk 1977; Public Affairs Research Center 1968).

16. The expression is taken from Clifford Geertz in *Local Knowledge* (1983).

17. This quotation is Sahlins' *disapproving* interpretation of Marx's tendency to view culture as determined by the mode of production.

18. Opposition to spruce budworm spraying brought together a populist alliance including MWA leaders, citizens of three towns subjected to spray drift, and a radical environmental organisation, PEST. (By this time the MWA was no longer a large or politically influential group.) At the height of agitation in 1978, the alliance was joined by the 'mainstream' Natural Resources Council of Maine. This temporary association of workers, communities and environmentalists was probably the closest Maine has come to having a Green movement (Lansky interview).

19. A suit pitting contract loggers against wood dealers in Georgia led to a 1974 US District Court ruling that would probably have permitted some small Maine contractors (those who sold timber directly to the paper companies) to organise a bargaining unit with the right to picket the mills. But since the MWA represented workers with many distinct relations to the paper corporations, it could not use this precedent. To the best of my knowledge, the only non-union loggers who bargain collectively with paper mills today are a few small woodlot owners who have formed a marketing cooperative (Falk 1977, Hoffman 1985).

The MWA has not disappeared without a trace. Some former leaders continue to be involved in forest causes, Friends of the Maine Woods (an ecological forestry group) and the North Woods Logging Association (a self-insurance company formed by contract loggers).

20. These calculations are based on timber prices published by the Maine Bureau of Employment Security and sales and cost data from the Paper Industry Information Office.

21. Regarding the illiquidity of land assets, it is rumoured that at least half a million hectares of industrial forest are currently for sale, but with no takers; and that International Paper got the extremely low price of $100 per hectare when it found a buyer for 50,000 hectares of previously clear-cut land (Anderson, Irland and Magnusen interviews).

22. In parts of western Maine, prime quality hardwood trees, like yellow birch and red maple, have been highgraded to supply the hundreds of small, specialised wood products factories which formerly dotted the countryside. In terms of volume, though, firewood is overwhelmingly the principle use for hardwoods. The 1970s 'energy crisis' induced a substantial conversion to wood heat in Maine homes. By 1980, domestic fuelwood was probably 15 per cent or more of the total harvest (Chaisson 1985). With some time lag, Maine consumers are quite sensitive to relative fuel prices, and the low price of heating oil since 1981 reversed the trend to wood heat.

23. The technology 'package' of a feller-buncher, grapple skidder, chipper and trailer truck costs roughly $500,000.

24. Many people in Maine forestry have visited Scandinavia or at least studied some aspects of its land use polices, forest management practices and labour relations. Positive comments about the state's role centred on long-range sectoral planning: regulated harvesting, replanting and timber stand improvement; protection of workers' interests; and subsidisation of management methods which enhance multiple-use forestry. Those who mentioned Scandinavian politics emphasised one or more of the following: well-organised forest workers, supported by national trade union federations; the large number and the political influence of small woodlot owners; and the pervasiveness of a resource conservation ethic. Each of these was seen as a countervailing force against corporate hegemony and preoccupation with short-run economic issues.

Interviews

Anderson, Richard: Commissioner, Maine Department of Conservation.

Austin, Phyllis: journalist, *The Maine Times*.

Benson, Joyce: Staff Sociologist, Maine State Planning Office.

Birdsall, Paul: horse logger, North Penobscot.

Bley, Jerry: Educational Projects Director, Natural Resources Council of Maine.

Butler, William: Manager, Firewood Cooperative (Portland); founder, Friends of the Maine Woods; former vice-president, the Maine Woodsman's Association.

Chase, Pat: logging contractor (biomass harvesting), North Whitefield.

Corcoran, Thomas: Professor of Roest Economics and Engineering, University of Maine.

Falk, Jonathan: former researcher, Yale School of Forestry; former organiser, Maine Woodsman's Association.

Hagan, Richard: Maine Bureau of Employment Security.

Hoffman, Benjamin: Associate Professor, University of Maine.
Irland, Lloyd: State Economist, Maine state Planning Office.
Judd, Richard: Assistant Professor of History, University of Maine.
Lansky, Mitchell: forestry journalist, Wytopitlock.
Magnusen, Henry: Executive Director, Maine Paper Industry Information Office.
Schonberger, Howard: Professor of History, University of Maine.
Seymour, Robert: Assistant Research Professor of Forestry, University of Maine.
Shipman, William: Professor of Economics, Bowdoin College; energy economist.
Soule, Haydon: Associate Professor of Agricultural Engineering, University of
  Maine.

Bibliography

Allen, Scott (1985), 'Maine's energy panacea', *The Maine Times*, 15 November.
Anderson, Richard (1981), 'Response', Maine Forest Service 1985: 118–20.
Andersson, Stig (1984), 'Forces and obstacles in the mechanisation of forest
  operations in Sweden', in Corcoran and Gill (eds): 115–19.
Austin, Phyllis (1986), 'Mining and forest', *The Maine Times*, 12 September.
Bailey, Dennis, Kim Clark and Bob Cummings (1986), 'Maine woods enter era
  of decline', *Maine Sunday Telegram*, four-part series, 20 July–10 August.
Bartlett, Robert F. (1984), 'Why Great Northern Paper moved to Portland',
  Maine Business Indicators, vol. XXIX, no. 4, July, Portland.
Benson, Joyce (1985), 'Natural resource industries: quality of life characteristics
  of workers', Maine state Planning Office, Staff Technical Paper, Augusta.
Bley, Jerry (1986), 'Clear-cutting in Maine: should it be controlled?', *Maine
  Environment*, May: 4–5.
Burch, William R., Jr. (1986), 'The rhetoric of wilderness', *Habitat*, vol. 3, no.
  6, June/July: 36–41.
Business Week (1986), 'The climate is right for forest products again', 13 January
  p.82.
Chaisson, Joseph (1985), 'Environmental issues associated with Maine's forest
  resources', unpublished report to the Natural Resources Council of Maine,
  Augusta, ME.
Corcoran, Thomas and Douglas Gill, eds. (1983), *Recent Advances in Spruce
  Fir Utilisation*, Society of American Foresters, Publication 83–13 (Orono).
Cottell, Phillip (1975), 'Human factors in logging productivity', in Irland 1975:
  48–72.
Cox, Thomas R. (1981), 'The stewardship of private forests', *Journal of Forest
  History*, 25 October: 188–96.
Cut and Run (1981), a documentary film produced by Howard Schonberger for
  the Maine Humanities Council, Orono.
Falk, Jonathan (1977), 'The organisation of pulpwood harvesting in Maine', Yale
  School of Forestry Working Paper No. 4, New Haven
Geertz, Clifford (1983), *Local Knowledge*, New York: Basic Books.
Goldschmidt, Walter (1978), *As You Sow*, Montclair: Allanheld Osmun.
Griffin, Ralph (1984), 'The clearcutting method of regeneration in spruce-fir
  forests', *Forest Technique*, vol. 84, no. 8: 11.

Hardison, Mark (1984), 'A Maine woodcutter talks about safety in the woods', Maine Department of Conservation.

Hays, Samuel P. (1959), *Conservation and the Gospel of Efficiency*, Cambridge, MA: Harvard University Press.

Hermelin, Joachim (1981), *Film and Remarks on Swedish Forestry*, Maine Department of Conservation: 31–7.

Hewett, Charles (1985), 'Whole tree harvesting: the potentials and the pitfalls', *Habitat*, vol. II, no. 8, July: 35–8.

Hoffman, Benjamin (1985), *Estimating Production of Forest Cooperative Members*, US Department of Agriculture, ACS Research Report 45.

Howlett, Duncan (1981), 'Response', in Maine Forest Service 1985: 88–90.

Howlett, Duncan (ed.) (1982), *The Small Woodlot Owner in Maine*, College of Forest Resources, Orono: University of Maine, Technical Notes No. 85.

Irland, Lloyd (ed.) (1975), *Manpower: Forest Industry's Key Resource*, New Haven, CT: Yale University School of Forestry.

———— (1981), 'Maine's timber supply', Maine Forest Service 1985: 39–54.

———— (1982), *Wildlands and Woodlots*, Hanover, NH: University Press of New England.

———— (1984), 'Future employment in the Maine woods', Maine Forest Service 1985.

———— (1986), 'Canada–US forest products trade: tragic tensions of a maturing market', paper presented at University of Maine Conference on Resource Economies in Emerging Free Trade, Orono.

Ives, Edward (1985), 'The life of Machias lumbermen', in Sheldon 1985: 5–6.

Kingsley, Neal (1982), 'Who owns Maine's woodlots', in Howlett 1981: 22–33.

Knight, Fred and James Shottafer (1984), *Technology Strategy for Maine: the Forest Products Industry*, The Maine Development Foundation, Augusta.

Kurelek, John (1984), 'The feller-forwarder concept and its application', in Corcoran and Gill 1983: 191–4.

Lack, Larry (1986), 'Toward a healthy Maine economy: managing the woods to benefit Maine's people', unpublished paper.

Lansky, Mitchell (1984), 'Lessons in forest destruction', *Rural Delivery*, December: 26–32.

———— (1986), 'Budworm-proofing the forest', *Rural Delivery*, April.

Lautenschlager, R.A. (1986), 'Badmouthing of herbicides called unjustified', *Habitat*, vol. III, no. 3, February.

Maine Bureau of Employment Security (1981), *Proceedings of the Blaine House Conference on Forestry*, Augusta.

———— (1984), 'Proceedings of the Blaine House Conference on Forestry', Augusta (unpublished).

Maine Department of Labour (1985), 'Census of Maine manufactures 1983', BLS 593, Augusta.

Maine Forest Service (1985), 'Biomass harvesting and whole tree chipping', Department of Conservation, Augusta.

Mikkonen, Esko (1984), 'Recent advances with off-road forest vehicle development in Scandinavia', in Corcoran and Gill 1983: 181–6.

Natural Resources Council of Maine (1985), 'The changing forest: looking at the future of Maine woods', August.

Osborn, William (1974), *The Paper Plantation*, New York: Viking Press.

Parenteau, William (1986), 'The rise of the small contractor: a study of technological and structural change in the Maine pulpwood industry', MA thesis, Department of History, University of Maine, Orono.

Public Affairs Research Center (1968), *Study of Problems Relative to Obtaining a Continuing Supply of Domestic Workers for Wood Operations in Maine*, Brunswick: Bowdoin College.

Sahlins, Marshall (1976), *Culture and Practical Reason*, Chicago: University of Chicago Press.

Scialabba, George (1986), 'Why voters always lose?', *Village Voice Literary Supplement*, November: 15–21.

Sennett, Richard and Jonathan Cobb (1973), *The Hidden Injuries of Class*, New York: Random House.

Seymour, Robert (1984), 'Can we improve Maine's timber supply?', Maine Department of Conservation (unpublished).

—— (1985), 'Where has all the spruce fir gone?', *Habitat*, vol. II, no. 8, September: 24–9.

—— J. Grace, P. Hannah and D. Marquis (1985), 'Silviculture in the Northeastern United States: the past 30 years and the next 30 years', paper presented at the Society of American Foresters Conference, Fort Collins, July.

Sheldon, Karen (ed.) (1985), *From Stump to Ship*, Orono: University of Maine Printing Office.

Smith, David C. (1972), *Lumbering in Maine: 1861–1960*, Orono: University of Maine Press.

—— (1985), 'Lumber and the framework of Maine's economy', in Sheldon 1985: 3–4.

Smith, D. M. (1981), 'The forest and Maine's future', Maine Department of Conservation: 79–87.

Summers, Eugene (ed.) (1983), *Technology and Social Change in Rural Areas*, Boulder: Westview Press.

Swedish Institute (1984), *Environment Protection in Sweden*, Stockholm.

—— (1985), *Forestry and Forest Industry in Sweden*, Stockholm.

Swift, Jamie (1983), *Cut and Run*, Toronto: Between the Lines Press.

Yacavone, Peter (1983), 'From stump through mill', in Corcoran and Gill 1983: 37–41.

Young, Harold (1984), 'Some non-traditional uses of forest material', Maine Department of Conservation, unpublished paper.

Young, John and Jan Newton (1980), *Capitalism and Obsolescence*, New York: Universe Books.

Index